GOD MODE

WE ARE WAKING UP

BOOK 1

Kivar Dhawan & The 144 Victors

אני האחד אני

אהיה האחד אהיה

गलेक्टिक लोगोस

कृष्णा ΣΗ ΣΨΗ سحور

釋迦牟尼

ᴵ ERAᴶ

ॐ

22

ॐ

ᴵ ERAᴶ

釋迦牟尼

कृष्णा ΣΗ ΣΨΗ سحور

गेलेक्टिक लोगोस

אהיה האחד אהיה

CHRISTIC GATEWAY BOOKS

Seven Hard-Headed New York Teenagers learn humanity's Hidden Metaphysical Knowledge in this Spiritual Comedy-Drama. This Story Explores The Universal Law of Oneness. We'll Explore the Serious Inner-Seeking of The Creator. Individual Responsibility. Self-Development. Expanding Your Awareness. Practical Uses for Metaphysics. Problem-Solving. Etheric Energy. Your Inner Youniverse. Salvation/Harvest. The Dimensions. Extraterrestrial & Higher-Dimensional Life. Energy Centers/Chakras. Sexual Energy. Grounding. Balance. Healing. Nutrition. Physical & Mental Health. Fear. Facing Challenges. Solutions. Service to Others. Desires. Thoughts. Feelings. Choices. Music. Dance. Art. Comedy & Playing.

(Your head hurt yet? Relax, it really is a Comedy. And we're gonna break it all down in regular words. There are gonna be some *bursts of rapid-fire information flow* that'll be like a mental roller coaster. Reading those parts can entrain your brain & sync your mind to higher vibrational rhythms. You can read this story in parts, 10 pages at a time. Have a GodMode n Chill session with your friends & take turns reading. Check out the GodMode pages on Facebook, Instagram & Youtube.)

Cover Design By James Will Power,
Kivar Dhawan, & Kevonte. L Anderson,
Edited By Kivar Dhawan
Copyright © 2016 By Kivar Dhawan. All rights reserved.
ISBN-10: 0692614257
ISBN-13: 978-0692614259
Christic Gateway Books, New York, New York

... In Service to The Creator
and The Younger Generations of Incarnating Souls ...

1

<u>HUMANS BE LIKE ...</u>
WAKING UP.
WHAT DOES IT MEAN?
NO, NO, SERIOUSLY, WHAT IS THIS
AWAKENING, CONSCIOUS, METAPHYSICAL STUFF ALL ABOUT?
PLEASE, EXPLAIN IT TO ME AS CLEARLY AS POSSIBLE.

Wednesday, February 2nd, 2017. Manhattan, New York.

It's the end of the day at Fleming's Junior High school. Seven seventh-graders from different classes have reported to detention. Earl, Vincent, Nadia, Scooter, Kareem, Din and Bindia have all been detained for different reasons. Mr. Lightman is the teacher who is assigned to detention today. He's thirty-eight years old, brown-skinned, and stands at six feet tall. His father is from India. His mother is from Egypt, where he was born. His birth name is Qamar Kapoor. The name "Lightman" came about after a corny joke fell flat on his students.

He's always goofing around with the students and messing with their heads. The students and the other teachers consider him to be weird. He wears jeans and a T-shirt to work everyday, and walks around with no shoes. He addresses the students.

MR. LIGHTMAN: Aright, who's here today? Earl and Vincent, welcome to your weekly detention session. Let me go ahead and schedule you guys again for next week. When do y'all plan on acting a fool again? Is next Wednesday good?

Earl is a dark-brown-skinned thirteen-year-old.

MR. LIGHTMAN: Earl, why are you in detention today?

EARL: Huh? I don't – don't even remember.

MR. LIGHTMAN: That ... just sounds about right. Okay. Vincent?

VINCENT: Huh?

Mr. Lightman shakes his head. Vincent is an athletic thirteen-year-old who walks, talks and dresses with confidence and swag. He and Earl are best friends. They bonded after discussing the loss of their fathers. Vincent's parents died in a car crash when he was eight years old. His father was an unorthodox and very unconventional Jewish man who lived and owned property in Harlem. His mother was an Italian artist who loved to paint and collect items from different cultures around the world. The deaths of his parents led to Vincent having a more nonchalant, slightly cold-hearted view of the world and other people. He's one of the most popular kids in school, and one of the smartest. He speaks boldly and uses his hands a lot to make sure he gets his point across.

VINCENT: Now, you know I don't belong here with these lames.

MR. LIGHTMAN: I know. Your teachers are always doing something wrong to you. Who is it this time?

VINCENT: Mr. Russo.

MR. LIGHTMAN: What'd he do now?

VINCENT: He's jealous of me.

MR. LIGHTMAN: Here we go.

VINCENT: No "here we go." It's true. The thing is —

MR. LIGHTMAN: What's the thing?

VINCENT: Let me tell you.

MR. LIGHTMAN: I can't wait.

VINCENT: Really? Really, bro? Are you gonna let me talk, or …

MR. LIGHTMAN: No, sorry. Tell me the thing.

VINCENT: You're always butting in with your whack jokes. You know that, right? You're one of those people. You just got to get the laugh, don't you? Mr. Lightman lowers his head, disappointed in himself.

MR. LIGHTMAN: Yes.

Nadia and Bindia laugh.

MR. LIGHTMAN: I'm sorry. Why is Mr. Russo jealous of you?

VINCENT: No, no, no. You do that thing, you know. Where somebody says something important, right? But instead of talking about that, you go off and try to make a joke after their first sentence. Then they laugh and forget what they're gonna say. And if they don't know you that good, they try to be polite and just let it slide. But you don't care. You're proud of yourself. You got your joke in. You got the laugh. "Ha, ha, I'm funny." And that's all that's important, right? Can *I* speak without being interrupted, please?

MR. LIGHTMAN: Well, I guess ... I've been ... owned, as you guys say. Epic fail right? I'll hold this "L" for now.
Earl and Scooter laugh.
EARL: This guy ...
VINCENT: Hold an "L?" You don't even know what that means! Stop that. Stop ... doing that!
MR. LIGHTMAN: I'll stop for now.
VINCENT: Good!
MR. LIGHTMAN: But I will continue tomorrow when you're in detention for mouthing off and raising your voice.
VINCENT: When did I do that?
MR. LIGHTMAN: You just did.
   Earl bursts out laughing and the others follow.
VINCENT: That wasn't — Yo! No! I wasn't serious! Sorry! I'm sorry!
MR. LIGHTMAN: No, it's my fault. I never get these things right — with the ... the "L" holding and all. I'm sorry. Go on about Mr. Russo.
VINCENT: Do I really have detention tomorrow? I was just joking.
MR. LIGHTMAN: Oh, man. You should've told me. Because *I* was being serious. If I had known you were joking, maybe you wouldn't be spending an hour here after school tomorrow.
VINCENT: That's foul, bro.
MR. LIGHTMAN: Bindia, why are you here?
VINCENT: Wait, we're still on me!
MR. LIGHTMAN: Mr. Russo is jealous of you. We know.
VINCENT: I didn't tell you the story.
MR. LIGHTMAN: Of course there's a story.
VINCENT: Of course.
MR. LIGHTMAN: What's the story?
VINCENT: Mr. Russo says that I'm ... like, exactly equal to everybody else in the class. And he knows that's not true. I'm better than them ... in most ways. He's old, and bald, and washed. I'm everything he ever wanted to be, so he uses his power as a teacher to get me in trouble. That's why I'm here.
MR. LIGHTMAN: Mm-hm. And this being better than everyone else — how exactly did you come to that conclusion?
VINCENT: What do you mean?
MR. LIGHTMAN: What makes you better than the other people in your class?
VINCENT: Pshh! What? I thought it was obvious, bro. I look hella good, I'm smart, and I'm funny.

MR. LIGHTMAN: Okay.

Vincent nods. Mr. Lightman nods back. Vincent looks around and smiles. Mr. Lightman smiles.

MR. LIGHTMAN: What?

VINCENT: Most people want to have those things and don't have them. I have all of them in one person, so I'm better than the average person. It's simple logic. I don't mean to sound conceited, but, I'm saying, there should at least be *some* rules that don't apply to people like me. We're better.

MR. LIGHTMAN: He actually said, "I don't mean to sound conceited", then goes on to describe himself as the definition of conceited.

The others laugh.

VINCENT: Besides that part. I know you understand what I mean, though. I'm smart.

MR. LIGHTMAN: Oh, yes.

VINCENT: I look good.

MR. LIGHTMAN: Of course.

VINCENT: And I make clever jokes that make people laugh. That's a gift, bro. Most people would kill to have even one of those things.

MR. LIGHTMAN: You know what? I actually get that logic.

VINCENT: See?

MR. LIGHTMAN: I'll, um, file a complaint with the front office. Mr. Russo should realize that you are just plain better than the other students. All of us need to recognize that once and for all.

VINCENT: Wait.

MR. LIGHTMAN: No, no, let *me* finish! You are the most important student that has ever walked the halls of this school!

VINCENT: Are you messing with me? Or are you kinda serious?

Mr. Lightman shakes his head in disbelief.

MR. LIGHTMAN: Who do you think you are?

VINCENT: I'm —

MR. LIGHTMAN: Eh! Don't answer that, Vincent. Please.

Mr. Lightman shakes his head.

MR. LIGHTMAN: Let me talk to Bindia. Sweet, little, innocent Bindia. What are you doing in here with … *them*?

Bindia is a skinny twelve-year-old Indian girl. She looks like a sweetheart, but behind her appearance is a cynical and miserable child.

BINDIA: I didn't want to participate in the passions and dreams activity.

MR. LIGHTMAN: What's that?

BINDIA: This stupid thing where Mr. Pryor makes us talk about what makes us feel passionate. Everyone gets all excited and makes all this stupid arty stuff. It's annoying! He's always saying, "Follow your excitement!" There is no real excitement. Life is just normal. Just live normal. He should just face it and stop trying to make up fake excitement with all these activities and events and stuff.

   She shakes her head and rubs her right eye.

MR. LIGHTMAN: I see. You don't have anything that you're very passionate about?

BINDIA: No.

MR. LIGHTMAN: What do you like to do?

BINDIA: Watch videos online, I guess. Texting.

MR. LIGHTMAN: Texting? I guess that could be a passion.

BINDIA: Why do you need a passion? Just live life like a normal person. It's just life. Why do we need all that extra stuff?

MR. LIGHTMAN: What about having fun with family and friends?

BINDIA: I do have fun with my family. I have fun. But ... then it's over ... and it's back to TV, and chores, and sleeping, and eating. What's to be excited about? It just comes and goes.

   Mr. Lightman chuckles.

MR. LIGHTMAN: Oh, come on. You're only, what, twelve? You can't be fed up and bored with life already.

BINDIA: I'm not. It's just like, uhh! Do this, do that. And meet this new person. And go ... parties, and birthdays, and weddings and ... "Let's have a ... little get-together today!" Then sleep, then school, then home. How do you old people do this stuff for so many years? I guess it's fun while it's happening, but then you know it's gonna end soon. And it's just not a big deal.

Mr. Lightman rubs his eyes.

MR. LIGHTMAN: Wow!

   He takes a sip of water from a bottle.

MR. LIGHTMAN: I feel so bad for the people around you if ... *when* you have a mid-life crisis. I feel sorry for them now.

BINDIA: It's just the same thing. Wake up, eat, go to school, play with my friends.

MR. LIGHTMAN: Fart, shower, blink, beat your heart. You have to enjoy the moment. You just said it. Enjoy things as they're happening.

BINDIA: I do, but then it's over. And plus, everything gets boring after a while.

  Vincent shakes his head.

VINCENT: "And plus."

BINDIA: Shut up.

EARL: Freakin' language police.

BINDIA: Always!

SCOOTER: He does it on Facebook all the time.

BINDIA: I know!

VINCENT: Learn to speak English. If people learned the language, I won't have to correct them. (Shakes his head) "And plus."

BINDIA: We're not in school, idiot!

VINCENT: (Looking around) Really?

BINDIA: I mean online!

VINCENT: You said it here.

BINDIA: Well, we're not in class!

VINCENT: (Nodding) We're kind of in a class, Bindia.

BINDIA: I said, "Not in class." Not, "Not in *a* class."

EARL: Not not?

BINDIA: And this is a class-*room*, not a class! Learn English!

VINCENT: You just don't want to speak properly. "This is not a classroom." That's what idiots say online to justify their stupidity.

EARL: You just scroll through comments looking for mistakes?

VINCENT: No, but it's annoying when people think they can just write anyhow they want.

BINDIA: They can!

VINCENT: And what's with the mixing numbers and letters thing? Using "3" for "E" and all that crap. Is that supposed to be cool? It hurts my head to read.

BINDIA: You hurt my head to talk to!

VINCENT: Nobody's making you talk to me.

BINDIA: Good!

VINCENT: Good.

BINDIA: Uhhh!

VINCENT: And why are people still saying, "First!" in comment sections. Is your life so empty that you need to win at a thing that's not even a … thing?

SCOOTER: It's just something people do.

VINCENT: Yeah, in the year 2000. Eehhhh. Up to 2005. I'll give it up to

2005. After that, aright. Enough. Cut it out. It's lame.

BINDIA: You weren't even alive in 2000. What kind of person are you?

VINCENT: The kind who knows the difference between "your" and you're."

BINDIA: Shut up!

MR. LIGHTMAN: Both of you.

VINCENT: "Then" and "than."

MR. LIGHTMAN: Vincent!

They talk a little more and then come back to talking about Bindia.

BINDIA: Everything gets boring after a while. What's the point of doing it?

MR. LIGHTMAN: *For the experience.* Maybe you're too locked into only one way of doing things. Maybe you can try new things. Make some changes.

BINDIA: Oh, that's even worse!

MR. LIGHTMAN: (Mumbles to himself) I made it worse.

BINDIA: It is so annoying when things are going good, and exactly the same all the time, and then something just changes all of a sudden. My mom does that. I like things to be the same.

MR. LIGHTMAN: You have to go with the flow.

BINDIA: That doesn't mean anything. It just means I have to waste time to learn something a new way, and … and then ... and then it takes long to get used to it, and … uhh!

MR. LIGHTMAN: Uhh!

Bindia tilts her head and smiles. Mr. Lightman shakes his head.

MR. LIGHTMAN: Wow.

Earl sits next to Bindia. He's hyperactive, speaks quickly, sharply, and moves around a lot. His attention span is short, and he constantly slips in and out of imaginative fantasies. He's extremely creative, has a vivid imagination, and has a Power with Words that he hasn't really recognized as yet. He has a small afro and uses a pick to comb it often. His father was in the army. He was killed during the 2003 invasion of Iraq. He lives with his single mother and his sister, Nadia.

EARL: Man, you just dunno how to have fun. You gotta live e'rday to da fullest, like me.

MR. LIGHTMAN: Gotta live what?

EARL: E'rday to da fullest.

MR. LIGHTMAN: Earl's day?

VINCENT: Every day.

EARL: E'rday.

MR. LIGHTMAN: Oh. Wow. You know there's — there's a "V" … in that

7

word. Yeah. And a couple other syllables you missed there.

EARL: Don't tell me how to talk. I know how to talk right. I talk like this when I'm chillin', and jokin'. I'm a clown. That's me. That's how I do. Ain't no rules to talkin'.

MR. LIGHTMAN: You know how to "talk right?"

EARL: Oh, my bad. I meant to say, "I know how to talk right-ly."

MR. LIGHTMAN: There you go.

EARL: I'm just playin', man.

Nadia is Earl's twelve-year-old sister. She's short, chubby, and dark skinned.

NADIA: He's playing around, Mr. Lightman. He does know how to speak properly. He's good in English.

MR. LIGHTMAN: I can't possibly imagine that.

VINCENT: Nah, it's true. He's a beast. He gets all nineties and hundreds on his English tests.

NADIA: And fails in everything else.

MR. LIGHTMAN: Oh. Well. I guess the bad is all mine.

EARL: Huh?

MR. LIGHTMAN: My bad.

Vincent shakes his head at Mr. Lightman.

VINCENT: That awkward moment when the aging teacher desperately tries to hold on to his youth by talking like his students.

BINDIA: Jeez. Don't start the "awkward moment" stuff now. It's old.

VINCENT: Man. If I say it, it's still relevant. It still got some life left. And they named a movie after it. That's something.

BINDIA: The movie's old.

VINCENT: Shut up.

MR. LIGHTMAN: So, you're really good with words, and you're just having fun.

EARL: Yeah. That's how I do. I have fun! That's my shwag.

MR. LIGHTMAN: Your shwag?

EARL: My swag.

MR. LIGHTMAN: What's that, the name of your bank?

EARL: My style, my mojo. I can't stand bein' bored and doin' things all proper-like all the time. Workin' all the time. Just gotta have fun and live e'rday to da fullest. Yolo!

MR. LIGHTMAN: Okay. The fullest. But why do you full so many of your days in detention?

EARL: 'Cause teachers dunno life is all about playin'. They like Bindia. She's bored 'cause she don't play enough.
VINCENT: Now, that's true.
MR. LIGHTMAN: And you're failing most of your classes because you play too much. And at the wrong times.
EARL: I don't see the problem. No work, no problems, nah mean?
MR. LIGHTMAN: You do have responsibilities.
EARL: You sound like my moms, man. I do hard work all the time but I hate to. I don't like to do boring stuff. I have fun. If I didn't live like that, I'd be like Bindia — all stuffy and bored.
    Vincent turns to Bindia. Bindia shakes her head.
VINCENT: Hashtag #GrumpyLilGirl!
MR. LIGHTMAN: So, why don't you play around in your English class? How do you manage to get work done there?
BINDIA: He likes Ms. Jay. And I am not stuffy and bored.
MR. LIGHTMAN: Ahh, Ms. Jay.
BINDIA: Stuffy ...
VINCENT: But he likes Ms. Bachman too and he sucks at history.
BINDIA: Am I stuffy and bored?
NADIA: Why do you like your teachers? That's creepy.
    Earl bops his head and rhymes his words.
EARL: Stuffy n' bored. Bruh, I can't take it no more. If I was like her, I'd fall asleep n J'snore. Havin' fun is a gift and I really like to use it. I play games, laugh, chill and I listen to music. Responsibilities make you old as dirt. I rather take it easy and let y'all do all the work. Jyeah!
MR. LIGHTMAN: That was actually some good rapping skills, Earl.
VINCENT: Your standards for good rap are looowwww.
EARL: Quit hatin'.
MR. LIGHTMAN: So, you *do* play in English class. The way you see the words, it's kinda like a game to you.
Earl shrugs.
MR. LIGHTMAN: But you should know that work and play needs to be mixed together properly. It's not good to just play all the time, or just work all the time.
EARL: I do mix work and play. I work really, really hard at playin'.
MR. LIGHTMAN: Huh? Like in English class?
EARL: No, Xbox.
    The others laugh hard.

MR. LIGHTMAN: What?
EARL: What?
MR. LIGHTMAN: You work hard at playing Xbox? That's how you mix work and play? That's a joke?
EARL: I *do* work really hard at playin'.
MR. LIGHTMAN: You're serious.
The others continue laughing.
NADIA: I'm weak! I'm weak!
MR. LIGHTMAN: This, "I'm weak."
VINCENT: It's stupid, isn't it?
MR. LIGHTMAN: You want me to call the Nurse? Don't faint in here, now. Who else is here? Din-Din! Why are you here again this week?

Din is thirteen years old. He's Chinese. He has a hard time controlling his temper. From grades three to six, he was bullied by the boys in his classes. Since then, he's learned to defend himself physically and verbally, but still carries the emotional pain. He's always defensive and feels like everyone is trying to disrespect him in some way.
DIN: Doesn't that ever get old?
MR. LIGHTMAN: What, "Din-Din?"
DIN: You've been calling me that for forever.
MR. LIGHTMAN: It *has* been a few years. I mean, I can get some new material if that's the problem.

Din feels like Mr. Lightman isn't taking him seriously.
EARL: Don't get him amped, Mr. Lightman.
VINCENT: That vein is gonna pop outta his forehead.
NADIA: He threw a chair at that girl today.
MR. LIGHTMAN: Okay, I won't call you "Din-Din." What happened today?
DIN: She started it. Mr. Carter even admitted that she started it. They always start with me. They all deserve what they get from me.
MR. LIGHTMAN: It's okay to get angry sometimes. But why do you always have to take it so far? Throwing chairs?
DIN: I hate when people say that! How come it's my fault how far I take it? If I was innocent, and didn't bother anyone, then some idiot does something to me, and I do something to them worse than what they did to me, how am I the bad guy? Because I did something worse? No, they're wrong, because I wouldn't have done something worse if they didn't do something in the first place.
Mr. Lightman nods his head in agreement.

MR. LIGHTMAN: Okay. Okay.

VINCENT: That awkward moment when you realize he has a good point, but you don't wanna tell him.

EARL: And all you can say is "okay, okay."

BINDIA: That awkward moment when you guys shut up with that!

VINCENT: No. That wouldn't be awkward.

SCOOTER: Not at all.

EARL: Yeah, you can't do it. Stop tryin'.

Bindia grunts. Mr. Lightman continues talking to Din.

MR. LIGHTMAN: But revenge doesn't get you anywhere. You just get yourself in trouble all the time.

DIN: She deserved it. Everyone deserves what they get from me. They made me like this.

MR. LIGHTMAN: Come on. *No one can make you anything.* You're only hurting yourself.

DIN: It doesn't hurt me to see someone who hurt me get hurt back.

MR. LIGHTMAN: Oh, you angry wittle man.

Din begins to breathe faster.

DIN: Wittle man? Who do you think you are? A big man?

MR. LIGHTMAN: Well, you —

DIN: Shut up!

VINCENT: When trying to be the funny teacher goes wrong.

MR. LIGHTMAN: Vincent, you'll have Din joining you in detention tomorrow. That's detention for you again tomorrow, Din. You want the rest of the week?

VINCENT: How can the detention teacher give detention anyway?

DIN: I don't care. You're a loser with no life. You just make corny jokes all day so that kids think you're the "cool teacher."

VINCENT: (Fake coughing) Hashtag #KindaTrue.

EARL: (Fake coughing) Def! Def! Definitely true! Definitely! (Clears throat) Allergies.

DIN: But you're not cool. You're an epic failure! That's why you never got promoted to anything better in all these years. And your clothes are old and cheap.

They're all silent, tense, and uncomfortable. Din breathes faster and harder.

MR. LIGHTMAN: You know, ever since they raised the price of that gum to 35 cents, I never brought one. And I see it all the time in the checkout line, but never pick it up. The thing is, I used to get it all the time for my girlfriend. I don't chew gum myself. But I used to buy it very often. Now, I just don't.

Earl, Scooter and Vincent snicker as they look at Din. His face gets red and he starts to boil.

MR. LIGHTMAN: And — and it's not the price, y'know. It's not. I mean, I can spare another ten cents. What's another ten cents? It's just a weird thing I realized. And, you know what? I'm not gonna start buying it again. I'm not. There you go. That's a life choice I made today, and, uh, I — I feel accomplished.

Vincent, Scooter and Earl snicker and burst out laughing.

DIN: That was not funny! You guys should be ashamed for laughing at that! You're not funny! You're all failures, and all of you will get what you deserve from me!

MR. LIGHTMAN: Din, come on. Okay. You're right. I *am* a failure. Okay? You're right.

SCOOTER: Failure?

Scooter's family is from Bolivia. He's the first to be born in the United States. He's twelve, wears glasses, and is considered to be a nerd by most. He's obsessed with finding information on many different subjects. He reads, watches videos, and does tons of research on whatever catches his attention. His parents are wealthy. He's always looking for business ideas, connections and strategies to impress his father. His parents are liberal democrats. Scooter is socially liberal, but to his parent's bewilderment, very conservative when it comes to finances.

SCOOTER: My Dad says you've been a professor at colleges, and you're a millionaire.

EARL: Say what now?

Mr. Lightman shakes his head. He's never mentioned that to any of these students.

SCOOTER: And you donate a whole lotta money to this school district. I think you're gonna regret giving so much of it away. You're like my father. I try to tell him. See, the way the economy is going —

MR. LIGHTMAN: Scooter.

SCOOTER: Huh?

MR. LIGHTMAN: Shut up.

SCOOTER: 'Kay.

VINCENT: Millionaire? Everybody makes fun of how poor you are.

EARL: Can't do it no more. (Pointing to Nadia) Bossip girl over here is gonna make sure the whole school know you ballin' by the end of the day. The end of tomorrow … day.

VINCENT: If you continue to dress like that, nobody's gonna believe you're a millionaire. You want that, though, right? You don't want us to tell anybody? I don't mind keepin' it a secret. The "Lightman so broke" jokes are funny as hell.

EARL: Plus, remember, nobody cares about the truth if the lie is more entertaining.

VINCENT: You people and these fake-deep Facebook quotes.

EARL: It's not a Facebook quote. It's a quote from a great wise man.

NADIA: He's not wise. He's a perverted and lawless man!

BINDIA: Are you really a College Professor?

SCOOTER: You've taught all over the country, right?

MR. LIGHTMAN: I have. I choose to stay here now because I love this community. I guess that makes me a failure. Oh … an epic failure. That's a higher grade of failure, I guess. At least I have that.

DIN: Not … funny!

Din stands up, picks up a chair, and prepares to throw it.

DIN: Is that funny?! Is anyone laughing?!

VINCENT: Din, no!

EARL: Chill out!

Mr. Lightman picks up his own chair and gets in position to throw it.

MR. LIGHTMAN: You wanna throw down?! Let's do this, bro!

The others laugh. Din cracks a smile, but tries to hide it and play it off. He puts the chair down, sits down and folds his arms.

Mr. Lightman puts his chair down and takes a seat, mumbling to himself.

MR. LIGHTMAN: Wanna throw chairs? I can throw chairs.

The others keep laughing, Nadia the loudest.

NADIA: I'm dyin'!

MR. LIGHTMAN: Throw a chair at me? (In Southern accent)
Ain't *nobody* got time f'dat!

Nadia SCREAMS in laughter!

NADIA: Stop! I can't with you, Mr. Lightman! I just can't! Oh, my goodness!

MR. LIGHTMAN: Alright, stop laughing. If someone passes by the door, they'll see I'm not qualified to do this detention thing.

VINCENT: You're not really a millionaire, are you?

SCOOTER: Yep.

EARL: You don't act all millionaire-ey.

MR. LIGHTMAN: Scooter, why are you in detention?

SCOOTER: For no reason.

Mr. Lightman pounds his desk.

MR. LIGHTMAN: Oh, the injustice!

SCOOTER: Mr. Simmons sent me here just because I said that a lot of poor people are just lazy. And I shouldn't have to pay so much in taxes. People shouldn't have to share the money they work hard for just to help people who don't wanna do it for themselves. It's not fair. What's the point of working so hard and making money if you have to give it away to lazy people? That's class warfare.

MR. LIGHTMAN: You told him that?

SCOOTER: Yeah.

MR. LIGHTMAN: Well, that's an opinion. You shouldn't be in detention for that.

SCOOTER: Thank you! Can I go?

NADIA: Nuh-uh! That's not the reason he's here, Mr. Lightman! He called *me* lazy, and poor, and ugly. That's why Mr. Simmons sent him here.

SCOOTER: I didn't call you ugly. Seth did.

Nadia is insecure about the way she looks. She's always wanted to be skinny and light-skinned, with a thinner nose. Every morning, she stares at her reflection in the bathroom mirror and drowns herself in deep emotional pain over what she sees as an ugly face.

EARL: Aye, Scooter, you better watch what you say about my sister.

SCOOTER: Or what?

EARL: I don't know 'cause you my boy. But I don't wanna have to pop off on you, bruh. Don't call her names again.

NADIA: Yeah. I am not lazy! And I am not poor!

EARL: Nah, we poor.

NADIA: We are, right?

EARL: Stop playing, girl, you know we broke! You could admit to that one. I ain't ashamed of our struggle.

NADIA: Well, I'm not lazy.

MR. LIGHTMAN: Or ugly.

NADIA: Uh, no. I can admit that one, too. I am ugly.

MR. LIGHTMAN: You're not ugly.

NADIA: You don't have to be nice and say that.

MR. LIGHTMAN: You're beautiful.

NADIA: Stop it. Why do people do that to me like I'm an idiot? Don't give me that, "Oh, we're all beautiful" nonsense. Or, "Let's all accept our bodies and appearance the way they are." Everybody who says that is already good-looking. Or they're lying to themselves. And plus, people —

VINCENT: And plus.

Nadia looks at Vincent up and down. She gives him the side-eye, then slowly turns back to face Mr. Lightman.

NADIA: People who look good are always trying really hard to look way better than they already do. So, what does that say about me. What does that say about how they really feel about me? Huh? Can't answer that one, huh?

MR. LIGHTMAN: What do *you* say about you? That's what matters.

She rolls her eyes.

NADIA: I say I'm ugly as dirt and that won't ever change. Go online and see what boys say is ugly. I know what good-looking is, and I know what ugly is. There is such a thing as ugly, and I am ugly. My nose is too flat and wide. My (her voice cracks) skin is way too black. And I'm fat. Look at my face. Everything is all … (swallows) lumpy and out of place.

She laughs nervously.

MR. LIGHTMAN: You are beautiful …

NADIA: "Beautiful In your own way?" Is that what you're gonna say? That means, "You're hideous, but I can't say it because I don't wanna hurt your feelings. So, you're beautiful *in your own way*."

MR. LIGHTMAN: Nadia! Why do you think that? Where'd you get all that from?

NADIA: The mirror.

The others laugh. Mr. Lightman shakes his head, sighs, then closes his eyes.

NADIA: What?

MR. LIGHTMAN: (Takes a deep breath) Nothing.

The others talk among themselves for a few minutes.

Mr. Lightman closes his eyes and focuses his attention between his eyebrows. He sees his Golden Inner Etheric Light flowing in his frontal lobe. As he breathes, the inner light forms various patterns as it flows in and around his head. Most of the vision of the inner light is blocked out because of the light in the classroom. There are blue and red seeds or filaments within the white and gold light. He breathes and moves his awareness from right to left, left to right within the space between his eyebrows. He feels a strong gathering of Primal Substance in his frontal lobe. He feels movement and slight pressure in other portions of his brain, in the back of his head, his nostrils, around his mouth, ears, cheekbones, chin, thyroid, collar bone, underarms, and in the center of his chest. He breathes in the light slowly. He feels the energetic harmony in the very center of his brain. This creates greater neurological synergy in both brain hemispheres. Although these actions are done in such a casual setting, this moment is anything but casual for Mr. Lightman. He has a feeling of providence, a "This Is It" moment. He has no idea what "it" is, but he feels the presence of The Creator. He let's go of his doubts and fears. He trusts himself and surrenders himself to the flow of the Infinite.

MR. LIGHTMAN: (Whispering to himself) How do I help them?

The children continue talking among themselves for a few minutes.

MR. LIGHTMAN: Well, I learned something today. You children have taught me something for sure.

NADIA: Really? What?

MR. LIGHTMAN: You all ... are beyond messed up! Goll-y! A bunch of mental cases!

They all laugh except Din. Nadia laughs with great joy and shakes her head.

MR. LIGHTMAN: Wait. I can get in trouble for saying that, right?

VINCENT: Definitely. I won't tell if you take my detention away.

Mr. Lightman looks at Kareem sitting at the back of the classroom. He's thirteen years old, new to the school. He's Muslim. He just moved to America from Egypt. He doesn't feel like he can fit in with the others. He has a middle-eastern accent and speaks pretty good English, even though Arabic is his first language. He's usually very nervous and shaky in new places and around new people. He stutters a lot and mumbles his words.

MR. LIGHTMAN: What's your name?

He's alarmed that everyone's attention is now on him.

KAREEM: Kareem.

MR. LIGHTMAN: And why are you here?

He fumbles with his glasses, rubbing around the lens.

KAREEM: Um. No problem. Just ... I'm here ...

MR. LIGHTMAN: You're here for nothing? What did you do?

KAREEM: Waiting. Yes.

He clears his throat a few times. His heart beats quickly and his muscles tense up. He feels a rush of anxiety swarming through his body.

KAREEM: I am waiting for …

He swallows and tries to talk again, but his mouth is dry. He gets up and walks towards the door.

KAREEM: I'm so sorry.

MR. LIGHTMAN: You can't leave. This is detention.

EARL: He don't belong here. He just scared of Marlon and his goons. They said they was gonna jump him after school.

MR. LIGHTMAN: Are you hiding ... in detention? Did someone threaten you? Come on.

Mr. Lightman takes Kareem outside and closes the door.

KAREEM: What am I doing here? This place is so frightening. How can I make it through the rest of the school year like this? What's the point? So much of the day, I worry about what they will do to me. That's why my parents bring me to America?

MR. LIGHTMAN: So, who exactly is bothering you? Marlon?

KAREEM: It's plenty more than that. They say bad things about Islam and my family. They think that I'm a bad guy because I'm Muslim. I don't know if they are waiting for me outside to beat me up. He said so. I don't know.

MR. LIGHTMAN: You can't live in fear like this.

KAREEM: I'm weary. I can't change that. It's been this way the whole time.

MR. LIGHTMAN: Do your parents know about this?

KAREEM: Yes. No.

MR. LIGHTMAN: They have to know what's going on. Would you like me to set up an appointment with them and the principal?

KAREEM: Will you be there?

MR. LIGHTMAN: No, the principle is gonna speak to them. Or maybe one of your teachers can be there.

KAREEM: The teachers just do nothing. I ask for them to stop it and they just let it happen. They let them bother me all the time. It does not stop. If you are going to be there, you can speak to my parents, please?

MR. LIGHTMAN: Oh. Uh, yeah. I can be there. I'm not Muslim, but I am from Egypt. It was a little tough for me also when I came here as a child.

KAREEM: I'm from Egypt, too!

He smiles.

MR. LIGHTMAN: Really? See? Already you're not alone.

Mr. Lightman pats him on the shoulder.

MR. LIGHTMAN: Are you gonna go home?

KAREEM: Can I wait a little longer?

MR. LIGHTMAN: Okay. I'll walk you out after detention.

KAREEM: Thank you very much.

Kareem feels a warm rush flow through him.

MR. LIGHTMAN: This is gonna stop.

Just then, a drip of water comes through the ceiling. Mr. Lightman looks up and sees a piece of rusty metal protruding through the ceiling tile.

MR. LIGHTMAN: That's not good.

KAREEM: What?

MR. LIGHTMAN: I hope that's not toilet water. No, it's a fountain.

KAREEM: There are a lot like that all around the school.

MR. LIGHTMAN: We've been having budget problems. Seems like all the money is going somewhere other than where it needs to go. Anyway, what part of Egypt are you from?

They continue talking and head back into the classroom. The others are having a conversation about how badly they want to live a different life. Mr. Lightman walks towards his desk.

SCOOTER: I wish I could leave this school.

MR. LIGHTMAN: Get a freakin' transfer.

EARL: I wish I never have to come to school.

MR. LIGHTMAN: Stay the hell home.

NADIA: I wish I could leave this country.

MR. LIGHTMAN: If I buy you the ticket, would you really go?

NADIA: There are too many good-looking girls here. I wanna go somewhere where everybody looks as bad as me. Or where I can look good. Some place where beauty doesn't matter so much. Yeah.

MR. LIGHTMAN: Oh, Nadia.

DIN: I wish I could leave this planet.

MR. LIGHTMAN: If only it was flat, I'd kick you off the edge.

DIN: What?

MR. LIGHTMAN: Where would you go if you left the planet?

DIN: To Earth 5.0.

MR. LIGHTMAN: What's that? An amusement park?

DIN: It's another planet.

MR. LIGHTMAN: Oh.

DIN: Everybody there is always happy. You can create the world any way you want.

MR. LIGHTMAN: You have that here already.

SCOOTER: No, we don't. Earth 5.0 is where real happiness is.

EARL: Yeah, it's ⌊it! You never have to work hard and do boring stuff if you don't want to on Earth 5.0.

NADIA: And everyone looks how they want to look. Everybody is beautiful.

SCOOTER: If you can really get anything you want there, I want everyone to make their own money. And there won't be any poor people to sponge off of me. No class warfare on Earth 5.0.

VINCENT: And on Earth 5.0, everyone would recognize me to be as great as I am. I'd get respect there. I'd be a boss! A king or something.

Mr. Lightman nods his head.

MR. LIGHTMAN: And how do you get to this planet?

DIN: I don't know. It's hidden somewhere in the solar system.

SCOOTER: No, it's in another universe or dimension or something.

MR. LIGHTMAN: Where do you guys come up with this stuff? On the Google? The Facetube or pecker?

BINDIA: Pecker?

MR. LIGHTMAN: What's the bird one?

EARL: Twitter?

DIN: Uh!

EARL: Oh-mi-Lrrd!

BINDIA: Okay. Yeah, Din is right. Your jokes are not funny. You know rightfully well it's not pecker, Mr. Lightman!

Mr. Lightman leans towards Bindia.

MR. LIGHTMAN: You, my friend, need to learn how to enjoy life. You need to laugh more — maybe even at corny things. All of you need to lighten up a little. This is the planet you're on now. You might be here for another eighty or ninety years. Might as well change the way you think and feel about other people, and about the world. And about yourselves more than anything.

EARL: Preach!

MR. LIGHTMAN: I'm not kidding. You guys need a good wake-up call. I just wish you guys, for one day, could see reality more as it is, without so much of the veil over your eyes.

BINDIA: I see reality like it is — hell.

MR. LIGHTMAN: Okay. I see the hell, too. But it's not the only channel *you* can tune into. You, Bindia, I mean. If you wanted to, you can choose to

19

tune into a different channel.

VINCENT: This guy watches way too much TV.

MR. LIGHTMAN: You can choose to view the world differently. Look inside of yourself.

Vincent smiles and shakes his head.

VINCENT: Oh, here we go. What does that mean? How can you … I hate when people talk like that. That's not a real thing to tell somebody who's going through hell.

MR. LIGHTMAN: I'm speaking of those of us who have a reasonably comfortable life where we have food, water, comfort, entertainment, books … access to the internet. It is literally possible to at least find what we call heaven. For some, it may be possible to search inside and live a heavenly life in this lifetime. Even without all of those comforts, it's possible. I know there are many other things that matter, like family life, personal stuff, your childhood, your upbringing, struggling financially.

Vincent points to Mr. Lightman.

VINCENT: That's what I was gonna say.

SCOOTER: What do you mean by "literally" find heaven? Literally?

MR. LIGHTMAN: That's not my point.

SCOOTER: But it was the most interesting thing you said. People say literally a lot for things that are not literal. You mean that it is literally possible for a person who is living now on Earth to find … heaven … the Kingdom of God that Jesus said? Literally? Like, really literally, though?

VINCENT: (Valley girl accent) Like, literallaaayyyy!

SCOOTER: Shut up.

EARL: What time is it?

VINCENT: Time for us to go.

Scooter looks at Mr. Lightman.

SCOOTER: No, wait, what were we talking about?

VINCENT: You gotta ask yourself, "If I forgot the subject that quickly, was it really that important?" Huh? Scooter? Was it?

SCOOTER: What were you saying? Oh, yeah. Can a human on Earth really see heaven for real life?

Mr. Lightman checks his phone for a while.

MR. LIGHTMAN: It is possible to experience what we call heaven.

SCOOTER: No, like, the real heaven. Have you been there? Or researched it? Do you really know it's there for sure?

VINCENT: Why the hell would he know that?

MR. LIGHTMAN: It's a little too deep to explain. But to keep it simple, I'll say that I know the heavenly state of mind.

SCOOTER: So, heaven is real.

Vincent opens his arms wide.

VINCENT: What?! Did you have to say that?! Do you have to be that gullible?! And you with, "I know the heavenly state of mind." All that ANNOYING love and light crap! The most annoying people on the internet. (Mocking) "That's deep." "Sending positive energy!" "I'm – I'm sending love and light!" "Everything happens for a reason." How 'bout that one? Are you on your *path*?! On your – on your spiritual *journey*? (Belittling) "Journey." If heaven was real, it would've been proven by actual science by now. How can all these Scientists miss something so big?

SCOOTER: I think that's true, though. By now, somebody would've found something. I've seen stuff on The History Channel, and it's always ... vague stories and ... stuff they prove to be normal. Like later, they find out it's just a normal thing. Like regular stuff that just seemed all amazing and spiritual. But it always has a ...

SCOOTER & VINCENT: Logical explanation.

MR. LIGHTMAN: Are you saying that if it hasn't been proven by mainstream science, it doesn't exist?

SCOOTER: Hmm.

MR. LIGHTMAN: Why would I wait for someone to prove something that's already a part of me? Something that I know personally and experience directly?

SCOOTER: Hmm.

MR. LIGHTMAN: There is a world that is ... let's say ... inside of our minds — for simplicity. This state is actually beyond our minds. There's a world inside of us that reveal much, much more about reality than the physical world you see with your physical eyes.

VINCENT: Here we go.

MR. LIGHTMAN: You would open up a whole new way of experiencing life if you were able to personally explore and experience more of the actual details of these worlds.

Mr. Lightman feels a sudden rush of emotion. His feelings shine through his eyes. He laughs it off as his feelings drift back and forth between love and fear for the future of his students and their generation. This sudden rush of emotion is unusual for him. He's long mastered the ability to rise above emotional attachment in these situations, but something is different now.

The unusual rush of emotion causes certain imbalances in his hormones. This tightens up many channels in his body and clouds his judgment as a Public School Teacher. It opens him up to being a Teacher of Light. He taps the center of his chest with his index finger, closes his eyes, takes a deep breath in, then out.

MR. LIGHTMAN: The great amazing life you all want to live is so close and in your face, that it's laughable that you can even miss it. It's laughable until I see that you missing it is *the* worst thing in the world. You're ignorant of your true selves.

He clears his throat and swallows.

MR. LIGHTMAN: I'm sorry. I don't mean just you guys. It's all of us — people. I have fun hanging out with you guys. I just wish you could see through these illusions of petty worries.

VINCENT: It's not that serious, dude.

MR. LIGHTMAN: It is for me. I take in the love and laughter I share with you guys. I do it with my friends and family. It's spiritual fuel — Vital Energy from laughing and interacting with people. I love how you guys feel free to joke around and take shots at me. That laughter is our energy, God's energy, loving energy. Sitting here and laughing with you guys is as "spiritual" an experience as meditating, or praying, or anything else that allows me to feel that direct connection to my Source.

NADIA: Jesus said that love is the answer.

Vincent scowls.

VINCENT: Dude ... this is detention. We don't need to be hearing all that right now. Plus I didn't give you permission to take my love. What if I need it?

Mr. Lightman chuckles. He wants to stop talking and change the subject, but the thick waves of emotional substance magnetically swirl around his heart He takes a few deep breaths and is able to quickly balance his conscious mind. He's able to reach this state with ease due to his morning meditation. In this morning's meditation, he was able to quiet his conscious mind enough and experience a few minutes of direct soul awareness. Now, the deep breaths allow him to easily center his mind and relax his body. His rational mind is wise and sharp. He knows that he shouldn't be talking to the children about spiritual and religious matters at all, but he goes on.

MR. LIGHTMAN: I take love into my heart everywhere I go. Even when things don't go the way I plan, I've trained myself to spot the lessons they present. I live the love, and focus on the love way more than the fears and the stress. That makes it a lot easier to live in this world. When the state of love is your dominant feeling, it's easier to find solutions and think clearly to face the fears and the challenges. I wish you guys could see reality more as it is.

NADIA: That's what Jesus taught, though. Love.

MR. LIGHTMAN: He did, Nadia. But, you know ... that way of looking at things can seem a little too positive and unrealistic to most people. But Jesus was right. Even with all the nasty and disgusting stuff we have to deal with in this world, heaven is absolutely *available* here and now ... for everyone in this room. Everyone has it within them to reach that state of mind. Unfortunately, most people don't because they're forced to live in survival mode for most of their lives. We live in a world that is designed to keep us in survival mode. But the Kingdom is within your mind, heart and body – literally. Literally, Scooter. It's been there the whole time. It's up to us as individuals to tune ourselves to that channel. That means facing our fears, facing ourselves, and realistically working through it all to get past everything that blocks the state of mind that they've called heaven.

SCOOTER: That sounds profound.

VINCENT: But it's not. It's fake-deep — Facebook-deep.

MR. LIGHTMAN: It means working through and getting past the judgment, blame, and negativity towards yourselves and towards other people. If you can really — I mean really do that, and live it for even one day, you'd be able to truly free yourself from the worries that make you want to leave the planet.

They're all silent. He looks at them one-by-one. He feels an emotional burning in his heart.

VINCENT: What the hell are you talking about?!

Mr. Lightman laughs.

SCOOTER: How do you do that? Like, with your mind? I mean how do you, like, really be like that – peaceful and stuff — for real life?

MR. LIGHTMAN: You have to come to know yourself in a way that's way deeper than you do now. Get to know your Source.

Scooter sighs and Vincent shakes his head.

SCOOTER: Oh, come on! What does that really mean, though? Like, how? Like, for real.

VINCENT: This guy wants specifics.

SCOOTER: If you really know it, say it like it is.

Mr. Lightman feels the unusual emotional tug calling him to be a Teacher

Of Light to these students, regardless of the potential consequences as a Public School Teacher. He struggles with this, knowing that as a teacher, he would be stepping way over the line by telling them his deeper metaphysical knowledge. He lets go. He surrenders to his intuition and to his greater purpose in life. He feels a strong connection to The Creator. He lets go of all the blockages of thoughts and feelings. He's comfortable and free. He just speaks.

MR. LIGHTMAN: The Source of Creation is what we all are at our Core. The deepest essence of it can be consciously experienced through silence. It can be felt emotionally through good feelings, through excitement, through genuine happiness. To tune into it better, you can consciously choose to express strong and continuous love out to the world, and choose to receive love continuously from the world. Just try it for a while. No need to be a saint. Or expect others to be. Do it as much as you can, day after day, week after week, until it becomes your dominant, default feeling. Specifically match your reactions, your thoughts and behaviors to love, and humility, and to being less judgmental of others. The things you think, the way you feel, the things you say, the things you do, the way you treat others, the way you respond to negative situations and people, the way you deal with tough issues, can all be slowly transformed to make your experience in this world much, much more heavenly — even when you seem to be in what you call "hell." That is how you learn to think and act from your Source.

KAREEM: Whoa.

SCOOTER: Okay, that sounded better.

BINDIA: No, it doesn't! That's only for really delusional people. No one can really be that way. All that positive-thinking stuff is for people with serious mental disorders.

EARL: I know, right. And what is the Source? You think and act from a magazine?

MR. LIGHTMAN: The Source of creation, what many people call God. It is The Creator of everything we know.

   Vincent holds his heart and pretends to cry.

VINCENT: Oh, God! Okay then. Which god? Huh?

MR. LIGHTMAN: The God that is love. It's really beyond description.

NADIA: Jehovah.

KAREEM: (Whispers) Allah.

DIN: My grand dad said that the Tao is beyond description.

MR. LIGHTMAN: Jehovah, Allah, Tao for Din, Brahma for Bindia. A writer

named Napoleon Hill calls it Infinite Intelligence.
SCOOTER: Oh!
EARL: Who dat?
SCOOTER: My dad made me read his book, *Think and Grow Rich*. It did talk
a *lot* about your mind and spiritual-ly stuff. I remember infinite
intelligence.
MR. LIGHTMAN: It's been called The Divine Mind, The Almighty, The
Heavenly Father, The Divine Mother, The Architect, The Force, Nature,
The One, The Prime Creator, Spirit, God. It is the intelligence which
created All That Is. I don't get stressed out about what anyone says you
have to call it. All of the names have power. I can respect everyone's
beliefs. Sometimes I call God whatever the people around me call God. A
great man once said, "You can't get physically wet from the word 'water'."
Y'know? The word "fire" can't burn you.
EARL: Nah, words matter. This dude named "Rob" jacked somebody for
their iPhone last week. Got caught lackin' and Rob robbed him.
VINCENT: (Laughing) You put that on Facebook last week!
EARL: You saw it on my timeline?
VINCENT: Yeah.
EARL: And you laughed. You liked it?
VINCENT: Yeah. Why?
EARL: You didn't like it.
VINCENT: I did.
EARL: You didn't. You always do that.
VINCENT: I just told you, I did.
EAR: You didn't like it, like it.
VINCENT: Bro, don't ever say "Like it, like it" to me. Like it, like it. What is
this, third grade?
EARL: You didn't press "Like."
VINCENT: I don't have to press like to know I like it. I know I like it.
Everybody else doesn't have to know I like it.
EARL: I see right through you, dawg. You just didn't want people to see that
you liked the joke. You are petty. You don't *ever* want to give anybody else
no shine.
Mr. Lightman raises his index finger, about to speak.
EARL: "Any" shine! Happy?
MR. LIGHTMAN: De-lighted!
VINCENT: Okay, I'm gonna "Like" it. It's not that serious!

25

SCOOTER: You don't like anyone else's stuff.

EARL: You notice that, too, right?! I don't want your fake "Like" now. You suddenly wanna "Like" it after I hater-shamed you?

NADIA: (Bursts out laughing) Hater shamed!

Mr. Lightman laughs and shakes his head.

VINCENT: (Holding his chest) I liked it on the inside. And it's what's inside that matters. Right, Mr. Lightman?

SCOOTER: Come on! What were you talking about, Mr. Lightman?

KAREEM: Hater sha — I mean about names do matter.

NADIA: (Cracking up) Hater shamed him!

After the laugher and commotion dies down, Scooter and Kareem convince Mr. Lightman to continue talking. He takes a few deep breaths and mentally centers himself.

MR. LIGHTMAN: As I said, the names do matter — a lot. But the Source goes way beyond names and descriptions.

VINCENT: Whoa, wait. You're Hindu, right?

MR. LIGHTMAN: No, but I was raised Hindu and Muslim. My parents were of different religions. As a teenager, I rejected both until I saw things clearly for myself.

VINCENT: So, when you saw things clearly, you went back to Islam?

MR. LIGHTMAN: No.

VINCENT: So, you're Christian now?

MR. LIGHTMAN: Nope.

NADIA: So, you're just spiritual.

MR. LIGHTMAN: I hear people say that one a lot these days. Uh, yeah. I'm spiritual.

NADIA: You don't sound too sure about that one either.

Mr. Lightman takes a deep breath and centers himself.

MR. LIGHTMAN: Well, no, I am. It just feels kind of weird to say that, "I *am* spiritual." Like it's something I'm practicing or trying to be. I've come to *know myself* as a spirit as much as I am a body and a mind. It's a good thing to practice spirituality. Or to research and know *about* it, and talk about it. It's a whole other thing to directly *realize* your Self as spirit in your mind, in your feelings, in your body, your organs and bones. Not as a metaphor or some school of thought, or — or some wise, beautiful saying that makes you feel spiritual for a while. I mean to really come to *know* that at the tiniest and largest levels of existence, you are literally one with all of Creation. Without the need of anyone or anything outside of yourself to

validate it for you. That is what the greatest spiritual teachers taught. I'm
not a Christian, or a Buddhist, but Jesus and Buddha taught that the deepest
and highest ... thing that we're looking for as humans – the Kingdom of
God, enlightenment, salvation, nirvana, whatever — is inside of us. I'm
sure they saw things around them just as bad as you see them now. But they
worked very, very diligently at changing their way of viewing the world.
They expanded their minds to see and know a lot more. They faced many
challenges and a lot of stress and ugliness in their lives. Some people make
them out to be these all-knowing men who had no fears or doubts. Quite the
opposite. They saw some of the most horrific things ever happening around
them every day. And they still, day-after-day, were able to realign their
minds and bodies just enough to see beauty and light in this dark world.
These men spent hours, days, years in stillness and silence in order to
explore themselves within and reach the levels of awareness they did.
VINCENT: : (Shaking his head, Belittling) "Within." Don't ever say
"within" to me. "Within."
MR. LIGHTMAN: They opened their eyes and came to know heaven within
themselves. Jesus was able to see that true happiness, heaven, is in our
midst — right here all around us. That had to sound so idiotic to the real
people who were experiencing a daily hell. He saw the hell also, but by
looking within and really opening his eyes, he was able to see the essence,
the Source underneath the stress and ugliness of the world. That Source
essence somehow matches up with feelings and acts of compassion and
love. Jesus and The Buddha worked hard to become what is called "God-
realized" men. That's what I wish for you guys to experience sometime in
your life. From that state of mind, major problems and things that stress
you out a lot can be dealt with in much easier and unexpected ways. You'll
see options, choices and solutions that you ignored before, or were too
afraid to try. Your view of yourself and the world changes so much that
many of the things you consider to be big problems disappear. And you
laugh at yourself for haven taken them so seriously in the first place.
SCOOTER: That's really profound, Mr. Lightman.
NADIA: But how are you a spirit? That sounds scary.
MR. LIGHTMAN: Well, we're all spirits. We're also minds. And on the
outside, we are physical bodies.
MR. LIGHTMAN: You do believe that you have a spirit, right?
NADIA: Yes.
MR. LIGHTMAN: Well, you don't just *have* a spirit. You *are* a spirit. You

27

have a human personality. You are a spirit before you are a body or a personality. We use separate physical bodies and different unique personalities. Those things make it seem like we're separate from each other. But behind all theories and philosophies, and interpretations of this and that, everything we see and know is one infinite and intelligent system. We are one spirit that has multiplied itself into many individual, seemingly separate spirits. If you've been taught to have a scary relationship with the word "spirit," and with spiritual things, then I guess it can seem scary. But I am That. I am one single point of attention for the universe. My parents did it, and the physical seed and egg did their thing.

NADIA: Ew?!

MR. LIGHTMAN: Now I am experiencing myself as a physical human being on Earth. I existed before coming into this body. We all did. But no matter how solid our bodies are, or how different we are in our personality, skin color or culture, we never stop being the original substance — the essence of The Source. We forget that we are spirit when we live a life that is overly focused on the physical world outside. We don't get to know the kingdom inside well enough. The Creator's essence binds all of our layers together with neatness, purpose, and intelligence. That essence is everything. It is all material objects. It is the empty space in between all material objects. It's the atoms, molecules, elements and minerals that make up our bodies. It organizes the mind and the geography of the brain and allows us to experience thoughts and feelings and all kinds of stimuli. We all have our own mental device to manage and experience the world however we choose to. I've learned to choose peace, kindness, and love most of the time. I was given a chance to find that. And I took advantage of that chance.

SCOOTER: How did you get the chance?

MR. LIGHTMAN: As poor as my family was, I had a great luxury — quiet time. I had time to daydream and contemplate about what I am and what this world is. Not everyone has that chance. But most of *us* do. I had a very, very rough start in life. When I got to the point where I had food, water, clothes, and a few moments a day of free time, I went in to seek knowledge of God. I didn't know that that's what I was doing at the time. I just wanted to know what I was and what was really going on. I knew there was more. I knew it was a lot deeper than … just what they told me in school and at religious services. I've been guided. And now I've spent years evolving consciously, balancing myself, and refining my understanding and my behaviors more and more. |

VINCENT: You're giving me a headache.

SCOOTER: How do you deal with the bad stuff, though?

MR. LIGHTMAN: You face it head-on. One main benefit of getting to know your Source is being able to face your challenges and life's ugliness with a balanced mind. At least as balanced as you can be. Don't hide from your emotions and your problems. Challenges will always be there. Face them. If you have to cry, cry. Bawl if you have to. When faced with a major issue, think first. Write ideas down if you have to before you approach it. If you have to have a difficult conversation with someone in order to solve a problem, do it. It might be awkward or uncomfortable, especially with people you've had a lot of difficulty with. See your own faults. Don't expect yourself or them to make things perfect, but do what can be done and say what can be said in order to resolve the issues as much as possible and free yourself. Then, you breathe a sigh of relief and move on with your life.

EARL: That's real.

MR. LIGHTMAN: And this is why, when you have a chance to have a good day, or to focus more on the positive, do it. The challenges will always pop up. *Focus on the negative head-on when you absolutely have to. Do not focus on the negative when you don't have to.* We do that *a lot.*

NADIA: Everyone does.

SCOOTER: Yep.

MR. LIGHTMAN: As you evolve spiritually, or if you quickly shift your point of view, many of the things you see as problems won't be problems anymore. At the very advanced levels of spiritual awakening, the idea of a problem is nonexistent.

SCOOTER: That's where I want to be.

MR. LIGHTMAN: I see the fear and negativity all around me. I face my challenges. I see that I always have an option to put my focus where I want to. I've been shown the kingdom, along with freedom of choice, so I just keep choosing to focus on the things that evolve me. Even the really difficult challenges aren't nearly as stressful as they were when I didn't know myself as well as I do now. A more peaceful state of mind is just one of the many gifts you get from exploring your inner Self and seeking what we call God, instead of only reading, debating, studying, and talking *about* God.

Kareem sits at the edge of his seat, fascinated.

SCOOTER: That is epic! All of that!

NADIA: But which god?

SCOOTER: Yeah!

MR. LIGHTMAN: Oh. I can tell you that. The one that ... The one that says to love each other. End of story.

SCOOTER: How's that the end?! That's not an answer!

EARL: Yeah! Don't all our gods say to love each ... Oh, I got you.

MR. LIGHTMAN: Exactly. There is One God. A better way of saying that is that there is only God. God is infinite. It has been interpreted and experienced in many ways by the people on this planet.

SCOOTER: Infinite.

MR. LIGHTMAN: Like I said, there's not much of a need to get into debates about the different names, and religious belief systems, and rules, and ways of doing things. For me, it's more about the way you interact with other people and with the natural world. Now, as I said, the names that we call God are *extremely powerful*, and they *do* matter. "Brahman," "Jehovah," and "Allah" are words that can carry a tremendous amount of power. But beyond all the names and descriptions, and interpretations of this and that, there is the original essence. It's an unnamed, un-interpreted, indefinable infinite intelligence which exists as all of us and everything we can ever know. We can come to know It in ourselves if we sincerely sought it out. All of the words, scientific theories, religious beliefs, rules, and explanations are built *around* It, they talk *about* It, trying their best to point *to* It. But You *Are* It. You *are* That. No religion, no new-age belief, scientific theory, no expert, scholar, no spiritual guru can give you That. It is you. They may help you to find it in yourself, but you are it already, and you can come to know it consciously within you. Like one of my greatest teachers, Alan Watts, says: "Anyone who tries to tell you that you can only find God through their interpretation is someone you should be cautious of." For someone to tell you that you need them or their organization to know God, "It's like picking your pockets and then trying to selling you your own watch."

They laugh.

SCOOTER: Because it's already yours.

VINCENT: Yes, Scooter, yes. That's the joke. A bad joke. Should be "your own cell phone." No one wears watches anymore.

MR. LIGHTMAN: The holy books, the religions, theories and beliefs systems are methods, systems and guides designed to help us to know God and know ourselves. If you truly and continuously live by the central messages of love and wisdom taught in your holy books, you can reach God-realization. Jesus personally knew the original essence. He knew that, on a metaphysical level, his mind was of the same stuff as the physical world outside.

SCOOTER: Metaphysical?

MR. LIGHTMAN: Google it. It relates to existence beyond the physical world.

SCOOTER: Wait, go back to Jesus.

VINCENT: Or don't.

MR. LIGHTMAN: Well I was saying that Jesus came to really know the original essence within himself and the physical world. He knew that, on the deeper level of existence, his mind was the same stuff as the physical world. That's how he was able to heal people by actually communicating with the atoms, minerals and cells in their physical bodies. On the level of the original essence, his intention and their faith made it possible for them to be healed.

NADIA: Yeah, "Their faith healed them," he said.

MR. LIGHTMAN: It did. He explained most things through stories and through religious and philosophical teachings. He didn't explain the exact quantum physics which shows that our minds and the material world are inseparable. He knew it, but he could only explain what would be understood by the people who lived at that time. I know you guys are learning about quantum physics, right?

SCOOTER: Yeah, that stuff is crazy!

NADIA: It's weird.

SCOOTER: It's there, but not there, and it is, but isn't at the same time. Backwards time and parallel universes.

EARL: I tune out as soon as Mr. Hughley says "quantum" anything.

MR. LIGHTMAN: It is a mind-twister. But it's very different when you come to know what it means personally for *your* mind and body.

NADIA: So, it has to do with God?

MR. LIGHTMAN: Well, of course. But that depends on how you view it. It depends on who you ask. The modern merging of spiritual knowledge and scientific knowledge helps to explain the exact same thing Jesus was demonstrating and teaching in his time. Quantum physics is now a part of mainstream science. They've given us a much wider point of view of what and who we are. Vision of the subatomic world allows us to see the ghost-like mysterious and magical stuff that creates our experience of reality.

31

This is often the point where many people get stuck because they are unable to go any further. Or they can make a huge leap forward to a much wider understanding of what reality is. Many people get stuck, though. Especially if they continue to believe that this entire process was caused accidentally ... by completely random events. Or with some accidentally-well-organized natural laws of physics doing their thing with no intelligence behind them. I mean, you'll get stuck if you're unable to open your mind and face the question of who or what created the atoms, the laws, or the original ... whatever that started the random process. For those who are interested in finding the Source of it all, you can admit that there's something unknown but obviously intelligent behind it all. Of course, that would result in a huge change in the way you see the world. That big of a change can sometimes be a painful road to go down, no matter what you believe. This stuff is too brilliantly organized to be the result of random accidents caused by other random accidents caused by other random accidents. Vincent, is your head hurting as yet?

VINCENT: No, Mr. Lightman, I'm doing fantastic! But you do say ... way too many words ... at once. Too many.

SCOOTER: And I'm understanding him. I feel smart.

EARL: Sound like you rappin' when you talk. You flowin'.

VINCENT: It's con-man 101. Confuse people.

DIN: It's not confusing to me.

KAREEM: Not to me either.

NADIA: Why are you the only one confused?

VINCENT: I'm not. I just know that that's what con-men do.

KAREEM: So, none of it is random, right?

MR. LIGHTMAN: From our limited human point of view, there is a whole lot of randomness. But this process is too intelligently put-together to have been created completely by random *accidents*. Wherever there is randomness, there is a higher level of intelligence that set the randomness into being. Subatomic particles behave like things we consider to be ... ghost-like. The subatomic world is an entire invisible world that we now know is right here, but was invisible to us before. Then there's the world of microscopic beings. Beings that were invisible to us before, but now we know they're right here. There is a high degree of intelligence in these worlds. Is it so crazy to think that there are other levels of our reality that are unknown? And that there are entire worlds and living beings that we don't see? We can use scientific tools to finally see deeper down into the microscopic world, into the subatomic particle world, and see farther out into outer space. I'm saying we can also use our knowledge, our minds and bodies to see the worlds within us and above us. It becomes clear that actual thoughts and behaviors of love, forgiveness, and compassion directly relate to the subatomic world, to the atoms and cells of our bodies, and to the solid matter of our world. When you make that connection ...

Mr. Lightman EXHALES SHARPLY as The Life-Force Energy known as Ka, Ruah, Chi, Kundalini, Holy Spirit, shoots up his spine, causing him to quickly straighten his back!

MR. LIGHTMAN: Uh!

NADIA: What? Are you okay?!

VINCENT: What the hell was that?! He had a seizure!

DIN: Shut up! I hate Vincent! You're not even listening!

MR. LIGHTMAN: I'm okay. What time is it?

SCOOTER: No time! Don't leave me stranded! I want to hear more!

VINCENT: (Peter Griffin Voice) Oh, my gawd! Who ... the hell ... cares?!

Din clenches his fists and breathes heavily, looking at Vincent.

KAREEM: You said that the religions and the science are guides. And they can guide us to the direct experience of God. Right?

MR. LIGHTMAN: So, you guys understood that.

SCOOTER: Yeah.

NADIA: I understood it.

DIN: Me, too.

Vincent yawns and shakes his head.

MR. LIGHTMAN: They can guide you towards knowing God. It also depends on the individual, their intention, their sincerity, and many other factors.

VINCENT: There's no connection or guide or none of that crap. Only you're making that connection in your mind. These new-agey fake Scientist-wannabes are psychos talking a lotta noise about things they don't understand. They're delusional. And the religious people are way more delusional with their invisible man in the sky who's always pissed off for some reason.

Nadia shakes her head at Vincent.

KAREEM: So, the … essence is God. And God is all things.

NADIA: The bible says that God is everywhere.

SCOOTER: I'm gonna check all this out. Makes God seem more real.

DIN: You have to really do it. Not just study it. My granddad says all this stuff, too. He's like a Buddhist Master ... for real.

NADIA: Well, I will study my bible even more now.

KAREEM: I feel Allah closer.

VINCENT: Are you guys serious?

SCOOTER: It's all the same thing, right?

Mr. Lightman nods and centers himself mentally.

MR. LIGHTMAN: All is one, but there are many portions within the one. And there are many systems that humans have created to seek The One. Each part and each system gives valuable information about God. Whether it's useful or not depends on the individual; their personality, their intentions, their level of commitment. In my personal experiences with individuals, I've seen the great religions do a lot of good for people.

KAREEM: Islam helps my family a lot. God is great.

NADIA: My mother's faith in Jehovah definitely stops her from having a nervous breakdown.

VINCENT: Jehovah? You're Jewish?

NADIA: Jehovah's Witness.

VINCENT: Oh, those are the religio-nuts that knock on your damn door. Freakin' worse than telemarketers.

NADIA: They're not nuts. Jehovah keeps my mother sane.

EARL: Yeah, she right on the edge, too. Whoo!

MR. LIGHTMAN: The names and the religions are for you guys to cherish and honor as long as you resonate with the teaching. But your religious beliefs, your interpretations of who and what God is ... and your specific rules and ways of doing things ... are not for everyone. They're for you because you agree to that system. There's no need to force your beliefs on anyone else, especially people who are resistant to it. The main point is that all of your belief systems call for you to love each other as their central message. If we focused on that, it would be enough to change the world.

Vincent yawns.

MR. LIGHTMAN: That's what got my attention. When you really go inside and thoroughly explore your being, there comes a point where you get too deep into the love itself to get caught up in the petty arguments. You get an automatic desire to be good to others and see them do well. Arguments over whose religion is right or wrong — it's been going on for thousands of years and it's taken us ... mostly further into ignorance.

VINCENT: Don't tell that to my Dad.

SCOOTER: Your father's dead.

Vincent opens his arms wide and nods.

VINCENT: Oh, yeah. Thanks, bro! Really? Really? Really? You wanna tweet that to the world?!

SCOOTER: I didn't mean it like that.

BINDIA: Your father died? What happened?

VINCENT: My parents died in a car crash a few years ago. But, anyway, when my father was alive, he was friends with people in other religions. He's Jewish. But he talked a lotta crap about other religions in private, behind their backs.

EARL: Yeah, my mom talks reckless about other religions, too.

KAREEM: My mother say it like Mr. Lightman. She say respect others religion. But my father always say she is crazy. And that she is a bad Muslim. He talks bad about other religions.

SCOOTER: My dad says the other religions do too many crazy things. He laughs at the way they have to meditate and hum, and do their weird dancing, and chanting and stuff.

MR. LIGHTMAN: They all have different ways of experiencing and expressing their connection to, ultimately, the same thing. It's a built-in magnetic pull towards the presence of God. Everyone has the God-given free will to move towards the Source in whatever way they feel, while allowing others to do the same … without infringing on their free will. I like the ritual prayers that Muslims do, and the way they worship and devote themselves to God. I love how Christians and Jews show great devotion and worship in their ways. I love how Buddhists and Hindus see God in the organs of our bodies, and in the depths of our mind and spirit. They see God in the flow of nature, in the trees, the rivers, the animals. They explore the everythingness of God.

VINCENT: Noohh. Void. You can't say "everythingness" at us.

EARL: "Everythingness" is wi-y-ld!

MR. LIGHTMAN: I enjoy the tribal aspects of many African cultures, and the Native Americans, and also the civilizations deep in places that are separated from our "civilized" world. They all have different ways of feeling and seeking the Source, whatever, whoever you consider that to be.

SCOOTER: Yeah, it *is* already there. So … y'know? It's like, we *are* here already! It *was* created already. Everybody agrees with that. So, like, what — Wherever we came from, that is whatever God is. Is that what you mean?

LIGHTMAN: That is precisely what I'm trying to say. Well-said, Scooter.

I'm actually shocked that you said that … in such a way. Very well-said.

Scooter turns to Earl and displays a goofy smile.

SCOOTER: I said it very well.

MR. LIGHTMAN: Throughout our history, humans have used our interactions with a greater power to help each other a lot, and to hurt each other a lot. But *if* a belief *does* guide someone to live more by the universal law of unconditional love, I'm okay with it. As long as you don't harm others or infringe on their free will. I'm all for it if it helps them to realize, "I am one with something much greater than my two eyes allow me to see. I feel it in my heart and know it in my mind. And that makes me feel good, and makes me want to keep feeling good, and makes me want to do things to make others feel good." I know most people don't actually talk like that, but that idea is at the heart of most religious belief systems. That means that even with all the differences in religious belief, whoever they got the original knowledge from wants us all to treat each other with love and respect. And that's my point for today.

Vincent raises his hands high and shakes them.

VINCENT: Thank the non-existent, invisible man! Can we go home?

SCOOTER: We still have, like, twenty minutes more.

VINCENT: Who argues to stay in detention longer?

DIN: My granddad teaches Buddhism at the senior center. He says to respect others beliefs.

KAREEM: That is like how my mother say it, too. Love and respect everybody the same.

NADIA: My mom says, "There's only one true religion." "All the others are false religions doing the devil's work."

VINCENT: (Sarcastically) Yeah, that'll bring peace. Bring an end to all these religious wars.

SCOOTER: That's a bit much, don't you think?

VINCENT: You're Catholic. You can't talk about what's a bit much.

MR. LIGHTMAN: The debates and arguments have played their part. But we're way too evolved to still seriously think like that; that God is on my side and against everyone else. I prefer not to dwell on the debates and arguments. For me, they are major obstacles that … stop me from … more … directly experiencing God in my life. And it stops me from seeing God radiate through other people.

SCOOTER AND EARL: Radiate. Jinx! Jinx!

NADIA: How can you see God in other people?

MR. LIGHTMAN: How can I not? You can't really know God in yourself, in a balanced way, if you don't realize God in all others.

   Mr. Lightman nods and centers himself mentally.

MR. LIGHTMAN: That leads to elitism. The worst poison on the human mind. That's the unhealthy and dangerous pride. You think you and your group alone have all the answers about this … Infinite Being we call God. That often comes with a desire to control and dominate others. When you experience God in a more balanced way, you see that God is in yourself and is in all others. We all stand closer to God when we stand in universal love, regardless of religious beliefs. Even as an atheist, universal love gives you the power of the universe. My focus is to experience the Kingdom of Heaven that is at least *available* to us here and now. People have spent thousands of years arguing about how to get there someday after they die, or experience it on Earth far in the future. For the whole of humanity, on this level, it'll be in the future. But individually, it's available for most of us here and now. It's just easier for some than others. Those who are able to realize it will radiate it naturally in all sorts of ways. Harmony is the most important thing. I've been *blessed enough with a chance* to seek the Kingdom within. I am blessed enough to experience heaven right now at 3:16 pm in this classroom with you guys.

NADIA: Aww.

   Mr. Lightman taps the center of his chest with his index finger.

VINCENT: Gimme a break with that noise.

Vincent laughs. Mr. Lightman laughs also.

NADIA: Vincent, shut up.

MR. LIGHTMAN: The words I use are too cheesy for people like Vincent, but if he felt the actual experience directly, trust me, he'd eat it all up in a heartbeat, and share it with everyone he loves.

VINCENT: You don't know me. Maybe I'd feel it and throw it away.

LIGHTMAN: Maybe. But I think that your soul's experience of oneness would be stronger than your personality. I know that your soul isn't such a douchebag.

Vincent smiles and shakes his head. The others laugh.

SCOOTER: You're saying that everyone can be, like, really happy, like, for real, real?

MR. LIGHTMAN: Well, the short answer is yes. Everyone. I am inspired by the people who beat the odds and become happy after facing nightmarish situations. It may seem insulting to some people for me to say that everyone can be happy. Insulting to those who are truly suffering. But, you can read a lot of stories where people who you'd think can't ever be happy turn out to be some of the happiest people in the world. There are so many factors to how someone goes through their process. What I can say is that I believe happiness is very available here and now *for everyone in this room.* We're all lucky enough to have a certain level of good health, safety, comfort … water, food … healthcare … many luxuries and material things to enjoy. All these things are not as available to many people around the world. Many don't even have the basics to survive. But *you* guys *do* have the basics, and so much more. I wish you guys could see passed some of the unhealthy pressures of this society to only be a certain way, and only see things a certain way, and only do certain things. If you were able to see past the pettiness and feel a deeper appreciation for these basic things, you'd be able to move closer to experiencing the state of heaven much more often in this lifetime. I promise you.

SCOOTER: That sounds so cool.

EARL: That's righteous.

Vincent shakes his head. He wants to say something, but can't think of anything right now.

MR. LIGHTMAN: I'm not waiting for death, or for any person, or belief system to tell me how to get to heaven. It's already been given as part of our mind's and body's makeup. The problem is that many people are often on their deathbed when they figure out that it's been available the whole time.

Kareem is intrigued.

KAREEM: Whoa!

NADIA: But, wait. You keep saying, "Kingdom of Heaven." That's from Jesus! You *are* a Christian.

DIN: No! My grandfather says —

VINCENT: If your grandfather is some ancient kung fu master teacher, how are you so messed up?

MR. LIGHTMAN: Vincent! Go ahead, Din.

DIN: Nothing.

MR. LIGHTMAN: Say what you were gonna say.

DIN: Nothing.

MR. LIGHTMAN: Don't let Vincent get to you right now.

VINCENT: Yeah, don't let Vincent get to you, Din.

DIN: (Clenching his fist) I was just gonna say that it doesn't matter what religion you are.

SCOOTER: So, why do you say "Kingdom of heaven?"

MR. LIGHTMAN: Because it's a term that you're familiar with. But I'm talking about a state, a Way of being, of thinking, and feeling. A Way of knowing yourself, and God, and others, and the world. I'd be able to describe the same experience using language from all of your religious belief systems, and from a scientific, or a more philosophical point of view. None of the names and descriptions can compare to the experience itself.

EARL: That's wavy!

KAREEM: Whoa.

SCOOTER: That's awesome.

MR. LIGHTMAN: You all experience that heavenly feeling a little at a time. It comes in many ways. It's that silence, that stillness, and that *flowing* in the stillness. It's when you get lost in a daydream and go off into that mysterious zone in your mind. Or out of your mind. You somehow, just for a moment, stop the constant thoughts and random chatter that goes on in your mind.

EARL: Yeah, that's crazy! That feels good for real.

MR. LIGHTMAN: What feels good about it?

EARL: I dunno. Just to stop thinking.

The others laugh. Earl shakes his head at them.

MR. LIGHTMAN: You laugh but that's exactly what I'm suggesting is good for you — very good for all of us. That's the main aim of the most basic kind of meditation. To go beyond the constant emotional reactions to your thoughts. You get a sense of that, uh … empty awareness. That's the experience I'm talking about. It's that zero point awareness. On the other end, it's the heavenly experience that also comes through high excitement, enthusiasm and passion.

EARL: Turnin' up!

MR. LIGHTMAN: Exactly! Like deep belly-laughing. Like really enjoying the good company of your coolest friends, good people, loved ones, and creating good memories with them. It's getting lost in the zone during really good music.

EARL: Oh-mi-Lrrd, I know the zone!

MR. LIGHTMAN: I know *you* know the zone. Who else has gotten lost or gotten into that state of *automatic flow* during a good song?

Everyone except Vincent and Bindia raises their hands.

MR. LIGHTMAN: No matter how you describe it, or if you don't ever describe it at all, we all know that heavenly state of being when we experience it.

Vincent gags and pretends to vomit.

MR. LIGHTMAN: And I don't mean this as some philosophy to ... to ... try and make you ... feel good, or ... It's beyond that. My explanations can be seen as philosophical, scientific, religious, or just nonsense.

VINCENT: Ding!

MR. LIGHTMAN: It's that ... I'd keep repeating myself because trying to find words for the actual experience isn't always easy.

NADIA: It's just love, though, right? God is love.

MR. LIGHTMAN: That's the truth.

NADIA: It's unconditional love.

SCOOTER: What's that, really? How is it different from regular love? Like how I love my family.

NADIA: And how husbands and wives love each other?

SCOOTER: You just love everybody all the time?

MR. LIGHTMAN: Well, it's the same love; just different forms of expressing love.

He taps the center of his chest.

MR. LIGHTMAN: Universal love goes beyond human emotions. It includes emotions, but it goes beyond. It's also magnetism, togetherness, unification and movement on an energetic universal level. *A human who experiences genuine universal love receives the ultimate freedom* from the mental prisons we've made for ourselves. Universal love brings *Understanding* in its truest meaning. It brings freedom from many of the unnecessary confusions that we live with. It comes with a profound *Understanding* of the bigger picture of what it means to be a person living on a planet with others.

VINCENT: What planet are you from?

MR. LIGHTMAN: It's not that you necessarily walk around being lovey-dovey and smiling at everyone all the time. It's more about being in a state of being where you become *So At Peace With Yourself And The World* that you just *Let People Be*. At that point, you don't just love others because your religion or your chosen holy book says it's the right thing to do. Or because you read it or saw it in a video, or heard it from a speaker or a teacher. Or because you believe that God is threatening you with eternal suffering or some other form of horrible punishment. You'll give and receive love because it's all you *want* to do.

SCOOTER: I never heard anyone say it like that before.

MR. LIGHTMAN: But you've known someone like that personally, right?

SCOOTER: No.

NADIA: My grandmother is like that.

EARL: Oh, yeah.

DIN: My grandfather, too.

MR. LIGHTMAN: He is a very peaceful man. I've seen him teaching tai chi at the senior citizen's center.

DIN: Yeah. And he doesn't let little things bother him.

VINCENT: And you're the opposite.

DIN: He talks about flowing, and matching … energies and stuff with his body and … nature.

MR. LIGHTMAN: (Quietly) Matching.

As he says "matching," he feels a tingle and a slight pressure on the top-back of his head. He gets a visual flash of a vague pattern. As he speaks to his students, he's unable to focus on exactly what is happening inside.

MR. LIGHTMAN: Your grandfather …

He rubs his eyes and around his mouth.

DIN: He's Buddhist. He says we all match up with the universe. Like, the pieces fit …

MR. LIGHTMAN: I see.

Mr. Lightman sees the pattern again. He doesn't know what it means and doesn't try to figure it out. He accepts it as a part of himself. As he speaks, some of his sentences flow with the pattern, causing him to communicate in a way that is unusual for him.

MR. LIGHTMAN: Well, that's what it means to be in alignment with God, with nature. From the higher point of view, it's not all about our ideas of right and wrong, good and evil. There are … energetic points, keys and locks within our reality. It goes beyond our human ideas. They're like tubes and points of information or data which can line things up in your life with the higher energies of what we call heaven. This heaven is really a higher kind of light that is layered under, over, above, below, and within the essence of the physical world. Heaven is really everywhere at all times. You guys can think of it like … We kind of live inside of a computer.

VINCENT: What?! What?!

Vincent looks around at the others.

VINCENT: What?!

MR. LIGHTMAN: Open your mind a little. Look at the galaxy, stars and planets. We're on a blue ball rotating around a ball of fire. Isn't that enough to open your mind to infinite possibilities?

EARL: On a blue ball going around a ball of fire. I never thought about it like that. You droppin' some real knowledge, Mr. Lightman.

Vincent shakes his head.

MR. LIGHTMAN: I heard Alan Watts put it like that. And I thought about it. It's such a strange situation to actually be in. No matter how much we may want to deny all these other weird and far-out things, we can't deny that this strange and far-out idea is the situation of our daily lives. We live on a blue ball and we're rotating around a giant ball of fire. It doesn't fit into our daily thinking as something that's "normal." It doesn't fit in with the bills and the rent and the daily frustrations. But it is the situation we've actually been in our entire lives. Everything we know is happening in this bizarre situation.

EARL: That's a fly way to look at it.

NADIA: That's cray.

BINDIA: It is weird to think about.

SCOOTER: It is like a computer system.

MR. LIGHTMAN: Look at the system of our bodies. That's a whole universe in itself — the atoms, elements, molecules, cells and organs. They make up our brains — a complex system which allows our minds to experience this physical world. Our minds are an invisible and metaphysical world in itself.

EARL: That's ⌊it!

MR. LIGHTMAN: Through our spirits, minds and bodies, we're sort of experiencing God's universal internet. So, you see what Din's grandfather means by matching ourselves with the universe. We're all compatible to the higher energies of heaven. We sync up. We receive downloads and uploads on many levels. Think about the metaphor of the invisible points and tubes matching our minds and bodies to the universe and to the energies of heaven. Remember, this is a metaphor, but you can see how it can be seen as literal also. For our physical bodies, the tubes, points, keys and locks — they sync the energies of heaven with the subatomic particles, the atoms, the cells and organs in our physical bodies. We can match the physical energies of heaven through the food we eat, and how well we take care of our bodies. Exercise, stretching, cleansing. Eating fruits and vegetables, the light of the Sun from the natural foods of the Earth. We can match the energies of heaven to our emotions through how much we stay in that state of love, compassion, joy, learning and forgiveness. We can match the energies of heaven to our minds and thoughts through what we *choose* to think about over and over — our patterns of thought. There are uplifting thoughts, positive thoughts, and thoughts of practical solutions.

EARL: Rrrradiant!

MR. LIGHTMAN: We can choose thoughts that lead to unnecessary fear, negativity, stress, blaming others, bringing pain to others, infringing on another's freedom of choice. These thoughts and the results they bring are all destructive to our devices — our minds and bodies. The only result that can come from sending negativity to another is negativity coming back to us at some time in some way. These are fundamental laws of our reality. Forgiving yourself and others, and really letting go of the pain is the most reliable repair service to balance and heal our minds, and align ourselves to the energies of heaven.

NADIA: That's why Jesus taught forgiveness.

MR. LIGHTMAN: It is fundamental. So you see, from the physical, emotional and mental to the spiritual, these tubes, keys, points and locks work neatly in a way that allows Earth and heaven, human and God to align on multiple layers.

EARL: Facto! Radiate it!

MR. LIGHTMAN: Of course it's hard to see how that can be true. Throughout our history as a planet, our beliefs, thoughts and fearful feelings have sent the whole thing into a painful and twisted chaotic experience. So, it'll take some time for everyone living on the planet to align with the heavenly state. Each one who finds the light teaches others. Teach as many as you can who are open to your message and willing to listen. Leave everyone else alone. It might get very scary, and like any great story or movie, it will seem like there's no way to achieve heaven on Earth. But the end result will be heaven on Earth. What we call heaven comes to Earth through our personal positive, compassionate use of our spirits, minds, hearts, and physical bodies. More and more of us must have personal responsibility for our use of God's energy in our minds and bodies. If the basic loving philosophy of every religion is followed in thought, feeling, word and action, on a regular basis, things will change. Not being perfect. Just better and more focused on compassion and love. If we literally lived by the lessons from Luke chapter 17, verse 21, our world would be raised to a higher state of vibration.

SCOOTER: Vibration. What's Luke 17:21?

NADIA: Jesus, said, "The Kingdom of God is in your midst."

SCOOTER: Midst? Like middle?

MR. LIGHTMAN: Exactly. In your center; your Core. He meant that it's all around us here and now and it's inside of us here and now.

SCOOTER: Jesus said that? The famous Jesus? Isn't that, like ... really profound?! Like, he said that thousands of years ago. Do priests in churches know that? How can people just pass that by like it isn't the most epic thing he ever said?

MR. LIGHTMAN: I'm glad you see it that way. It is one of the most profound verses in the bible ... to some of us. Not something to be analyzed and interpreted forever. It's something to be recognized and lived directly.

SCOOTER: That's cool!

EARL: Oooh! Radiate it, Mr. Lightman! Preach!

MR. LIGHTMAN: It's a huge lesson that is very misunderstood. And even if it is paid attention to, it usually ends up being ignored or left behind. It requires exploration into the unknown, into the mysterious. If the one learning it is not balanced, it can lead you off-course. And you'll miss the whole point.

SCOOTER: What do you mean?

MR. LIGHTMAN: Well, for example, if you approach it with too much intellectual analysis without *enough* intuition and love, you can get too caught up in arguments about details and specifics about interpretations and what something should and shouldn't mean for everyone. Or the technical scholarly, book-based explanations of what is possible and impossible — all based only on current mainstream scientific evidence. If you look for heaven with too much intuition without wisdom and analysis, maybe you'll have a better shot at finding it in yourself. But without *enough* wisdom and analysis, you can get caught up in the obscure nature of the mysterious — the vagueness. You may end up going off on things that, without some rational grounding, can leave you lost in the shadows.

SCOOTER: Wow. But isn't getting lost a part of the whole thing, though?

MR. LIGHTMAN: How do you know that? You are precisely correct!

SCOOTER: (To Vincent) I'm precisely correct.

MR. LIGHTMAN: Scooter, you are tuned into this message. The seeking into the mysterious and getting lost *is* part of the process of seeking God. Actually, you usually get lost over and over and over again as you gain knowledge and experience. The experience of getting lost, then finding our way, is the experience we signed up for as human beings. It all occurs in

44

cycles — small cycles within bigger cycles. Seeking the highest heavens within yourself requires a sincere and genuine look at your ... Self. Your deep-down, far-in Self — Body, personality traits, gut reactions, social interactions, unconditional love, blunt and honest communication, and so on. It requires *The Real Inner Work*.

EARL: Uh! Knowledge dart!

MR. LIGHTMAN: The great thing is, once you dedicate yourself to knowing yourself, there is a whole lot of fun and enjoyment along the way. You'll face challenges, but if you can regain balance every time you fall, if you can keep your eyes on the prize, happiness will be there all along the path! If more people learned what they are, and lived —

VINCENT: Don't you mean *who* they are?

MR. LIGHTMAN: I meant "what" we are. Who you are is just as fundamental as what you are. But, isn't it weird that we live entire lifetimes, doing all these different things, and not too many of us really take the time out to ... actually figure out *what* we are? Who has time for that, right? Again, many are in survival mode. Got to eat, make money, take care of the bills, continue the struggle, I know. But *if* there was something major to make time for, wouldn't it be to at least, before you die, to know *what* you actually are? Why is that not a thing in this culture?

VINCENT: Hmm. Well, what are we?

MR. LIGHTMAN: One way of putting it is that you are the universe. The far-in, deep-down you of you, is the universe. From a more down-to-earth point of view, you are one player, one point of attention for the universe. Just like each of the trillions of cells in your body is one point of attention for you. You are one point of attention in one galaxy, one star system, one planet, one region, country, state and city. You are the universe experiencing itself from one unique point of view that no other has. There are eight other self-aware points of attention for the universe in this room with you. Each of us is the universe experiencing itself through unique points of attention. Of course, the question, "What are we?" can't be summed up like that alone, but it's a start. You are a microscopic copy of God. Of the universe. The universe is in the image of God. Your bodies, your minds, your souls, are all made in that image. If you explored yourself deeply enough, you'd be able to see what Jesus saw, what Buddha saw. You'd know yourself as they did.

VINCENT: (Shouting sarcastically) Okay, Mr. Lightman! Thanks for that one!

Mr. Lightman chuckles. He takes a deep breath.

MR. LIGHTMAN: If more people were able to learn what they are, and live from the center of what they are, there would be a chain reaction in society. That knowledge would spread. Why? Because the one who realizes the One in themself would radiate the One out to those they come into contact with. At least one of those would seek within enough to find and radiate the One out to others. The essence of God would spread like a hashtag or a meme. Not by preaching to people or convincing them to join you in your point of view. This is about you, the individual, and only you, radiating the essence of God through your thoughts, words, feelings, and behaviors. It'll rub off on others in some way or another. If they ask, you'll teach them your point of view. If they don't want to know, or are not open to it, you don't teach them. Whatever their choice is is the right choice for them at that time. *You're going to be your best self as much as you can be.* Your truest personality is magical and magnetic. God lives through you when you can be your own true honest self with love and compassion. Be yourself, radiate love freely without judgment of others and the essence of what we call God will spread in ways that we are unable to imagine.

SCOOTER: Yes!

EARL: Bruh!

Din laughs. Kareem nods in agreement.

MR. LIGHTMAN: As it goes far enough for a long enough period of time, the world would slowly transform. Our personal identities, personal lives, relationships, communities, social order, art, music, medicine, inventions, everything we do as humans, would be improved, and lifted to a level that allows for an unimaginably higher level of living.

Scooter shakes his head in awe.

MR. LIGHTMAN: On a deeper level, this isn't based on our human ideas and interpretations. It breaks down to simple physics, God's physics. It's a complex and colorful system of different streams of energy interacting with each other within the fabric of existence. And it's all designed by our Creator — whoever and whatever you consider that to be.

SCOOTER: You've researched this stuff?

MR. LIGHTMAN: I have. But I'm only telling you this because of my personal experiences. Without the experience, I would only have what I've heard others say. And what I've read. I would be able to accept these things, and I'd have faith that they were true. But I couldn't know them as my truth unless I disciplined my mind and body well enough to actually experience these things myself. Even then, this is only *my* truth, my opinions. It just so happens that many others across the world are experiencing the same things … and have been for thousands of years. And it just so happens that Jesus, The Buddha, and other advanced spiritual teachers who you guys haven't heard of, experienced and taught many of these same things. And it just so happens that quantum mechanics is now able to better explains many of these extraordinary things that were previously considered to be unexplainable. You can do your research yourself.

SCOOTER: I will! I will!

MR. LIGHTMAN: This is my truth, and you don't have to believe anything until you have good reason to.

VINCENT: None of us do.

SCOOTER: I do.

VINCENT: Except the sheeple, of course.

SCOOTER: The quantum physics brings it all together, right?

MR. LIGHTMAN: It does. As it's presented, it reveals infinite possibilities … in every sense of that term. It reveals much more of our reality. It can assist us in knowing more of what we are, and in changing our ways. You can see for yourself that, as corny as it sounds — and I hate to say it like this – but *love is the answer.*

Mr. Lightman sees the pattern in his mind again. His thoughts, feelings and words flow with the pattern and he flows.

MR. LIGHTMAN: The energy of love, peace, forgiveness, excitement, and all their variations send out and bring in the spiraling spiritual light from the universe, galaxy, sun, and planet, into the spiraling DNA molecules in our bodies. The light carries information just like the light in our TV's, cell phones and internet. Except this is a Higher Light with higher information which gives signals to our cells. These signals cause natural impulses and bring out natural feelings which stimulate us to seek, think, feel, do and say the things that can eventually bring us to know ourselves. Most people in our world don't make it to the highest levels of self-awareness. But this time is like no other time on Earth. Information, deep revelations, and the vibration of this planet are at an all-time high. Your generation of religious leaders, teachers, doctors, inventors, artists, musicians and Scientists will make huge leaps in our conscious evolution towards a God-realized humanity.

EARL: Rrrradiation!

NADIA: Shut up and pay attention!

MR. LIGHTMAN: We're in the beginning of a major transition, so it's still very hard to see how things are getting better.

SCOOTER: That's ... like ... the most epic-est of epic things I've ever heard! How can this be real?! Is it real?! For real!

MR. LIGHTMAN: I know it to be very real. Many others do also. More people will express it publicly as we go forward. But you can't know it by me convincing you, or telling you about it. You have a chance to know it way better than I do, at a much earlier age than I did.

Mr. Lightman is surprised at the way he's speaking, and by what he's saying. He's known these things for a while, but has never made many of these connections of ideas and understandings. He wonders if he's explaining it the right way. He wonders why he's still talking about these things to his students at all. Vincent looks into Mr. Lightman's eyes and remains silent for a while. He shakes his head and smiles.

VINCENT: How do you know these things?

NADIA: Oh, now you believe!

VINCENT: Believe what?! It sounds like a good con job. It's interesting though. How did you find this stuff out?

MR. LIGHTMAN: I asked over and over, then received over and over. I seeked continuously and I continue to find. I "sought," I should say.

NADIA: That's Matthew 7:7.

MR. LIGHTMAN: Yeah. You know the bible.

EARL: She memorizes verses like an idiot —

Nadia SNAPS her fingers and yells at Earl!

NADIA: Who you callin' —

EARL: Like an idiot savant! You're smart! I'm sayin' you're good at memorizing the bible like a genius or something. Calm down! Idiot savant means you're smart! Damn!

Earl turns to Vincent and laughs.

EARL: Hashtag #NadiaBeLike ...

NADIA: Don't hashtag me! Shoot!

MR. LIGHTMAN: That's good that you're so into knowing God. You go, girl.

EARL: Trust me, she gone.

VINCENT: You make it sound believable. But why hasn't the world been able to change into this ... whimsical heavenly place?

MR. LIGHTMAN: It involves a whole lot of different components. And there are natural metaphysical factors which create a resistance to our evolution.

The resistance may be seen as bad. But from the higher perspective, it's no different than gravity. Everything has their reasons for being the way they are. In this world, this resistance manifests as uncertainty, confusion, feeling separated, fear, stress, evil, control, repressing certain behaviors, forcing certain behaviors, and domination. We've made it through very dark times as a species. But you guys live at a time that is unique and amazing. There is still a lot of darkness, but we've never had this much light. A better world is coming. The transformation into a much better world will come at a pace that we will decide. It will take our effort and our will to learn, love, forgive, let go, and empower ourselves.

VINCENT: Sounds good. It always ... *sounds* ... good. But that means nothing. And all of us know that.

MR. LIGHTMAN: I understand your point of view. I really do. It won't happen while we're all living comfortably. It'll likely be forced to happen after we're faced with very frightening challenges that force us to come together, depend on each other and go within to see what's really going on. We're hard-headed and won't change until we're at the very brink of destruction. But, at our core, we are very loving people.

BINDIA: Now, you're going too far. Most people are not loving.

MR. LIGHTMAN: Yes, we are. You guys are.

VINCENT: Sounds like you watched way too many science-fiction movies and internet quantum videos. And read too many positive thinking books. You're all screwed up.

MR. LIGHTMAN: Okay. Even if you choose not to believe in any of that — it's just a bunch of nonsense. Okay. For you, personally, doesn't it just feel better to experience love more than to experience hate or anger? We can all agree that it at least feels better to have loving experiences than to have fearful, negative, angry, or hateful experiences. Is that true for you, Vincent? Bindia? Even the people who we consider to be the most evil usually love something or someone at some time. Love is universal. If we agree that it feels better to be loving than to be negative, and we see a chance to choose between the two, why choose to continuously be negative?

VINCENT: Sometimes anger saves you.

MR. LIGHTMAN: Okay. But I'm speaking of day to day life ... in general. Your personal life with your family, friends and coworkers. Is it possible to choose ways to create more positive daily experiences for yourself? Of course, we're supposed to feel anger and frustration, hatred and misery in our lives — that's a part of this experience. But don't you notice in our society, and in our personal lives that *we choose to focus way too much of our attention on petty and negative things?*

SCOOTER: Now, that's true!

EARL: Yup!

NADIA: Mm-hmm.

Vincent nods.

MR. LIGHTMAN: Of all the things you can experience for the rest of your life, if you could choose to give and receive love and positivity more, or fear and negativity more, which would you choose?

NADIA: Love and positivity.

MR. LIGHTMAN: Vincent?

   Vincent looks up at Mr. Lightman with wide eyes.

VINCENT: Oh, are you still saying stuff?

MR. LIGHTMAN: Seriously.

VINCENT: Love. But what does it have to do with all that spiritual quantum God energy vibration mechanism nonsense?

MR. LIGHTMAN: *It doesn't have to be about that for you if you're not interested in that.* However you choose to express love, and whatever you choose to believe about it is for you and you only. As long as we all agree that love is the one that we'd want to give and receive ... *more* ... since we have a choice.

VINCENT: But we have both.

MR. LIGHTMAN: I said that we're here to experience all of it. From the highest ecstasy to the lowest depression. But for your own sanity, knowing the benefits of goodness and love, in general, why not just choose to experience love more? What do you have to lose, except *excess* stress and pain? If your way of life is comfortable enough to the point where you have more of a choice than many others, why would you purposely choose to experience negativity by treating people badly, and judging them negatively?

VINCENT: But it's impossible to love everyone all the time.

MR. LIGHTMAN: It's not about that. Love more people more of the time. Do it for real, over and over for a long enough period of time, and your point of view will shift. So many other things will change. You'll be able to live in this world of positivity and negativity, and experience a lot more positivity. There will always be challenges, so you have to hit refresh, hit restart, over and over.

Scooter tilts his head and nods, really trying to get it.

MR. LIGHTMAN: Try it in those difficult situations, with those difficult people, day-after-day. It won't be easy at first. You'll probably fail the first few times, or the first ten times. But if and when you do it and get it right, you'll make progress in mind, soul, light and life. You'll decide from there if you want to make it a regular part of life, or if it's just too much work.

EARL: People will take your kindness for weakness.

MR. LIGHTMAN: You are spot-on. I can tell you personally that you will be challenged in that way. You'll have to be wise and responsible. You'll still protect yourself against those with predatory behavior towards you. You can acknowledge the ones who take advantage of your kindness. You can acknowledge that the darkness is there. But, okay ... forget even going that far ... for now. Start simple. Just focus on loving behavior more of the time. When it's easy. Start there. Your experience of this life changes so much when your main focus is on treating others in a positive way. You don't have to make it your only focus right away. Just make it your main focus, your default focus to treat your neighbor as yourself.

EARL: My neighbors steal.

NADIA: Sneakers. Packages.

NADIA AND EARL: Wi-Fi!

Mr. Lightman laughs.

BINDIA: That's too deep to really do, though. Like, in the real world. Some people are sooooooo hard to get along with sometimes. Love doesn't really work with everybody.

EARL: Yeah, that's hard.

NADIA: But I never heard anybody say this kind of thing before.

MR. LIGHTMAN: What do you mean? You've heard it a million times. "Love is the answer." "Think positive." All that stuff.

NADIA: But not like how you're saying it.

EARL: It's still impossible.

MR. LIGHTMAN: It is hard. It's very hard to deal with difficult people when you try to *force it from outside of your center*. It's hard when you have to … try and believe that God demands you to obey and be good, or else you'll be punished. It can be very difficult, if not impossible to live life with the energy of pure love when you have to force it or have it forced on you. When you try to make God happy only by falling into line because you're afraid, you'll probably find it much harder to live in a continuous state of love. But if you learn what I mean by, "Living From Your Center", you'll find it easier.

KAREEM: Your Source.

MR. LIGHTMAN: Yes, Kareem! Get to know your Source. It is the central point that I'm making for you guys today. When you live more from The Being That You Are — *The One* who is behind your names and personalities, you'll have a more natural desire to experience love as much and as deeply as possible. You'll be dealing with those same so-called annoying, impossible, difficult people. But you'll see more options for solutions. From inside your center, it's a much smoother sail through this world. I promise you that. You've done it. When you're already in a good mood and things are going well, even annoying people are much more tolerable, aren't they?

EARL: We were just sayin' that the other day!

NADIA: Yeah! It happened with our cousin! We were saying that!

MR. LIGHTMAN: You respond more peacefully to the same thing that would set you off when you're not in a peaceful state of mind.

NADIA: That's so true. I get it.

SCOOTER: Who's behind our name and personality?

MR. LIGHTMAN: The One Universal Self. *The One Identity* of All That Exists. The I am. You are that I am before you are Scooter.

SCOOTER: I am?

MR. LIGHTMAN: We all am ... are. It is the perfect part of you. The human personality, on its own, is designed to be imperfect, and out of sync with the higher light of God. That's not because of some evil force or some punishment. It's the way it's designed in order to create a particular experience in this physical world. The separate personality falls short of Higher Light because that's its function.

NADIA: (Whispering) Falling short of God's glory.

MR. LIGHTMAN: The soul is a much purer expression of the Higher Light, of God's glory. And you are the soul before you are the personality. If you are able to identify with soul *and* personality as you seek self-knowledge, your experience of this world will change in a balanced way. When you open yourself and express yourself in love like Jesus did by example, the universal part of you that is already perfect radiates through your unique, imperfect personality. This is where it becomes so much easier to deal with difficult people and very challenging situations. So much easier.

Bindia opens her mind a little more and listens a little closer.

MR. LIGHTMAN: Then, for those who are seeking, you can get to really know your Self beyond your human self. Most people will experience it as something divine. Some will experience the deeper Self in a completely non-spiritual way where they just feel "in the zone," living as their fuller, truer personality. The mind becomes much clearer and much more efficient. However you experience it, you'll most likely feel like this is what existence is all about. The far-in, deep down Self feels like home to all beings because it literally is home — as home as home can be. It's the ultimate feeling of being home. As you get to know it, your behaviors, views, beliefs, and choices change for the better. Your personality shines brighter. And you can make major positive changes quickly in the world around you as you desire. Of course, I'm speaking generally. There are so many factors on so many levels that are involved with each unique individual.

SCOOTER: And we do this by being loving?

MR. LIGHTMAN: That is the root and the essence of it all. Unconditionally love yourself, the planet, animals, plants, and everyone else. As I said, it doesn't mean what you think it means. It means, generally, just ... chill ... out and *let people do what they do without always judging and criticizing.* Even those who you say are your enemies. You don't have to go and be extra lovey-dovey with every person you see. Just get to know your Self. And get so involved in the joy or the duty of playing your part in the world that you are able to just leave them alone. Let them be who they are. Let them mess up. Let them see it wrong. If you can help, try to help. If not, you don't have to put so much energy into them. Sometimes, you might see the absolute need to interfere. It's your choice. You'll be right some times. But don't sweat the small stuff. Don't be petty. Live for the deepest love and the highest light. You'll notice how much small stuff you make into a big deal. We do this a lot!

NADIA: We do.

EARL: Especially online.

MR. LIGHTMAN: Get rid of that excess baggage and let other people do their thing in their way. And don't judge them. Even in your own mind, let them be, and be your Self. Your highest and greatest work involves you and God, you seeking God, you getting to know God and your Self. That is top priority. Focus on you and God in love and wisdom, and you will be doing your best to fix all that you see that's wrong with the world. Those who manipulate, control, discriminate, hate, dominate, lie, kill, rape, scam, steal, and harm others will get it all back over and over until they learn their lessons the hard way. You don't *have to* focus on them *as much as you do*. That's not saying you don't have to at all. Maybe it's your duty to do so, but take a look at yourself truly and eliminate the *excess* baggage. You are carrying around a lot of it. Most people are just like you. People going about their own process and making many mistakes — some small, some big. We've all made mistakes and will continue to. You make yours. They make theirs. Let them be. As for those that you care for, you don't have to just let them go crazy and ruin their lives. But as you live more from your Source Self Center and express more of your Natural Self, it'll be easier for you to face the issues. You'll be able to see so much more. You're able to look directly at the issues and have a better chance of seeing solutions! To better help where you can, and not interfere where you don't have to. And it'll be easier for you to simply let go if you need to let go. There's even a point of spiritual development where you'll know that you're helping the world without saying or doing anything in the physical world at all.

KAREEM: This is so wise. Like a wise man.

DIN: What about masters like my granddad?

Mr. Lightman sees the pattern again and feels it sync neatly within his awareness.

MR. LIGHTMAN: They'll be many who take seeking to much, much deeper levels than most. These are the ones who really, really just want to know their Source — with no ulterior motive. They just want to know themselves. If you have this deep, deep desire to know, and you are able to seek with enough balance, the gifts are literally limitless. Learning *What* you truly are and what the world is helps you to see from a wider point of view — that this is a personal, social, national, global, planetary, interplanetary, galactic, universal and metaphysical process. These are some of the people who become advanced masters — Adepts. It sounds so complicated, I know. It is complex, but it doesn't have to be complicated. Seeking with love, guided by your highest excitement and enjoyment is a key to making the complex part of it much simpler. You'll see that you only have to do your part. Others will do their part. Let people be. And don't judge them.

Earl claps his hands. The others applaud! Vincent smirks at them.

EARL: This is some high knowledge right here!

VINCENT: He is very high!

MR. LIGHTMAN: You can't fool the universe by being positive on the outside, but still being negative on the inside. Your Source Self doesn't fall for that. You're not gonna fool the metaphysical energy of the universe. Most people on this planet, for thousands of years, have lived that way. I did it. Especially when I first started to come into this knowledge. I'd put on a good show on the outside while having a very negative environment on the inside. This is the norm, I would say. Most of us have watched our parents do this from an early age.

EARL: Hell, yeah.

SCOOTER: Yep.

BINDIA: Uh-huh.

MR. LIGHTMAN: As you seek to know your Self, you can accept that part of yourself, along with all of your other negative qualities. Accept that it's there, forgive yourself for it, and work on bettering yourself through more love, discipline and self-knowledge. You don't have to try to be a saint. Some may be able to just let it go instantly. That ... is magical, and life-changing. If you can let go of your excess baggage quickly, do it. Don't lie to yourself though. That's easy to do also. But many people can just let go of something that held them back for a long time. More power to you if you can do that. In other areas of your life, you'll most likely have to do it one day at a time, one situation, one person at a time. As for people who are different from you, live from your center and you'll see that they are a part of you, of God. Just let them be. I mean those who worship differently or live differently, or are of different races and cultures. If you can Live From Your Center and radiate God's glory through your personality, you'll realize that when they do their "weird" stuff, worship their way, live as they do, they're radiating God's energy also. Just in a different way than you do.

Kareem nods, swallows, and really thinks about how much easier his life would be if others understood this message.

MR. LIGHTMAN: The way you see things isn't always necessarily the way things are. That's actually a ... central point also. Wisdom can help you to see your own limitations, weaknesses and darkness. When you see them, you can work on them to find abundance, strength and love. Wisdom helps you to adjust and expand your knowledge of your Self, your environment, and your situation. Wisdom combined with love allows you to be balanced, allowing, fair, accepting, forgiving, and to truly treat others as equals. When wisdom and love are balanced in thoughts and choices, you'll be accepting and forgiving, but you won't be a pushover and allow others to walk all over you. Remember, you do not love others in order to do anyone else a favor. You do it because that *Is* the stuff existence is made of. This is for those who truly seek God or the higher light. You can resist loving your enemy for as long as you want, but love is The Way you'll end up going eventually, no matter how many years or lifetimes it takes you to get that point. If someone oppresses you, steals from you, or discriminates against you, you'll only evolve spiritually by seeing God in them. Why? To try to be spiritual and saintly? No. It's because God *Is* in them. *And you see that because, as someone who seeks expanded awareness, you want to live in the undeniable truth.* Obviously, they're not acting in a Godly way, but it doesn't change the *fact* that you and them are one, and pieces of God. Love is The Way. Wisdom can help you to acknowledge that they do hate you, they do harm you, and you do have to defend yourself. And you may have to fight if necessary. Love and wisdom in balance helps you to find solutions without fighting. Love helps you to see that if you do have to fight, the one that you're fighting is a part of you and a part of God. Not because you're trying to be a good person. Because you seek greater awareness to know the truth. It can be no other way. They are a part of God. Now, how do you move forward from that point? If love guides you, you will find a much higher standard of solution than you would if you acted only out of hate and resentment. It can be tough to be the good guy. Tough to be the one who is actually seeking the higher light in a very sincere way. Don't let resentment for those who harm you drain your spiritual energy. It's up to you, the one who seeks greater awareness, to find the highest quality of solutions. That is *your* challenge.

EARL: This is serious stuff.

MR. LIGHTMAN: When you live in a state of unconditional love, you'll be more chilled out. You'll be able to enjoy life a lot more. When you're tuned in, you'll be better able to see pitfalls and avoid them. You'll face challenges with a more balanced attitude and find amazing solutions.

SCOOTER: That's amazing. And how do you talk like that? Are you a preacher or something?

EARL: Hurts my head. Flowin' and zig-zaggin' like we goin' on a idea trip. Trippin' on ideas.

Mr. Lightman laughs.

MR. LIGHTMAN: I don't know. You said to be specific.

KAREEM: I think it's ... (Clears throat) right.

Kareem swallows and lowers his head. Scooter looks at him.

SCOOTER: I think it's right, too.

Kareem lifts his head and nods in agreement.

EARL: Yeah, but really … That ain't happenin'. Like, realistically …
  Vincent laughs and mocks Earl.
VINCENT: Like, re-ah-lis-tic-all-eeey!
EARL: Re-al-is-tic-a-lly, though ...
VINCENT: Like, in ac-tu-a-lity …
EARL: Yeah, like, for all intensive purposes ...
VINCENT: Intents and purposes.
Earl looks at Vincent, then back at Mr. Lightman.
EARL: What was I talkin' about?
  He thinks. He looks around the room with his mouth open.
EARL: Oh-kay. Never mind.
SCOOTER: I think you're right because —
EARL: OH! OH! YEAH!
NADIA: Why are you yelling?
EARL: I remember what I was sayin'. I don't think you're right. I mean, I think you are right but, I think it's impossible ... to be in the love ... Man, forget it. I dunno what I'm talkin' about no more.
VINCENT: It is impossible to live like that. With unconditional love.
BINDIA: Yeah, especially in this world. It's not realistic at all.
DIN: You guys missed the whole point.
SCOOTER: Yeah, y'all haven't listened to anything he said.
MR. LIGHTMAN: Nadia, what does the bible say about what's possible with God? What did Jesus say?
NADIA: Matthew 19:26, He says "All things are possible with God."
EARL: But that's way too hard.
MR. LIGHTMAN: Too hard? I guess your bible reads, "All things are possible with God, except certain things that are too hard, like unconditionally loving others."
  They laugh. Mr. Lightman closes his eyes for a few seconds.
KAREEM: It is very hard, though. When you are angry with a person, you can't be loving to them.
NADIA: You have to have loving thoughts, right? Be positive.
BINDIA: I *hate* that positive thinking stuff. Like, oh, my God!
NADIA: Girl, can you, like, not say God's name in vain?!
VINCENT: Hold up! Dude's name is "God?"
NADIA: God is not a dude!
BINDIA: Positive thinking is totally a-nnnnn-oying!
MR. LIGHTMAN: Honestly, I hear you, Bindia. The way it's often presented

can be annoying and cheesy. It's even more annoying when you're in a bad mood. But, *if* you really want it to work for you, it will work very, very well. It changes lives. If it's efficiently used by you, the individual, it can change your life. Your thoughts direct your life. Thought creates everything. Thoughts create everything. That is so important. It can't be stressed enough.

Vincent raises his hand.

VINCENT: Well, I *can* be stressed enough … by this conversation.

MR. LIGHTMAN: The content of your thoughts creates the content of your life. This is another central point of everything I can teach you guys in this whole discussion. The power of your thoughts. Positive thinking — the term is kind of drained of its power now that it's "a thing," a trendy thing. If you approach positive thinking in a superficial, trendy way, you can get caught up in "trying to think positive." And you'll probably end up just as miserable as you were in the beginning — maybe even more miserable. Some people try positive thinking for a while, until things get too stressful. It's easy to be positive when things are good, but when you're pressed, and challenged with a potentially stressful situation, it goes out the window for most people. "Real life" situations, and dealing with "real people" during your day is usually enough to make people give up on trying to think positive. Again, forcing it may work for some, but not most. Again, let genuine, real enjoyment and feelings of fun, love and compassion be your starting point. Play your favorite music. Do someone a favor. Help a stranger. Talk to someone who actually "gets you." Watch a comedy show. But my main advice would be to go into your center. Daily meditation is the best tool … for me. There are many others, all having to do with silence, peace, love and enjoyment. Willpower and discipline is central, of course. But I don't have much hope for you guys when it comes to that.

EARL: That's cold.

MR. LIGHTMAN: It helps if you speak and act positively. And let yourself really enjoy good things. Letting joy be your guidance would be my advice to you guys. Let that feeling be your guidance system. Then let discipline and positive thinking grow out of that main feeling of feeling good. Because, for many, it is difficult if you keep looking at it as an intellectual task, like, "I'm trying to be positive." I mean, you will have to try and give a good effort as you practice it. But what you're aiming for is to get to the point where you can let the positivity be your natural, dominant feeling *most of the time*. SCOOTER: See, this is the truth. Because I see people who are angry ... and they act like they're really being positive. It was some show I saw where the guy was yelling and cursing at another guy, and he was saying that he's doing positive thinking.

MR. LIGHTMAN: "Doing" is the key word there. He might have just started and been practicing, so he was trying to do it, instead of being it and feeling it in himself. If you're doing it and not being it also, you probably won't get too far. You'll get too stuck in the world of thoughts, in your mind. You'll get caught up on ideas and definitions. You put ideas and definitions ahead of the actual experience. When that happens, you live in a more artificial way.

SCOOTER: That's interesting. How do you mean "artificial?" I think I know, but ...

MR. LIGHTMAN: Well, being more positive is much easier when you allow yourself to experience the richness of life in a more direct way. Like when you were babies, or younger children. At that time, you were not relying on thought *too much*. There was more feeling, and flowing, and being. Being is where the magic of life is.

KAREEM: What do you mean?

MR. LIGHTMAN: How did I get myself into this conversation?

NADIA: (Singing) Because you love us.

KAREEM: I would like to know. Please? What is being?

Mr. Lightman takes a few slow breaths, breathing deeply, allowing the air to go down into his diaphragm, then back up. He feels the oxygen flow through the individual regions of his brain, especially his frontal lobe. He feels the energy flow through his chest, back, collar bone, temples, around his mouth, his chin, upper lip, nostrils, and eye sockets. He closes his eyes and sees The Light flowing into his head as he breathes.

SCOOTER: You said, "Being is where the magic is."

KAREEM: "Magic of life."

MR. LIGHTMAN: I was saying that we live in our minds too much sometimes. We focus too much on thought and not enough on the deeper, richer flowing and being.

SCOOTER: But you just said that thought is everything.

MR. LIGHTMAN: Thought is the beginning. Thought creates, organizes and guides. It sets the tone and manages, and makes major decisions. But you don't want to live in your thoughts *too much*. You want to flow, feel and be and live in the moment.

EARL: When you say being, you mean the zone?

MR. LIGHTMAN: That's exactly what I mean. You get so caught up in The Moment that you don't have much room for thinking or analyzing. There's little to no awareness of what happened earlier, or what's gonna happen later, or the technical parts of what's happening now. When you're *totally engaged only in what you're experiencing right here and right now*. Even if it is a memory of the past, or a thought of the future, you're totally in it. I think that's a good example.

SCOOTER: It is. I understand exactly what you're saying.

MR. LIGHTMAN: Of course, as I said, thought can create and organize. You need proper thinking so that what you do in the moment isn't reckless and destructive.

NADIA: That's what I was gonna say.

MR. LIGHTMAN: This is why balance is a way of life. Balance in everything is the way. Now, when I talk about being, though, there is a state beyond "the zone," beyond the fun and joy. It's the deep inner stillness and silence of the mind. Then there are states beyond that stillness in the mind. But that's not what we're talking about. Another example of being is when you get lost in a daydream.

NADIA: Earl does that all the time.

VINCENT: All the time!

MR. LIGHTMAN: When was the last time you just stared at the clouds for no reason, or got lost in the beauty of something — anything? Or got lost in the goodness of the taste of food so much that you don't even think about it at all? You just experience how good it is in the moment. You slip into the eternal moment, the eternal now. It's when you're so enveloped in an experience that there's no room for an intellectual opinion … in *that* moment. Or the intellectual opinion doesn't take away from your experience.

KAREEM: I understand how you mean.

MR. LIGHTMAN: Again, thought and intellectual opinions are necessary to create, to set the tone, to organize, to move you forward. You don't want to stop thought and get lost in the zone when you're crossing a busy street. And brilliant thoughts often come to you immediately following a moment of bliss. But you don't want thought to keep getting in the way when you're enjoying a blissful experience. You would want to reduce thought enough in order to live in the richness and *be* in the real world. Thoughts are real, but you create an artificial world when you live in your thoughts at the expense of being and feeling love in the moment.

KAREEM: I get it!

MR. LIGHTMAN: I'm glad you're getting it.

SCOOTER: It seems like all the different things are needed. Like, one isn't better than the other.

MR. LIGHTMAN: That is precisely correct, and another central point

SCOOTER: (To Vincent) I'm precisely correct with a central point.

MR. LIGHTMAN: We are always being. We are beings. Thinking, feeling, speaking, and acting are all a part of being. They can enhance and coordinate being. They each play their part, and are necessary. And, keep in mind, positive thoughts are absolutely necessary to living a positive life. But you don't get all the benefits of positive thinking if you're going to speak, feel, and act negatively. You defeat the purpose and end up with negative consequences. And you'll end up thinking negatively eventually.

BINDIA: That sounds a little better than that other positive thinking crap they talk about on TV.

Bindia smiles. Vincent scoffs.

SCOOTER: So, we have to use them all.

MR. LIGHTMAN: Yeah. You're already using them all, all the time. It's just for those who are fed up with being miserable and angry, or negative — *if* you want to experience life in a different way, you have to change how you're using them. Change what you're focusing on *most of the time*. You can try to use them as tools. Use them to enhance the experience of whatever you're focusing on. Or to navigate through difficulties and challenges towards solutions.

BINDIA: It's sickening to hear that positive thinking stuff. It's fake.

MR. LIGHTMAN: Well, if it's genuinely making life better for the individual who's using it, then it doesn't matter what you or I think. People can go from being on the verge of suicide to living a fulfilled life just by changing how they choose to use these parts of themselves.

SCOOTER: Is it possible to think too much? I think I do sometimes.

MR. LIGHTMAN: It is. But that depends on the individual and their situation. And their reasons. I can't *tell* someone that they are thinking too much, but yes, I think it is possible to think too much. As I was saying, we often live in our thoughts so much that we miss out on the actual experience of what is happening. And that is what the most basic kind of meditation is used for. In basic meditation, you ease resistance and stop getting caught up in the constant flow of thoughts. You allow your mind to be still, then remain still, and just allow yourself have a direct experience of Being a Conscious

Being. Thoughts still flow by. They'll distract you at first. The more you remain still, the more you'll ... **sink in** ... or *fall in* ... into the deeper region of your being. For some people, it's easier to practice this lying down first before sitting down. Sitting allows energy to flow through your body in a very important way, but some beginners may find it easier to enter the meditative stated while lying down. Basic meditation has countless mental, social, spiritual and physical benefits.

EARL: I know what you mean, though, on the thinking thing. Is like, I was daydreamin' in math class yesterday, right? And I was —

The others laugh.

EARL: What? What?

VINCENT: The fact that that wasn't a joke to you is crazy.

Nadia shakes her head.

EARL: Yeah. So, then I was just like, "Why do people even need words for everything?" Is like, I like words and all, but I was like, the words aren't the real thing that they are called. Right? The real thing the word is about is realer than ... I mean ...

MR. LIGHTMAN: Go on.

EARL: The words are just the words, but not the real ... I lost it. I ...

He squeezes his eyes and rubs his head. The others laugh.

EARL: That sentence alone kinda ... looped around in my head and I didn't know where I was goin'.

They continue to laugh.

MR. LIGHTMAN: You got enough of it right, Earl. That is *exactly* what we're talking about. It's a perfect point. Words and language can get in the way of reality sometimes. The words are not the reality. They explain it, and help us to communicate, express, and shape and mold our reality. Now, I know more than anyone that the power of words is absolutely fundamental to creating our reality on so many levels — subtler layers especially. But we're talking about something else —about getting *too* caught up in the world of thoughts and ideas. Again, I'll say that it is very important to experience existence more directly ... without all the *excess* chattering of words, ideas and man-made *definitions* in your mind. You use words to create your experience. But there are much deeper areas of our being where words can't follow. Where you experience the world itself more directly, beyond the words and ideas that *describe* the world. I love that you can see that, Earl.

Earl feels proud of himself.

MR. LIGHTMAN: You know what that says about the way you learn?
EARL: Yeah.
MR. LIGHTMAN: You do? Tell me.
EARL: It means that all of us should daydream in math class 'cause the work be mad hard.
NADIA: I'm done with you. I can't! I can't even!
EARL: What?!
The others burst out laughing! Mr. Lightman shakes his head.
EARL: What? Man, I felt smart for a minute.
MR. LIGHTMAN: You are Brilliant.
EARL: Oh, good. I'm a brilliant idiot.
MR. LIGHTMAN: My point is …
   The others keep laughing. Mr. Lightman laughs with them. Nadia looks at Earl and shakes her head.
MR. LIGHTMAN: My point is that I wish you guys experienced the world more as it actually is.
KAREEM: I like your way to understand the world. It's the right way.
MR. LIGHTMAN: Well, the things I've described have worked for me ... and many others. They've satisfied me according to my personality, my desires, my questions, my intentions and my ways of seeking. They've given me the answers I've sought. I can't say that it's "right" for everyone. It's certainly not to be considered the "right" way. If a way works for you in fulfilling what you seek, with enough balance, without unnecessarily harming yourself, and without infringing on others, it's the right way for you. The greater point I'm trying to get through to you guys is that *what you are* at your core isn't about my way or anybody's way. It just *Is* what It *Is*. My way of explaining it to you may be helpful, but it's very, very dull compared to your own ability to seek the Source in your Core and radiate it out to others. That is your birth-right. It is who and what you are. Your personal inner experience with your Source. Not me, or anyone else can say they own That. No religion, no clever explanation, no teacher, video, book, or interpretation, no theory, or belief system can own That. Again, they can be used as guides, as tools and systems for you to use in order to come to know it in yourself, but You Are Your Own Spiritual Authority in this physical world.
VINCENT: I like that.
MR. LIGHTMAN: What you are goes so far, so deep. Definitions and beliefs are fundamental to creating your experiences, but they are still outside of

the deep-down *Core of what you are*. A person having the deepest experience of their Core Self may feel connected with nature, with strangers, and with … a thing that they can only sense, but can't grab and hold onto with their mind. Even if they don't believe in a Creator or a God, or spirit in the same way that you and I do. They can feel it and know it and express it in their own way. Because they are It.

SCOOTER: Even an atheist?

MR. LIGHTMAN: Yes. Sounds weird, right? Atheists are able to find the Source within them. Not believing in an Intelligent Creator can create many imbalances and many locked avenues when it comes to seeking knowledge about reality. But, in this world, it can have advantages also. Many atheists are free from religious dogma, painful and unnecessary guilt, superstition, vague spiritual concepts, and certain limiting thoughts, beliefs and behaviors. These things can create mental prisons that lock people inside a box of limited experience. But, as I said, many atheists are also locked into their own prisons that put certain limits on knowledge and experiences. But the Source isn't phased by a believer or an atheist. Or any kind of spiritual seeker. It is what it Is. It Is all of us.

VINCENT: I like that.

MR. LIGHTMAN: Remember, we've found many ways — some more accurate than others — many ways of *pointing to* that mysterious One. But what it actually *Is* can't always be easily grasped and organized in a way that we're accustomed to. So, remember that who and what you are isn't what Mr. Lightman says. It isn't just about Mr. Lightman's way of explaining things. Very often when someone tries to rigidly *make it a "way,"* they end up with a very distorted description of what It actually Is. As time goes on, if you guys seek within, you'll have experiences of feeling and knowing your Source directly. At those times, you'll have no memory or use of anything I said here today. You'll just flow in the experience.

SCOOTER: Good lord!

MR. LIGHTMAN: Teachers, science, religion, and the great wisdom of our holy books can be very useful in guiding us and clarify things we already feel inside. As you progress, if you seek enlightenment, you'll eventually have to learn to rely on the Source in you as your primary teacher, and let the worldly learning tools be secondary.

Scooter is speechless and has a goofy smile on his face.

SCOOTER: Okay, really. How do you know this?

VINCENT: You're acting like he's special or something. He's not.

MR. LIGHTMAN: That's another major point. Before learning anything more about any of this, get that idea of a "special" person out of your mind. No matter how well someone speaks, or how much knowledge they give you, don't ever think of them as being any *more* special than you are. You can consider others special. If you consider someone to be a special person in your life for your reasons, it's okay. I do. But don't give any teacher, guru of priest any kind of specialness over yourself because they know more or have experienced more. Don't put anyone on a pedestal.

NADIA: Was Jesus special?

MR. LIGHTMAN: To me, yes. I consider him to be special considering what he was able to accomplish. And some of my personal experiences with him. Jesus, Heru of Egypt, The Buddha, and a few others were able to take their advanced knowledge of the Self very much farther than the majority. The truth is that they only came to show us how special *we* are. He came to show us ourselves. Not to make us worship them or put them up on a pedestal. Their message was shown clearly by their words and behaviors.

KAREEM: My mother say Jesus is a great teacher.

VINCENT: A Muslim woman says that? And your father lets her?

KAREEM: Yes.

VINCENT: What does he do to her?

NADIA: Vincent!

KAREEM: My parents are normal. Not everything about Muslims is like how you see on TV.

   Mr. Lightman nods at Kareem and smiles.

KAREEM: Jesus is a great messenger in Islam.

MR. LIGHTMAN: Your mother understands Jesus' teachings with her heart. Jesus showed us our own potential power. He was able to do what he did because he remembered his connection, his oneness with all of us, with nature, and with the Source.

SCOOTER: If we can make oneness in the world …

MR. LIGHTMAN: No, Oneness Cannot Be Created, It Can only Be Realized. Oneness is all that there already is. You can't *make* oneness happen because it already is the nature of existence. The Creator is One, and we are all That One. There's no thing else to exist that is not part of The One.

KAREEM: So, you ... do not try to say it is so. It is just so.

MR. LIGHTMAN: Exactly.

KAREEM: I like that way of thinking.

SCOOTER: Yeah, me too. It feels better than the usual stuff.

MR. LIGHTMAN: Well, maybe that's because we all knew it since we were babies. It's built-in. And it isn't competing with the "usual stuff." The usual stuff is part of the oneness of all. This viscous and immature competition to be the only right one is a major obstacle as we seek to know ourselves.

SCOOTER: We need to be more humble, right?

Mr. Lightman looks at his watch.

VINCENT: Yeah, time is going slow because talking about oneness and quantum Jesus is boring!

EARL: (Laughing) "Quantum Jesus" is Wi-y-ld!

KAREEM: So, we must be humble?

MR. LIGHTMAN: Well, humility allows you to know God within yourself in a positive way. When you come to know that power inside, it's easy to become arrogant. But look at Neo in *The Matrix*. He was a badass. He knew his skills and his power. But he never boasted about it to a level that was arrogant. He admitted when he didn't know what to do and when he was scared. With all that power, he was still able to see his limitations ... without letting that take anything away from his power. That's an example of power and oneness with humility.

SCOOTER: That's true. Nice example.

MR. LIGHTMAN: And try not to think in musts and have-to's. Allow yourself to be humble and loving. Put the love first and you'll usually end up being humble, giving, accepting. You'll likely realize that you are perfectly average and extremely special, just like everyone else. The average *is* extremely special. It just depends on how you're looking at it. Spirit is the most amazing thing that can be experienced. Yet, it's our natural, normal selves. It took me a long time to see that. You guys can be like me and try hard for years to learn and understand it. ***Or you can make that shift quickly and open your hearts*** to unconditionally loving each other and the world. And you'll just ***get it***! I hope you guys get it someday. I love you guys.

VINCENT: Don't ever say ... That is creepy! Keep it to yourself.

Mr. Lightman laughs.

EARL: Are we done? I wanna get on *Xbox Live*.

VINCENT: Yeah, I've been killin' y'all in *The Rizing*.

EARL: Killin' "y'all?" Not me. Earl don't lose.

VINCENT: I meant everybody else. I'ma beat you in some game some day ... and it's gonna feel good.

EARL: Well not today. Keep feelin' bad. Loser.

MR. LIGHTMAN: What's *The Rizing*?
EARL: That's the most realistic game I have ever seen!
VINCENT: Yeah, it's like, really real!
EARL: Almost. I mean, I can't front, it got some mistakes. Like when somebody is on the other side of the door, and they stand real close, you can see their arms come through the door. I wish we could get a game that's all-the-way real.
SCOOTER: Yeah, like where you could really get into it like you're there in full 3D.
MR. LIGHTMAN: You mean like where you are in the game and you can see the environment all around you?
VINCENT: Yeah, *that* would be dope.
MR. LIGHTMAN: Maybe you could become one of the characters. Not just play as them, but really become them, and interact with the others inside a 3D world.
SCOOTER: Yeah!
MR. LIGHTMAN: Things look solid. You could touch, taste, hear, smell and see everything all around you.
VINCENT: Now, that's dope!
MR. LIGHTMAN: Yeah! They have that game. I've played it.
VINCENT: Yeah, right. You serious?
SCOOTER: Is this a game only rich people can get?
MR. LIGHTMAN: No. It's the most realistic game ever. You're inside of the game, but you forget that it's just a game. The objects seem solid, even though they're just made of vibrating light and sound.
EARL: Huh? What's the name of that?
MR. LIGHTMAN: It's called, "Real life on planet Earth."
Vincent pauses, then realizes Mr. Lightman is messing with them.
VINCENT: Man!
They all get it. Earl shakes his head.
EARL: Got 'em! Got us! Oh-mi-Lrrd!
MR. LIGHTMAN: This is the ultimate game, though. And you guys are the players. You'll be on this Earth for a while. Love each other.
They're all quiet for a few seconds. They think about it.
VINCENT: Who prefers Earth 5.0?
SCOOTER: Me.
BINDIA: Yeah.
EARL: Me, too.

VINCENT: You said some good stuff, but it's not realistic. (Condescending) "Love is the answer." Man! This is detention, dude. Not Oprah.
Mr. Lightman laughs. He stretches back in his chair and relaxes.
MR. LIGHTMAN: Ahh. Heaven.
He chuckles and shakes his head.
MR. LIGHTMAN: "Not Oprah."
He smiles, shakes his head, then nods.
MR. LIGHTMAN: Definitely heaven.

2

INVOLUTION INTO THE ILLUSION
WHO AND WHAT IS GOD?
THE ONE INFINITE CREATOR
A TOUR OF THE DIMENSIONS
SPIRIT INVOLUTION & SOUL EVOLUTION
DIMENSIONS, HEAVENS, GODS & ANGELS
HIGHER SELF, SPIRIT BECOMES SOUL, ASTRAL PLANE
KNOW YOUR MIND/BODY/SPIRIT DEVICE
SURF OUR MULTI-DIMENSIONAL INNERNET
INTERPLANETARY COMPUTER NETWORKS
EXTRATERRESTRIAL & INTER-DIMENSIONAL TEENAGERS
3RD TO 4TH DENSITY PLANETARY TRANSITION
ILLUMINATI CONTROL. GOVERNMENT COVER-UPS
HISTORY OF EXTRATERRESTRIAL CONTACT ON EARTH
SEEK THE CREATOR WITHIN. SEE THE CREATOR IN ALL

As the students sit in the classroom, a single particle of light called a photon dwells near the ceiling. The photon pulls the magnetic waves of fear, pain, and confusion that are emitting from the hearts of everyone in the room. The photon receives this energy as a form of intelligent energy and magnetism, not as emotional pain. Through the electromagnetic waves sent out by the pulsing hearts of the children, the photon receives a calling for answers to many questions. The photon then begins a spiraling motion. It then enters a vortex which is within its own center. It vibrates quickly and gets hotter. It remains in the same location of the classroom, but tunnels through the elements, molecules, atoms and subatomic particles that make up the empty space in the room.

It folds into itself more and more, tunneling deeper and deeper into the fabric of space-time all the way to the highest dimension a photon of its kind can exist. From there, the photon sends the children's calling through a signal that reaches even higher dimensions. The signal is now outside of the linear space-time and time-space experience of the physical Earth. The signal travels through an interplanetary computer network which connects to many different parts of this solar system and The Milky Way galaxy. The signal teleports from planet to planet, then star to star until it reaches a star system called Arcturus. Arcturus is located in a constellation called Bootes, which is about thirty-seven light years away from Earth. Meanwhile, in our solar system, a Great Council of eighth-dimensional Senior Beings has just finished a very important meeting. The members of this council have dedicated their entire existence to service of The Infinite One, service to beings in the physical dimensions, and service to the evolution of all civilizations in this small portion of the Milky Way galaxy. An eighth-dimensional spirit has just left the meeting with the council. This spirit has agreed to take on a great mission. The spirit was told to return to its home star of Arcturus and its mission will begin. When the Arcturian spirit returns to Arcturus, the signal from Mr. Lightman's class collides with it. The collision is more of an energetic merger. The Arcturian spirit gets disoriented and confused. Its consciousness is scrambled and it vibrates uncontrollably between dimensions. There are a group of Arcturian Elders nearby. These are large, luminous beings. They don't interfere. They know that this is part of the spirit's mission.

As the Arcturian spirit's consciousness vibrates between dimensions, it gets the attention of some individuals and collectives whose consciousness are in tune with these dimensions. Ascended Masters, Christic Beings, Angelic Orders, Cosmic Teachers, Guides, Guardians, Archangels, and a small community of extraterrestrial humans all see this happening. All of these beings play their part in helping to organize, teach, protect and guide the social welfare of many societies, planets, and star systems. They operate on the more subtle layers of our reality. Overall, their duties help to maintain balance and to serve in the evolution of all beings in this portion of the galaxy. A few of those who can be called Orders come to help the disoriented spirit.

They have to determine the best action to take in order to help this Arcturian spirit. They consider the spirit to be a young spirit because of its lack of experience within the universe. They see that the memory of the young spirit has been almost completely wiped out. They want to heal the young spirit and send it back to the dimension it came from. They notice that the young spirit's energy field has a very strong pulling towards the lower dimensions. Their duty is to help the young spirit without interfering with its destiny. They decide that the best way to do that is to let the young spirit experience infinity, and then experience the pure and empty awareness of The Creator. With that, they assume that the young spirit will become balanced, and direct itself to wherever it chooses to go. They bless the young spirit and allow it to go deep, deep, deep into itself where it t a p s i n t o Infinity||...|||||>>|||||>>|||...|||..||||...|||||....|||..||||...||>>>>>>....|||||..||||| || ||| | | ||| ||>>>... ... ... I A ^^||||U |||WE ||||US|||SHE|||HE|| THAT|||

The young spirit then experiences what may be described as pure and empty Mental Awareness. This awareness cannot be accurately described using words. From the human perspective, it can be said that this awareness Is All That has ever been, All That Is, and All That will ever Be. This awareness creates and becomes every thing, every essence, every dimension, universe, galaxy, star, planet, spirit, soul, mind, body, human, animal, plant, mineral, element, molecule, and every atom in existence. In this state, it is all things and it is no thing. Through Infinite Intelligence, it can be said that this awareness is The Creator, The Creating, and The Creation of all. It is beyond concept, description, name and gender. This Is *Your* Source which sparked our existence and experience. We use these words and ideas now only to *talk around it* and *talk about it*, in an attempt to point towards it, but we cannot grab hold of it or define it in a directly-factual way using words. This Source has been given many names and labels including "God," "Source," "Oneness," "The Absolute," "The Supreme Self," "*The Self*," "The Prime Creator," "*The One Infinite Creator*," "*The Infinite One*," or simply, "The One."

{144V: We use the term "Creator" and" Source" most often for two reasons. *One is to help you, the reader, to remember your nature as a creator with the ability to receive an amazing Idea at any moment, and use it to create something, an invention, business or social movement that can improve your life and the lives of others.* The second reason We use the term "Creator" most often is due to the personal choice of the human Scribe, Kivar, to include Devotion in his seeking. And the term "Creator" just helps to inflame his being with devotional energies. We use the term "Source" to help remind the reader that all spiritual, religious and scientific seekers agree that there is a creation. So we agree that there is a Source of creation. That Source doesn't have to be in a context related to organized religions. Source means source and That Is That}.

The Infinite One is total unity of Existence. In this state, it is what can be considered "no thing," but holds the potential for every thing — one and many, here and there, then and now, darkness and light. This is The *Identity, The Self* of All That Is. *This is What You Are.* In this state, there is no time, no space, no other. All That Is is a kind of unchanging, intangible state of timeless awareness.

The young spirit then begins to flow within the breath of The One and resonates outward from this center of being. This allows a sense of finity where the experience of "other" can be had. As the young spirit goes from the infinite to the finite, it gains a sense of The Creator's Original Thought, which is to realize and experience the *Idea of Finity and separateness*. This idea allows The One Self to experience ItSelf as multiple Selves. These selves are Co-Creators. Each Co-Creator exists within The Infinite One. Each Co-Creator is given the attributes of The Infinite One, but The Infinite One is always greater than all of the Co-Creators combined. As it radiates further out from the center, the young spirit flows through many layers of Co-Creators and their creations. At this level, all Co-Creators have the free will to create their own universes, life forms, laws, substances, body types, lessons to learn, ways of learning, stories, joys, dramas and challenges. These components create infinitely unique experiences. The experiences of each Co-Creator, their co-creators and their co-co-creators are all experienced by The One Infinite Creator. The young spirit knows that no matter how far out or how deep down existence goes, All That Is is The Infinite One.

The young spirit returns to the star Arcturus. Arcturus is a Solar Co-Creator which is strongly connected to our Solar Co-Creator, The Sun, also known as Sol. The young spirit gains some balance in its consciousness and returns to the state where it is resonating within many dimensions simultaneously. The young spirit resonates through worlds which contain beings that have been called Angelic Creator Gods, Archangels, Angelic Beings of all kinds on many levels, Devas, Cherubim, Christic Beings, Avatars, Seraphs, and many other beings of light. The young spirit resonates further out through many more worlds. As it does, its state of consciousness changes over and over. What is considered to be reality changes repeatedly. The young spirit radiates the signal that holds the data from the photon.

The beings who are helping the young spirit are all aware that it is destined to go into the lower octave of The Creator's essence. The lower octave of The Creator's awareness is made up of seven main levels of consciousness. The Creator experiences these lower layers of consciousness through Galactic Co-Creators such as The Logos whose physical body is the Milky Way galaxy. And through Solar Co-Creators such as the Sub-

Logos Arcturus or Sol. The helpers are aware that the young spirit is still not balanced enough to safely go into the lower seven levels. They come up with a plan. They combine their unique essences to create a specific arrangement of essences. The arrangement creates a program. They attach this program to the consciousness of the young spirit. The young spirit will use this program as a kind of mental browser. The browser will allow the young spirit to have a specialized experience. This specialized experience will help it to explore the lower dimensions without incarnating into them. They are aware that this will be an extremely stimulating adventure for the young spirit. The program will allow the young spirit to collect data and slowly become more aware of the worlds it explores and the beings within them. In a state of confusion, the young spirit will commune with the beings who are incarnated in the dimensions below. The young spirit will follow the calling to Mr. Lightman and his students. It will collect new experiences, learn new lessons, and attempt to provide a great service to humanity on Earth in a way that is not known as yet.

A cosmic guide leads the young spirit to a black hole within the star of Arcturus. The young spirit enters the black hole and experience what seems to be a tunnel. Within this tunnel experience, there are many exit points. These exit points lead to many different kinds of universes with many complex combinations of consciousness, essences, energies, laws, entities, and substances. Other exit points lead to other stars and galaxies within this universe. Some of these portals connect to the minds of beings in the lower worlds who have raised their level of awareness to match the energy of this dimension. The young spirit is very confused, but continues to flow through the tunnel. As it approaches the exit, there is an indefinable sense of timelessness.

The young spirit then experiences a process of changing over and over again. The changes occur in cycles — larger cycles to smaller cycles. Within these cycles, the young spirit senses that The One is Infinite, The One is Unity, The One is awareness, The One is Love, The One is All. All is the Expression of The One. All is Love. All is Sound. All is Vibration. Love is vibration. Vibration is the Expression of Consciousness. Vibration is expressed as "Many Things." Every Thing is Vibrating Love. Vibrating Love is the Energy of all things. Vibrating Love Energy is the expression of The One Infinite awareness.

As Consciousness Vibrates, there is Movement. Conscious Vibration can Move at different speeds. Another word for speed is frequency. The frequency of Conscious Vibration Creates Photons, Particles of Clear Light. The speed of Vibrating Consciousness slows down. Different speeds of Vibrating Consciousness create different Colors of Light. All of existence from here on out/down is Love and Light, Light and Love. There are infinite variations of simple, basic, very complex, and exponentially complex arrangements and patterns of vibration, frequency, love and light.

Within each major pattern of vibration are infinite sub-patterns of vibration. Within each major frequency of vibration are infinite sub-frequencies of vibration. All vibrating frequencies of energy are finite expressions of The Infinite. Generally speaking, the closer the vibrating frequency of a thing is to the state of unity, the stronger or higher the vibrating frequency of that thing is. The further the vibrating frequency of a thing is from the state of unity, the weaker or lower the vibrating frequency of that thing is. The young spirit realizes that its Self is one point of vibrating consciousness within The One Infinite vibrating consciousness.

In sheer confusion, the young spirit *VIBRATES CHAOTICALLY. IT GETS HOT, HOTTER, HOTTER*, and begins an *INTENSE PULSING, THRUSTING MOVEMENT* deeper and deeper into the essence of The Creator. The essence remains the same, but there are new patterns of vibration which lowers the bandwidth of the young spirit's awareness. This causes the young spirit to vibrate at a slower speed. This slower speed allows the young spirit to vibrate in sync with the lower octave of reality. A very simplified description of an octave could be: A pulsing, cyclical field of One consciousness, vibrating at seven different speeds, creating seven main colors, and seven different levels of consciousness. An octave is created and used by One to create an illusion which allows One to experience One Self as an "Other" One. An octave may also be called a "cycle," a "density structure" or "density frame." In this octave, the original essence is denser than it was in the one the young spirit came from. There are seven main levels of denser and denser essence in each cycle. The essence of each lower/outer level appears "thicker", denser, and more compressed than the level above/within it. A level may also be called a "density." The spatial terms "lower" and "higher" helps, but do not accurately describe the differences in these cycles and levels. There is a blossoming, unfolding, curvature to all this that We are not including in our description. Overall, as We attempt to describe all higher dimensions, We must restate that words are a very poor tool for transmitting the nature of the actual perceptions of experience in these "higher" layers of our beingness.

A level of density is created when the essence vibrates at a slower frequency and forms the photon, the basic particle of light, as a new color. The light creates atoms which contain the blueprint for the illusion of solid matter. The primary color of the light in this level is Violet. Although the essence is more dense than it was in the level above, the atoms that make up this level are far, far less dense with matter than the atoms that make up level three which is the physical world. The atoms at this level are much more dense with light, but less dense with matter than the atoms in the physical world. The atoms in the physical world are denser with matter and less dense with light. The eighth density level which the young spirit came from is the first level of another cycle of seven densities. After that, there are seven more levels in another cycle. The young spirit is now vibrating at the highest level of this octave. This is the seventh level which can be called "seventh density."

Within each density level, there are seven sub-levels. Vibrating at each density level, there are worlds within worlds within worlds within worlds. These worlds are experienced and inhabited by conscious and energetic beings who create "perspectives" of the "world." These perspectives and worlds can be called dimensions. For simplicity's sake, it may be stated that there are seven primary dimensions in this density frame. Within each primary dimension, there are an infinite number of potential dimensions. Although there is a difference, the terms "dimension" and "density" are often used interchangeably.

Spirits incarnate in the lower density levels and then evolve upward in awareness from one level to the next. In this cycle, the first density level of vibrating essence is the void of nothingness and the canal which gives birth to all physical matter — minerals, water, air, and fire. The second density level is higher in awareness. It is the level of biological life — microscopic beings, plant and animal awareness. Spirits incarnate as human beings in the third density level.

The young spirit exits the black hole and arrives at the center of another star in the Bootes constellation. Within the essence of this star lives a great being called Ribak. There are thirteen planets revolving around this star. The planets and the civilizations on them vibrate at different density levels. The young spirit uses its mental browser to take in the information of this world. The Great Spirit Ribak is a Sovereign Spirit which contains many, many group souls. All spirits are sovereign in their own right. Ribak can look through the eyes of the group souls within itself as well as the individual souls within the groups. Ribak's awareness exists within a timeless state that cannot be grasped by a third-density human mind.

Each group soul within Ribak contains individual souls. Ribak is the total and complete Identity/Self of all evolving group souls and individual souls within itself. Within the illusion of linear time, it can be said that Ribak has completed the lifetimes, lessons and experiences of all the lower dimensions and knows itself in its totality. Ribak has integrated all experiences of spirit and soul, and may also be called a sovereign soul. Each spirit which has used and integrated soul energy may also be called a soul.

The young spirit knows its consciousness is placed in a certain vehicle, a body which is made of vibrating violet light, and is in the shape of a torus. The primary bodies of the souls within Ribak are angelic and humanoid. These bodies are made of the purest attainable light in this octave. Each soul is made of seven centers of concentrated spinning energy which creates its body. On Earth, the most widely-used term to describe these energy centers is "Chakra." By going through many challenges and serving others, these souls have learned many lessons. These lessons expanded their awareness more and more, allowing them to refine and purify their energy centers to the purer love and light of Source.

Within the illusion of linear time, it can be said that all of these souls were once physical human beings living on a physical planet, going through hardships and not knowing what awaited them in the heavens above. They have all lived in solid matter, and learned more and more how to raise the matter into themselves through their centers. They learned how to move, seek light, survive, develop a personality, and socialize with others. They learned how to choose between a life dedicated to giving to others or a life dedicated to selfishness. They learned how to love each other. They learned the connection between compassion and the illusion of solid matter. They learned how to control matter with their minds, then learned to be one with matter and light, then learned to illuminate their matter and project it outwards. They've mastered the use of matter, choice, universal love & compassion, Understanding, wisdom, and Unity. They've learned all they needed to learn in the lower dimensions and are now radiating pure light as guides in service to the souls who are living in those dimensions.

The young spirit is unable to properly comprehend this. The mental browser that it's using to experience this world allows for a very limited and distorted perception of what's going on. It's similar to someone with no knowledge of any electrical device trying to browse the internet for the first time. There are many parts to be used and understood. As it moves through this world, many pieces of random information pop into its awareness. The information comes at light speed and holds knowledge about this world and the beings within it. The bombardment of data makes it impossible for the young spirit to stabilize its awareness and get a grip of what is happening. The word confusion is an understatement to describe what the young spirit is experiencing. Every time the young spirit tries to grasp a piece of information, it's hit with trillions more. It's similar to a schizophrenic human being having an uncontrollable episode. The difference is that the young spirit experiences no emotional discomfort. The concept of emotion is unknown to the young spirit. The overload of data creates a large amount of harsh static within the young spirit's awareness. The dissonance causes misalignment with The Creator's center, and creates extreme levels of distortion in the young spirit's perception of reality. Ribak helps the young spirit to find the messaging system in its mental browser. Using this system, the young spirit can store the most important incoming data about this world. Ribak sends the young spirit a welcome message.

I am Ribak. Welcome, Beloved.

You are about to experience a fictional exploration of my own exploration of my Self. I am what you may call a Sovereign Soul. Within the space-time illusion, I exist within the essence of a star in the Milky Way galaxy. Like you, I exist in the image of The Infinite One. The main difference is that I know much, much more of what that actually means than you do. I am infinity, I am awareness, I Am One, and We Are Many. I am awareness, I am energy, I am Love, I am vibration, I am sound, I am movement, I am magnetism, I am Light, I am geometry, I am Wisdom, I am Electricity, I am space, I am time, I am physical matter, I am spiritual, I am soul-ar, I am mental, I am emotional, I am angelic, I am human, I am animal, I am biological, I am mineral, I am elemental, I am molecular, I am atomic, I am subatomic, I am awareness. I am The One exploring my Self as all these things. I create vast realities and deliberately limit my awareness as I travel from spirit to matter. I speak to you, the young spirit. I speak to you, the physical Human on Earth who is reading this information now. Please, hold ...

Hold on as I shift attention. I am now in Foreverness and Togetherness in the essence of your solar system. While I have your attention, The One Who Is would like to leave a message for you through this text.

I Am
The One I Am.
I Am the essence of everything you know.
The physical world you see around you
is the most solid level of my essence. Look to your left. I Am That.
Look to your right. I Am That. Close your eyes. I Am That. Open
your eyes, look around. Listen, move your fingers,
feel your pulse, taste something sweet. And Look! I Am That, I Am
That, I Am That, I Am That, I Am That, I Am That, I Am That.
Within the physical illusion of separation, there have been many
posers and tricksters speaking and acting in the Name of The One I
Am. There have been much mystery, many blunders, and great
confusion about my True Identity and my true intentions for humanity
on Earth.
Within your perception
of time, in your coming decades,
I Will Be What I Will Be, I Will Become
What I Will Become, and I Shall Prove To Be
What I Shall Prove To Be. Eternally, I am The One I Am.

I am Ribak. I am again within the Ribak star system. As you can
imagine by now, I am one with your Sun, with all the stars in the galaxy,
and I am one with you. As I was saying, I am a Sovereign soul. I use
thought to create the illusion of separation with myself. We use
pulses of love, tones of sound, colors of light and segments of time to
dip down into the illusory matter and experience it as you and those
around you. I am one and I am united, but I learned to truly appreciate

this by experiencing separation and manyness. I learn to love in an infinite number of ways. I descend into matter, then raise the matter up into the light. I exist outside of your seconds, minutes, hours, days, weeks, months, years, centuries and millenniums. We experience oneness, perfection and contentment at all times. Nothing can ever be wrong. That is why we need to live as you — to help us explore ourselves in challenging situations. I thought, "What would it be like if I were to feel stuck in a physical body on a physical planet with millions of others, with no memory of what I am, moving through years of time in a difficult environment?" What if I were to forget my perfection and my oneness? What if I could experience myself as a single point of awareness who feels separate from the whole and separate from the other single points of awareness? What if I fully believed myself to be the single mother struggling to pay the bills, the father who lost his son in the war, the parents watching their child starve to death, or the teenager who's getting bullied at school? How would I react if I were to forget that everything is always perfect, that I am one with The Creator, and that The Creator is me and everyone I know? How would I react if I felt really frustrated, angry, scared and stuck in a chaotic and insane physical world? You guys help us to know that by choosing to forget the big picture and choosing to explore the network of mind, soul and body, and choosing to be born into the physical world. You chose to be where you are now. You are our many different points of attention. You are microscopic cells within me as I am a microscopic cell of The Word, Who is a microscopic cell of The Infinite One. To you, a lifetime seems like many years of joy and pain. From my point of view, this is simply a pulse, a breath out, then in — Spirit to matter to spirit again. With all the pain you see around you, it is insulting to say to you that everything is perfect. But I promise you, everything is perfect. Eventually, you will know your oneness with me and with The Infinite One. You will be back to this timeless state of awareness only to realize that you never left. It's confusing, I know. You are about to take a trip through my body, through the dimensions, the densities, the heavens, the planes, the layers of this reality. Much has been written about the heavens. Many humans have explored regions of these etheric worlds in their own inner universes/minds/bodies. On your planet, descriptions of these higher worlds have been transmitted through religious, spiritual, metaphysical and philosophical texts. The information about these worlds varies from individuals, cultures and schools of thought. There are specific terms used by some and not used by others. There are different ways of counting and categorizing the layers.

144V: Even the idea of learning lessons and seeking The One Self/Creator is not the only way to view the evolution of souls. The idea of seeking The One and learning lessons comes through this book according to the human Scribe's point of view. Some of you may evolve to higher levels of awareness without consciously seeking Oneness or God. The terms density, dimensions, and the framework we describe can be found in your myths, religions, magical and mystical systems with different breakdowns, framing, concepts, and using different terms. How you see it all depends on many factors. My Goodness, there is so much being left out as I transfer this message *to you. We're dealing with sovereign souls, oversouls, and individual souls. We're dealing with multiple dimensions, and with my simultaneous awareness of infinite timelines and parallel realities. Then there's the Comical Truth that, when viewed from a broader point of view, there's No Complexity at all. The absurd level of simplicity to all of this is the big universal joke, the Main game — God pretending to not be God — Infinity playing with the Idea Of Finity. When you Stand Over all of it, It's Just You, Creator of all, in one moment, just being what you are and doing what you do. Don't try to understand it all right now. You don't even have to believe it. Just continue this "fictional" exploration along with the young spirit who is moving through my essence ... In joy ...*

The young spirit takes in this message and gains a bit more understanding. It knows that the souls within this dimension are evolving and will all know themselves as a sovereign soul. They have grown, balanced, practiced and perfected every aspect of being within this frame of densities. They have worked their way through the confusion and the pain of feeling separated from Oneness. They've experienced the forgetting, the suffering, the believing, the faith, the outer seeking, the inner seeking, the trials, the learning of lessons, the remembering, the connecting, the awakening, and the knowing of the Self. They are perfectly-purified souls who know themselves in their totality, and are preparing to ascend through the infinity to be reborn into the eighth density where the young spirit came from. Although the young spirit came from the dimension above these sovereign souls, the young spirit has not collected the innumerable valuable experiences and lessons of the lower dimensions. These souls no longer have unique appearances. They all look the same. They are made of pure light. These souls no longer have unique personalities. They have integrated it all, and now only serve by being and radiating Light. By coming into seventh density, they've chosen to give up all sense of individuality and now turn to the indescribably ecstatic experience of completely consciously re-membering themselves as The One. That is the experience they've sought as they spiraled toward the sunlight as plants, as they grew, learned and survived as animals, as they sought understanding and love as human beings, and as they sought wisdom, unity, and total oneness as more evolved souls. This is what all souls are always seeking at every moment of their existence. Whether they acknowledge it or not, all plants, animals, self-aware beings, awakened self-aware beings, extraterrestrial beings, angels, demons, and all beings of light are always seeking their Source.

As the young spirit takes this in, its frequency of vibration slows down. It now vibrates in tune with a lower portion of the seventh dimension. It greets a new class of seventh-density souls who are still learning their final lessons before they fully know themselves as a sovereign soul. The young spirit experiences a cycling sense of being one and being many. It gets a sense of this entire world being in the shape of a torus. At the center of this world, there are repeating PULSES OF LOVING ENERGY WAVES THRUSTING outward from the center. The essence of Source radiates through the waves in all directions.

Suddenly, a wave of many incoming messages comes into the young spirit's awareness. The confusion gets worse. There's a sense of being one, being many, being small and being large. As the young spirit thinks about what is happening, it experiences the thoughts of the other souls and a "greater" soul thinking with it. Suddenly, there are no other souls to think with, there is only one. It's a bizarre experience to be itself, the others, then only one. The young spirit wonders, "Who is this One?"

I AM!

A LOUD BLAST OF HOT, ENERGETIC RHYTHMIC BEATS PULSE AND ECHO out in circles throughout the entire world. The young spirit hears the sound, then realizes that it itself is the sound, and the sound is it. It hears the voices of the other souls humming to the rhythm of the sound. It joins in on the humming. The greater soul sends love to itself and hums the sound "Ah-oh-m", which fills the "smaller" souls with love. These souls send and receive the love to and from each other. Together, they hum the sound "Auh." This sound keeps them and the greater soul feeling Good.

The young spirit experiences a strong pushing and pulling that squeezes it together then stretches it apart over and over. The Goodness continues and reveals the truth. The truth sets the young spirit free. There is a slight moment of CLARITY as the young spirit expands and realizes itself as all the other souls. They all expand and realize themselves as the greater soul. The greater soul expands and knows itself as a soul that is even larger than itself. That larger soul knows itself as The One. That larger soul knows itself as The All. All souls know they are

THAT!

The RHYTHMIC BEATS PULSE AND RESOUND A THUNDEROUS ROAR. The larger soul sends love to the smaller souls by humming the sound "Aum." They return the love by humming the sound "Auh." The greater soul feels the love of togetherness, peace and harmony of all the smaller souls. It sends love out to *The One, a being who is even larger than itself. All are silent. All is one. All is The One. The young spirit is at peace with itself, the other souls, the larger souls, and The One. But it wonders ...Who is The One?*

I AM!

The THUNDEROUS RHYTHMIC BEATS PULSE AND ROAR harder and faster. The humming gets louder and louder. The push and pull gets faster, faster, then stops. All is silent. All is empty. All is one. All is Good.

The young spirit's frequency of vibration slows down. It vibrates in sync with a lower portion of the seventh dimension. It greets a new class of souls. The souls who are vibrating at this point in the seventh dimension are learning very advanced lessons about themselves and Existence. Some of the souls here are physical humans. These beings are able to consciously experience the seventh-dimensional worlds without being incarnated at the seventh-density vibration. Some of these humans are Christic and Buddhic beings, newborn human babies, toddlers, adolescent children, Prophets, Seers, Sages, Mystics, Shaman, awakening Starseeds, as well as those known as Blue-ray, Indigo, Crystal and Rainbow souls. Other physical humans experience this world temporarily in ways that seem to be accidental. Every human being that consciously touches this state of awareness for even a second experiences a profound, ecstatic experience that usually changes them dramatically.

All seventh-dimensional souls in this world work to assist those in the lower worlds. They are neutral, and have absolutely no judgment towards anyone in the lower worlds. Their love is universal and unconditional. They are so appreciative of the feeling of closeness to Oneness that all they need to do is live as the light, and radiate the light.

Their appreciation of Oneness catches the attention of the young spirit. The young spirit experiences this oneness, but doesn't share the joy and appreciation for it as the incarnated souls do. Their thankfulness for simply being One is beyond what the young spirit is able to experience. The young spirit has gained enough awareness to know that this deeper appreciation of oneness must be due to their experiences of living in the lower worlds.

It decides to consciously lower its frequency of vibration and go into the dimension below this one. As one being, all of the seventh-dimensional souls send love to the young spirit. They open a portal for it to travel to the sixth dimension. Before it does, it turns its awareness back towards the souls and holds ...

The young spirit then turns and enters the portal. Inside, the young spirit senses many groups of expanding solar systems, galaxies and universes. The sheer size and number of everything is too much to take in. The young spirit is guided to one of the thirteen planets in the Ribak star system.

This planet is called Julāhā. As the young spirit approaches Julāhā, it VIBRATES CHAOTICALLY and begins an INTENSE SPIRALING MOVEMENT deeper and deeper into the essence of Source. The RHYTHMIC BEATS and

PULSING WAVES OF LOVE become LIVING LIGHT ENERGY. The light organizes the waves of love into perfect, complex geometric patterns. This light of the sixth dimension is the intelligent energy that creates everything that exists in the lower dimensions. All substances, laws, situations, souls, beings, stars and planets are created by intelligent fractal patterns within the geometry of this sixth-dimensional light energy. This process creates the infinite combinations of energetic patterns within the universe.

As the young spirit becomes sixth-dimensional, it becomes the actual ingredients and process of this intelligent design. The young spirit exists as triangles, pyramids, circles, spheres, squares, and cubes. The basic geometric patterns become more and more complex as the vibration and movement of the rhythmic beats blaze on.

The original essence of The One sings forth a new tune and vibrates at a slower frequency. The essence becomes denser. This is the sixth level of density in this frame of seven densities. Vibrating at this slower frequency, the original essence is expressed as radiant Indigo Light. In a state of confusion, the young spirit explores this world using its mental browser. It knows that the blazing sound in the world above has created and become this world of living light.

The young spirit sees that its sixth-dimensional body is made of etheric light. The torus that was its body now has a more solidified head. The young spirit opens its Single Eye and is now able to see with its mind's eye. Of the seven energy centers/chakras, only two are activated within the body of the young spirit. One is the crown center which is the violet body which holds all of the energy centers. The other activated chakra is the single eye chakra which is its indigo body. The indigo body is layered inside of the violet body. The indigo body also contains seven chakras. This etheric body creates the form for all other lower-dimensional bodies, including the chemical and physical biological human body.

The young spirit has not yet activated the five lower energy centers. Those centers have not integrated any energy through experience, so they are not activated. The bodies of the other souls are packed with a lot more data and information in their mouths, throats, hearts, arms, torsos, abdomens, navels, hips, legs and feet. They have access to many memories, experiences, personalities, and physical forms that the young spirit does not. Using its single eye, the young spirit's sense of Self is as a single point of awareness that is connected to other souls existing within their own points of awareness.

The young spirit is taken into a ship that is near Julāhā. This ship is not made of physical matter. It's made of conscious living light. This light is the combined awareness of almost 7,000 souls. The young spirit immediately feels at home because these souls are from the star system Arcturus. They are a small portion of a much larger civilization. Their civilization used to reside on a planet in the Arcturus system. Now, they have moved their consciousness out of that planet. They travel in groups in search of those in need of their service. These souls are all incarnated in the sixth-dimension. The young spirit experiences a sense of home and belonging, but has no conscious memory of being an Arcturian spirit.

The Arcturians are known as one of the most spiritually advanced civilizations in the Milky Way galaxy. Different societies of Arcturians exist in the fourth, fifth, sixth and seventh dimensions. In Arcturian consciousness, every aspect of living is connected to soul evolution and radiating Oneness. Family life, friendships, social interactions, helping others, health, education, finances, business, art, sexuality, playing, laughter and games are all connected to the appreciation and inner seeking of the complete conscious timeless experience of Oneness.

Arcturians are taught to see Oneness in themselves, in all others, in the environment, and in all aspects of life. Their deep connection to The Universal Energy of Christ helps them to learn in love and teach in love. The Christ energy helps them seek, teach and learn with a strong appreciation of existence and experience. The Arcturian souls know that the young spirit is here for an important reason, but don't know exactly what it is. They scan their sibling's awareness and sees that it's here to receive information about this world. Some of them volunteer to teach the young spirit about sixth-dimensional beings and the sixth-dimensional world.

The Arcturians of this ship can be considered to be young sixth-dimensional souls. This youth is not necessarily according to age or time. They are young in terms of experience within the sixth dimension. They are vast, wise and advanced beings of light, but have not progressed very far into the sixth-dimensional experience as yet. They vibrate at a frequency that syncs with the lower layers of the sixth dimension. According to frequency within this dimension, they can be compared to teenagers. They are able to project their consciousness anywhere they desire. Right now, they have chosen to project themselves to Ribak as a conscious ship. Here, they are serving, studying, teaching, and learning from their experiences on the thirteen planets of the Ribak star system. They are on a mission to learn a few major lessons in their own evolution.

The young Arcturians on the ship are working and studying on all of the thirteen planets in the Ribak system. Of the thirteen planets, five are currently vibrating at a fifth-density level. Planet Julāhā and two others vibrate at the sixth-density level. Two other planets vibrate at the fourth-density level. One of the planets vibrates at the third density level and is transitioning to the fourth. Just like planet Earth, their population is going through a lot of darkness, rapid social changes, and great suffering and warfare. One planet vibrates at a second-density level. Only vegetation and animals live there. This planet has a stunningly beautiful variety of unique plant-life and animals. The last planet in the Ribak system has not developed beyond the first-density level. It's only made of gases and minerals, including many precious stones and crystals. All of these planets, no matter the dimension, are visible to the eyes of 3D humans. This is because the foundation for all planets is the minerals of first density. On a sixth-density planet, the incarnated beings and their activities cannot be seen by 3D humans, but the physical minerals and gasses which make the planet's foundation are visible. To most 3D humans, the planet would be considered unpopulated.

There are lessons to be learned from all of these planets, and the young Arcturians are taking in all they can. They have lived through the lower dimensions, and have ascended to this one by learning many, many complex lessons about choices, compassion and wisdom. Now, they are one unified mind. They are many individual souls who are consciously combined as one group soul. For all souls, the sixth-dimension is a level of perfected maturity and accepting complete responsibility for all choices. They now see the big picture of existence, and each individual soul is responsible for the group as a whole.

These souls have an expanded awareness which is outside of linear time as humans experience it. They are able to experience any and everything in the physical world at will. Being made of the living light of the universe, they hold matter within them, and are able to experience the material world in their own bodies through thought alone. Using thought, they are able to travel within the universe that is their own body. They do this by knowing that the seven energy centers within themselves are the densities and dimensions of their own inner universe. They are able to instantly create and become any environment, body, form, situation, or state of existence that can possibly be imagined. They are able to live from any point of view in those experiences — be it one individual, two individuals, a group, an animal, plant, table, tree, or chair. They do this in order to filter and extract only the purest experiences and lessons of love and light within the third dimension. They use physical experiences to learn lessons in unity. They enter their physical scenarios with specific mental/emotional/physical filters. These filters create a blueprint for the experience and help them to face the challenge in an honest way in order to learn the necessary lessons in an honest way. They extract every single bit of every needed lesson in the unity of love and wisdom.

These beings are also able to project their consciousness to any location in the galaxy. They do this by thought. This is usually done with permission from their local council in order to serve a struggling planet, or with permission from the souls on the planet they wish to enter.

They follow the rules of the local and larger councils. These rules were put in place for many reasons, but there is one reason that stands above all. Galactic laws are followed in order to preserve the Free Will of the planet or people being served. This is because Free Will is a Fundamental Law of Creation given by The One Infinite Creator and the galactic Co-Creator. Every being is created as a copy of The One with free will to experience its reality as it desires. All positive and mature beings who serve others hold this law up high as one that must be respected and carefully followed. As advanced and mature as fourth, fifth and sixth-dimensional beings are, there is a long history of them making mistakes in their attempt to serve less evolved civilizations, such as those on planet Earth. Many higher-dimensional beings who have evolved from the third-dimension have not experienced darkness to the extreme degree it exists on Earth. Many are naïve to just how dark and evil beings can become on certain planets. Although they have lived and suffered as physical human beings, their experiences of separation and hardship did not come close to the levels that exist on planets such as Earth. They enter into service unable to completely grasp the specific social distortions of certain planetary populations.

In the past, they have given advanced technology to some of these third-dimensional planets in order for them to feed everyone and create equality in the social and economic structures. The technology was often accepted and used by those in power to create weapons of war instead of for the good of all. The local councils and the central council learned from these experiences, and are much more cautious when deciding how to help a planetary population. Often, higher-dimensional beings spend a lot of time just observing a planet trying to find just one individual who is open to the message of oneness and able to properly take it in and teach it to others without becoming corrupt with power. Often, higher-dimensional beings observe a population for a long time and end up having to leave without serving in any specific way.

The young spirit is greatly stimulated after learning these things. It's still very hard for the young spirit to grasp concepts such as physicality, separation and suffering. All of these things are experienced as geometric arrangements, tones of sound, and colors of light. It continues to learn. It takes in some lessons about the young Arcturians within this ship.

It learns that they have all fused their individual minds together to form one mind, one being — a Group Soul. The Group Soul experiences itself as what may be called a Social Memory Complex, or Social Memory Network. A social memory network is created when the entire population of a planet is able to consciously put their minds & souls together and seek Oneness in harmony. Many of the beings who are known as gods and deities on planet Earth are social memory networks. A social memory network can contain thousands, millions, or billions of intelligent souls/minds. As a social memory network, they are aware of themselves as a group mind, as one being. They still have their sense of individuality, but all is done for the good of the one total being. They divide into smaller groups to travel and serve different planets and solar systems in the galaxy. No matter how far they seem to travel from each other within the space-time illusion of the physical universe, they are always aware of themselves as one single being in one body experiencing itself. They work with unified thought and collective action. Every being is connected to the thoughts, experiences and memories of every other being within the one. They are one and many simultaneously. As they continue to learn and evolve, individual thoughts and experiences are sent, received, shared, and used to evolve the whole. When an individual soul learns a lesson that is fundamental for conscious evolution, that lesson goes viral instantly. In this way, they are able to learn, teach, experience, and work together in order to evolve towards the total conscious awareness of Oneness in a loving, wise, unified and efficient way. In love and wisdom, they are united in their goals and tasks. They serve The One by serving the beings in the lower dimensions while seeking ascendance into the seventh dimension. To the primitive 3D human mind, the beings of the sixth dimension would be seen as superior all-knowing gods. They are far more advanced in consciousness than 3D humans, but are not perfect. They can become imbalanced, but due to their harmony, are able to instantly learn the necessary lesson and balance themselves. These souls have lived as physical human beings in the third dimension. They have graduated through the 4th and 5th dimensions, and are now sixth-dimensional beings.

In their service, these Arcturians work with other groups to serve those in need. Each group, and each group within the group, serves according to their area of specialty. They help to organize meetings, solve issues, work through challenges, and bring balance to many societies and planets in the lower dimensions. As they help and teach others, they learn more about the universe, themselves, and The Infinite One. With each lesson learned, there is expansion in consciousness of the one being. With each expansion, they evolve closer to the seventh dimension. They move from seeing the big picture towards seeing the whole picture. They move towards having more clarity and a greater and greater sense of perfected eternal oneness as The One. No matter how advanced they are or how much they seem to know, the infinite timeless nature of creation continuously reveals just how much is still unknown. Mystery is always present in the consciousness of all higher-dimensional beings. All thoughts and motivations within a social memory network are united, divine, and universal in nature. All beings within a social memory network know the others as other versions of themselves. They are able to look at many beings in the physical worlds still suffering the effects of feeling separate from each other and from The One.

The young spirit suddenly experiences a sense of simultaneous timelines and parallel realities. It's not able to comprehend this. From these lower layers of sixth-dimensional existence, it sees that the souls in the physical third dimension are fragments of the spirits in this dimension.

This confuses the young spirit. It tries to comprehend how this can be. The many cycles of time are extremely difficult for the young spirit to grasp. From the young spirit's point of view, it seems like these spirits of the sixth dimension fragmented themselves into many souls, incarnated into the physical third dimension, experienced separation from The One, then evolved consciously, ascended their way back up through the fourth and fifth dimensions, and are now united again in the sixth dimension, and are able to look back at themselves living as physical third-dimensional human beings. The young spirit uses many pulsations of loving time-waves trying to take this data in. It reviews this idea over and over, correcting mistakes in its own understanding with every review. The young spirit sees a connection between consciousness, fragmentation, the dimensions, and cycles of time. It tries to distinguish the workings of time and space between the group souls and individual souls within the one sovereign soul.

The young spirit concludes that the spirits in this dimension are fragments of consciousness within the consciousness of a spirit in the dimension above. It's a continuous process of one spirit creating fragments of itself to experience life in its own inner universe. Those fragmented spirits within the greater spirit have their own free will and create unique experiences that the greater spirit was not able to experience on its own. The experiences of each fragmented spirit and soul is experienced and collected by the greater spirit.

The young spirit sees that all beings are fragments of The One, and that all of the fragments contain the blueprint of The One in them. The young spirit's awareness expands as it receives more light and understanding. It sees that the dimensions have been designed so that The One, co-creators, and co-co-creators at different levels can interact in an infinite number of ways within space-time and time-space. In the sixth dimension, the beings are not bound by the illusion of linear time flowing from past to present to future. The young spirit learns that these sixth-dimensional beings create moments of time and fields of space within their own light bodies as they desire. Every moment of time is created as needed to learn all of the absolutely necessary lessons from every bit of the third-dimensional experience. Through the eyes of a sixth-dimensional being, the illusion of the third dimension is used to learn the most valuable lessons and seek a wider universal understanding of the unity of love and wisdom. At this stage in their soul evolution, unity is the way of life. From the sixth-dimensional point of view, the third-dimension holds many of the best experiences for evolution.

As these young Arcturians learn all necessary lessons in the Ribak system, they will learn more about themselves, existence, and The One. They will expand their awareness and speed up the rate at which their consciousness vibrates. If they can properly use all of their lessons learned in Ribak, their consciousness will approach the middle layers of the sixth-dimensional vibration. When evolving sixth-dimensional beings reach the middle layers, they receive a powerful resource/gift. This is the gift of a portion of the being which is known on Earth as the "Higher Self." From this point of view, the Higher Self may be thought of as the expanded Spirit which is also called Atma, Ka, or Oversoul. The Higher Self gives sixth-dimensional souls the ability to travel within their own consciousness and look at themselves as they lived in 3D physical human form when their planet was third-dimensional. With this, they are able to observe and interact with themselves as they lived on any day, month or year in any of their many physical "past" lifetimes. They are able to affect the experiences and the direction in which their lives went. With total respect to the free will of their "past" self, they attempt to guide themselves towards spiritual awakening in "past" lifetimes.

The sixth-dimensional beings on planet Julāhā are currently vibrating at the middle layers of the sixth-dimensional vibration.

They have earned the gift of the Higher Self. The young Arcturians aboard the ship observe those on Julāhā. They learn what they can about the Higher Self. From the point of view of a sixth-dimensional being who is the Higher Self, there is no actual "past self." Their human self is living in the physical world here and now within their own consciousness. The only differences are in the perspectives of consciousness and time. Sixth-dimensional souls are able to see the many cycles of time within their own consciousness. The gift of the Higher Self gives the sixth-dimensional souls the ability to re-enter any of the smaller timelines. By doing this, they can guide their "past" human selves as they live/lived in the physical third-dimensional world. From the point of view of their physical human selves in the third dimension, the souls in the sixth dimension would be considered their evolved future selves.

On Earth, this future self is called different names by different people. Some refer to the future self as The Atma, The Ka, The Oversoul, The Christed self, The Holy Spirit, Spirit, or The Holy Guardian Angel. Most physical human beings struggle to believe in such a thing. Many who truly believe it struggle to understand this concept. Many seekers, adepts and masters who make conscious contact with their future self struggle to grasp and hold the understanding of this in a clear and balanced way. The physical humans meditate, pray, and use many other techniques to contact, know, or consciously become their Higher Self. Many humans learn the language of symbolism and co-incidences in their daily physical life in order to contact and interact with their Higher Self. When humans display genuine compassion or experience high excitement, these sixth-dimensional Higher Selves are able to interact with them in a more conscious way. The Higher Self interacts with its past human self by programming potential experiences in order to give clues, symbols, and reveal amazing co-incidents in their daily life. They do this to help the human self realize more truth and/or make important choices which will help them to progress in their soul's evolution. There are advanced individuals on the mystical spiritual path or the magical spiritual path who are able to raise their awareness and completely know themselves and the Higher Self as one. As the Higher Selves serve their human selves, they learn many necessary lessons which they themselves need in order to evolve. When a human self asks the Higher Self for guidance, the Higher Self attempts to guide as much and as best as it can without infringing on the Free Will of the human self. Often, the Higher Self is unable to help in any valuable way, and must let the human self make critical mistakes. If the human self is extremely dedicated to growing and evolving consciously, the Higher Self may use specially-reserved tactics in an attempt to steer the human self away from making a critical mistake. The act of asking allows the Higher Self to interact more with the human self. The Higher Self works so that all can evolve and move closer to the timeless awareness of the presence of The One. Many humans who subscribe to certain organized religions are taught to reject the silly idea of things such as a Higher Self.

In these cases, the Higher Self acts accordingly to uphold the free will of the human self.

Physical humans who believe in this expanded self live day-to-day through the challenges of the physical world. They consciously call upon their Higher Self for guidance and protection. Some starseeds, adepts, magicians, mystics and awakening ones who are more advanced are able to consciously completely embody, become, and express the Higher Self in their physical body and human personality. When called upon, the Higher Self can actually program specific life experiences for their human self that can potentially guide the human self to learn lessons and move forward on their path.

In order to aid their human selves, these oversouls use the power of thought to affect the geometry and mathematics of third-dimensional space and time. They are able to create potential situations and schedule potential experiences. If the human self is unable to intuitively receive the message, or choose not to engage in the programmed experience, lessons go unlearned. The Higher Self is very, very patient, compassionate and understanding of the limitations and ignorance of the human self. After all, it is they themselves who are living/has lived in those physical and difficult situations. The tools used to guide the human self are custom-designed to get the attention of that specific human personality. If the human is a gardener or interested in gardening, the Higher Self may let them know that it's time to grow in a certain area of their life by creating clues pertaining to soil, roots, seeds, plants or trees. The Higher Self may create a feeling of déjà vu or create a difficult challenge that turn out to be a blessing in disguise. The Higher Selves do a great deal of their service to their human selves through dreams. Another way these oversouls aid their human selves is by sending rays of light with huge amounts of information which help humans to gain knowledge to the nature of themselves, their planet, the universe, and The One.

The humans translate this light using their mental abilities and spoken languages. Usually, humans are not able to comprehend the information well enough to properly translate the full message into words. Some receive the light and translate it very clearly. Some use the information from the Higher Self to help others and serve their community and planet. Others use their inner light to gain power over others, to control others and only serve themselves. Most humans receive the light from the Higher Self and use it without consciously knowing about the Higher Self. They passionately express the purity of the light naturally through socializing, conversations, parenting, raising a family, dealing with romantic relationships, teaching, writing, music, dance, comedy, painting, drawing, building, speaking, playing sports, storytelling, inventing, healing, creating products, organizations, social movements, or just generally living life from a much higher state of awareness. A small amount of humans in the physical world are able to activate and balance their seven main energy centers enough to enable them to consciously visit these higher dimensions with perfect clarity and understanding.

Being from the eighth dimension does not make the young spirit superior to the souls in this dimension or the lower ones. All spirits who are descending down the densities for the first time must learn step-by-step how things work in each lower/outer layer of The One's essence. Those souls who are ascending upwards from the physical world have learned many lessons about Existence that many higher-dimensional spirits have not learned. Physical humans who have experienced the deepest darkness and suffering, and have learned from these experiences, possess particular knowledge that beings who have only lived in higher dimensions don't have.

The young Arcturians teach the young spirit to use its etheric indigo body. The young spirit learns to consciously form itself into basic geometric shapes. It learns to use the intelligent light energy of which it is made. The young spirit sees that the incarnated souls are able to use their etheric bodies to project physical matter outwards. It sees that the others have a vast collection of personalities, bodies, experiences, memories, feelings and thoughts to create with. The young spirit isn't able to experience those levels of stimulation and complexity in its being. It decides to enter the planetary sphere of Julāhā. The Arcturians give thanks and comfort to the young spirit as it moves into the sky of Julāhā.

Those who are incarnated on Julāhā are very tall, and their bodies are made of the living sixth-dimensional light itself. They are visually similar to the Sixth-dimensional Arcturians, but are more evolved in their consciousness. Their bodies of light are invisible to 3D human eyes and technology. They have mastered the use of the physical space-time illusion, and are able to refine, perfect, filter and distill the purest experiences of the physical world. As they perfect every aspect of the physical illusion in indescribably subtle ways, they evolve closer to graduation into the seventh dimension.

Like humans, these beings are able to experience reality within the invisible inner world of their individual minds. This inner world where the mind is experienced is often called an Inner Plane. The inner plane is a world of energy which is extremely subtle and is the inner invisible reflection of the outer visible world. The outer world is experienced in the more fixed, particul arized space-time while the inner world is experienced in the more fluid, wavy time-space. Time-space is the world within the mind of each individual being where there is no direct interaction with "others." In time-space, a being is in a fixed point of spatial experience, but able to move all around in time. And able to mentally/emotionally experience any and every possibility in the physical lifetime, but unable to make physical changes. Within the conscious experience of a being, time-space is the world and experience of the portion of a being which is not incarnated in "tangible" form. Space-time is the world and experience of the portion of the being which is incarnated in "tangible" form. In space-time, beings experience One Fixed Moment in Time, Seeming to Move From a Past to the Present to a Future. But they are able to move all around in physical space. If space-time is the world of matter, time-space is the world of antimatter. In the sixth dimension, the difference between these inner and outer worlds isn't easily distinguishable and verbally describable.

Beings in the 3D physical world also experience the outer and inner planes, space-time and time-space. Humans who are incarnated on Earth exist in physical bodies on the physical surface of the planet while simultaneously living on the subtle layers of the inner plane in their mind and imagination. This inner plane is known as the Astral/Emotional Plane. On the astral plane, physical humans are able to feel emotions, think, imagine, visualize, have dreams, analyze, make plans, experience the past through memory, and can experience all potential futures. Each human mind is connected to the astral plane. Each human being possesses an astral body which allows them to experience the components of the astral plane. On Earth, the existence of the astral and the mental planes are well-known. There are an innumerable amount of beings living on the astral plane of Earth. These beings interact with the humans who are physically incarnated on the planet. These beings are not physically incarnated onto the planet because they have no physical bodies. They interact with the Earth humans through mental and emotional experiences only. In the same way, the young spirit exists on the inner planes of Julāhā, but is not incarnated onto the surface of the planet. From the inner plane, the young spirit can interact with the incarnated beings of Julāhā. The inner plane of this dimension is referred to by some as the Spiritual Plane or Unity Plane.

Within the spiritual plane, the young spirit joins the social memory network of Julāhā. The incarnated beings are able to live in a clear and conscious way on the outer living light surface of the planet, and on the inner spiritual plane. At this level of awareness, all of it is unified. They also use the inner-mind time-space experience to mentally project their consciousness to distant locations in space-time. The social memory network of Julāhā is the combined minds and souls of all beings who are incarnated on this planet. The name of this social memory network is "Jabik." Jabik is The One being who is the combined consciousness of all souls on Julāhā. Jabik consists of over 500,000 souls. The young spirit is welcomed into Jabik, and it is given love and comfort. The young spirit explores the sixth dimension. It learns that Jabik began to provide service to the human beings of Earth in the year 1999.

The beings of Jabik all work very closely with Arcturian individuals and social memory networks. When observed by physical human eyes, Julāhā would be seen only as a physical sphere containing dangerous gasses. Physical human beings would be unable to see the vast cities made of golden white light, and the over 500,000 beings that dwell upon this sphere.

The young spirit suddenly receives a specific kind of incoming data from the beings of Jabik. It is the energy of deep love and appreciation for unity with each other. The young spirit sees the energetic, geometrical and mathematical information of the appreciation for unity, but isn't able to experience the intense feelings of satisfaction as those of Jabik do. Jabik is filled with joy, delight, bliss and perfect ecstasy in every single thing they do. They know that this appreciation and joy comes from remembering unity after forgetting it. They remember being born into physical human bodies when Julāhā was a third-dimensional planet. They were born into a scary and dangerous world filled with many hardships. They lived stressful lives in survival mode for thousands of years before evolving. As their civilization matured and learned to love each other, the experiences of joy and bliss became more valued than ever before. They see that the young spirit only knows what it has learned in the highest dimensions of existence, and has not as yet experienced emotional stress and difficulty. All negativity within the young spirit is experienced as asymmetrical geometric patterns and incorrect mathematical equations. Since light, unity, and oneness is all the young spirit has known, there is no darkness, stress and separation to compare it to. Therefore, the appreciation for light and unity is nowhere near as intense as those who have experienced suffering.

The other souls show the young spirit the history of planet Julāhā and the being Jabik. The beings of Jabik were once physical human beings living within the limitations of the material world. They had no idea that it was even possible to sync their minds together in order to influence matter and achieve harmony, peace, abundance, bliss, joy, and oneness with each other and The One. They experienced ignorance, fear, wars, separation, control, domination, and economic inequality. Christed beings incarnated upon 3D Julāhā and taught them to love each other. This was difficult, although nowhere near as difficult as it is on Earth. It was only by truly exhibiting enough universal love and compassion that they gained true Understanding and earned their salvation.

As Julāhā transitioned from a third-density to a fourth-density planet, those who exhibited enough compassion and understanding died and transitioned to the new fourth-density Julāhā. The fourth-density planet was layered over the third-density planet just like the fourth-density Earth is layered over third-density Earth at this time. Those who failed to live sufficiently in Love, Compassion, and service to all needed to repeat the third dimension. After death, those souls were required to incarnate on a different third-dimensional planet in the galaxy where they had to re-live the same difficult situations and learn the lessons they failed to learn before. The individuals who graduated to fourth-dimensional Julāhā learned to perfect their Love, Compassion and Understanding. They learned the hidden truths of the illusion of linear time and space. They learned of the light within the matter and the sacred geometry within the light and matter, and how this works with their own mind, bodies and souls. As a fourth-dimensional planet, it took them a very long time to harmonize with each other and form the social memory network. When they achieved planetary harmony, the social memory network was formed. After millions of years of being a fourth-dimensional planet, Julāhā transitioned to a fifth-dimensional planet. The members of Jabik remained harmonized enough, and remained a strong social memory network. On fifth-dimensional Julāhā, these beings used the ways of wisdom to learn their lessons and evolve. Planet Julāhā increased in vibratory frequency and became a sixth-dimensional planet. All of its inhabitants became sixth-dimensional beings also. These beings of living light are the very same beings who lived as ignorant, separated humans in the third dimension. Many didn't make it from third to sixth on this planet.

All third-dimensional humans will eventually evolve through the dimensions and densities at their own pace. Some will need a few incarnations, others will need many. Others will need many more. Salvation from third to fourth depends on Universal Love, Compassion, and adequate service to all, which is freely given love. This is a very simplified example regarding the transition and evolution of souls through the heavens. In the very "end," all souls in the universe eventually return to the timeless awareness of total oneness as The One. By experiencing the darkness and the choices of the third dimension, the Love and Understanding of the fourth dimension, and the Wisdom and Light of the fifth dimension, these sixth-dimensional beings appreciate Unity much more than any being from a higher dimension who has not yet experienced darkness, separation and duality.

The young spirit goes on to learn a lot about unity on this planet. All beings communicate by sending and receiving thoughts through the etheric light which they are made of. The young spirit explores more and finds a fun program that would determine a sound vibration for its unique frequency of vibration. The sound that emerges is "Aum." The young spirit resonates with this sound and identifies with it as a designation.

Aum observes the other souls as they live their lives. Some of the souls of Jabik go to planet Earth. They experience much joy and bliss by visiting indigenous civilizations. They visit drumming circles, shamanic rituals, churches, temples, synagogues, concerts, award shows, and many other locations where light and sound are organized to create beautiful rhythmic patterns. The souls of this world exist as light and sound, and are able to take any form they desire in any period of linear time and space they desire. They can radiate themselves as sound vibrations. They love to join the vibrations emanating from the vocal chords of singers, from plucked guitar strings, beaten drums, and anything that can be made a musical instrument in the physical world. The sixth-dimensional souls radiate as electrons within colorful exploding fireworks and pyrotechnic shows. They radiate themselves as colorful lighting effects within things such as paintings, digital screens and light displays in gadgets, stained windows in churches, and colorful body paint used for rituals and play. They reflect their beingness as the bling itself in shining jewelry. They work within many precious minerals, stones, crystals, and other solid geometric structures. They love the experience of actually being the vibration of human laughter. It's one of their favorite things to do for fun. They only radiate with humans who are open to their presence. For example, if a person's chosen beliefs do not allow for the sharing of love and light with these sixth-dimensional souls, they would simply not share their beingness with that person. Aum observes these souls as they radiate their love and light in concerts, karaoke bars, houses, bedrooms, showers, garages, and music studios. They radiate as internal and external planetary sounds, birds chirping, lions roaring, and the sensational vibrational patterns in all of nature. They experience joy within the light of exploding stars, pulsars, colorful nebulae, gas and dust patterns, and many other phenomena within the Milky Way galaxy.

They radiate within solar flares, satellites, lightning storms, electronic devices, computer networks, emails, text messages, phone calls, static electricity, bioluminescent animals and plants, toys, and the current within wires and power outlets. They radiate their beingness only in locations where they are welcomed, or locations where the inhabitants are neutral to their presence. Between the years 1999 and 2017, they've seen a large increase in the number of people who are becoming more aware of the presence of extraterrestrials and higher-dimensional beings. These sixth-dimensional beings don't feel the lower vibrations of fear and separation being vibrated by the physical humans they dwell with. The frequency of fear is out of sync with the refined living light.

Aum follows them as they respond to the many human beings on Earth who call upon the light for guidance, service, worship, healing, methods of teaching and learning, ritual purposes, and authentic magical workings which focus on freely giving love and service. The living light of this world is also automatically drawn directly into the physical bodies of those humans who intensely seek expanded awareness within themselves. In this case, the light which enters the human being is the original light which created all things. The light within the human body is the light which the human already is. It is the light of the soul itself. After mentally, emotionally, physically and socially seeking, rearranging, maturing, and balancing themselves, some human beings activate their indigo energy center, and are able to physically see, know and be the living light of the sixth dimension using their pineal gland. This begins a major period of the person's life where they may experience a level of heavenly bliss, inner knowing, and astonishment that is unknown to the majority of humans. They also experience personal challenges, tests and trials, great learning, and an overall evolution of the human mind, body, and soul towards The One within which the individual realizes is itself.

A member of Jabik shares a message with Aum. This is a quote from the most popular holy book on planet Earth, The Bible. "The light of the body is the eye: If therefore, thine eye be single, thy whole body shall be full of light." Matthew 6:22. This knowledge was cherished by the beings of Jabik when they were physical, separated, and living in fear. Aum sees that some humans on Earth have interpreted this literally and have actually activated the living light of the universe within their own pineal glands. Others have applied it morally, socially, religiously, magically, and symbolically. Aum sees that activation of the pineal gland fills the physical being with the living light, and intelligently provides necessary guidance for further seeking. With the living light of the universe literally felt and seen inside of their brain, the more aware seeker usually becomes able to invoke the light at will in order to work with it to achieve major purposeful divine accomplishments. After being properly called upon, the light can organize things, events, situations and people that aid in the creations and great works of the individual. Beings who desire to work with love use the light to heal, teach, create with genius-like abilities, and perform miracles that help others. The light slowly removes the division between the limited human personality mind and the divine mind of the universe.

Beings who are out to satisfy themselves only are also able to call upon the light through intense inner seeking. These beings are considered to be negative beings who are on a spiritual path of providing service to themselves only. These humans choose to become wise, but not loving. They purposely activate their energy centers in a way that creates a great imbalance within themselves. They activate their red, orange, and yellow energy centers, skip the green heart center, then seek to activate the blue and indigo centers. Without the green-ray energy of the heart center, they are still able to expand their awareness, become very wise, and invoke the light, but do not feel love and compassion for others in the process. When the light enters the body of a negatively-oriented selfish human being whose heart energy is blocked, it is usually used to manipulate, harm, control, confuse, and mentally enslave others. On some planets, including Earth, the negative ones discover the light and hide it from the majority of the population. They arrogantly use the deeper knowledge of The Creator against the majority. Aum is shown an example of this on planet Earth. Aum only sees this as geometric designs, colors, sounds, and mathematic equations. Aum is unable to actually see the physical world as humans know it to be.

After gaining enough experience, Aum is ready to experience existence while vibrating at a lower frequency. Members of Jabik warn Aum that if it goes too far down without proper knowledge, its experiences can become difficult and stressful. The concepts of stress and separation are concepts that Aum can't experience directly at this point. Aum sees these concepts as asymmetrical geometric designs, off-key musical tones, sloppily-arranged colors of light, and incorrect mathematical equations. Aum gives thanks to Jabik. Aum travels back to the Arcturian light ship. The young Arcturians see that Aum is ready to experience the fifth dimensional reality.

They send Aum to a fifth-dimensional planet named Akhen. Akhen is the planet which is furthest away from the star Ribak. Aum will be placed into the inner planes of Akhen. In this dimension, the inner plane is known as the Mental Plane or the Devachanic Plane. Those incarnated on Akhen can raise their awareness to experience the spiritual/unity plane of the sixth dimension. Five angels on Akhen were observing Aum on the spiritual plane. They create comfort as Aum experiences another inter-dimensional shift.

As Aum enters the mental plane, it VIBratES CHAoticaLlY and creates an up and down wavy motion. Aum PULSES FORWARD. Aum wiggles and waves deeper and deeper into the essence of Oneness. Aum's frequency of vibration slows down. The geometry of its body goes through many changes, becoming many patterns including the Merkaba vehicle. This pattern is made of two rotating interlocked tetrahedrons, one pointing up, the other pointing down. As they rotate, they create a field of energy around and within them, allowing Aum to experience a particular mixing of energy for a more specific type of conscious experience. The new geometric patterns allow Aum to more comfortably travel between the densities. The original essence of Source now sings a new tune which syncs Aum to the fifth level of density. Aum is now able to enter the worlds of the fifth dimension. In this dimension, the vibrating speed of the original essence creates a brilliant blue light.

Aum has vibrated into a state of existence where it will learn to live as a soul. For this experience, Aum vibrates primarily in fifth-density and uses aspects of the fourth, third, second and first-density energies.

Aum rests within the mental plane of Akhen, and is able to interact with the beings who are incarnated on the surface of the planet. The Mental Plane is an extremely unique portion of The Infinite One. It is a primary state of being for all souls who are experiencing the physical worlds. It is a primary sense of home. It is the divine point of mental awareness for all souls as individuals and as one. The Mental Plane of Akhen is, of course, very different from the Mental Plane of Earth. Like Earth, there are seven sub-layers/sub-planes within the Mental Plane. There have been many different philosophies, systems of arrangement, schools of thought, and subjective experiences presented about the experiences and inhabitants of Earth's Mental Plane. In the Ribak system, the Mental Plane is where human souls on the physical planets return to after death. They spend time here before incarnating again into another physical body. This death process is mainly handled by the Higher Self using the sixth-dimensional Indigo body. The death process also involves the Higher Self helping the transitioning soul through the fourth-dimensional astral plane.

This plane is inhabited by many different kinds of beings, including many of those that humans may think of as advanced angels. There are different classes of angels with different roles within the inner planes of the different densities. Some of the beings and angels on the mental plane are those known on Earth as gods. These gods are huge, luminous, and highly advanced. A small amount of humans in the physical world learn to consciously live on this plane with clarity and understanding. Many of these people are known as adepts, masters, gurus and starseeds. They are individuals who have reached the very advanced stages of spiritual development while living in a physical body. They're the ones who have understood and used the deepest roots of the spiritual teachings given to their planet by spiritual teachers such as The Christic and The Buddhic beings who have walked among them. These individuals have disciplined and purified their bodies and minds enough to the frequency of spirit, and to the highest understandings of oneness, compassion, wisdom, love and light. In the past ten to fifteen years on planet Earth, more awakening individuals have learned how to tune their minds consciously to the mental plane of Earth. This is due to the planet slowly transitioning into the fourth-density vibration.

In this dimension, spirits who are descending down the dimensions for the first time are able to use a more condensed expression of The One essence. This special condensation of love and light is a thicker substance that spirits are able to use for a certain purpose. This substance is the energy of the soul. One of the main uses of the soul is to allow spirits to experience physicality. The soul is made of the energy of spirit and the energy of semi-physical matter. The soul is known by some as "The Significant Self." Souls serve a very unique and valuable purpose by being the link between the higher and lower portions of being. Soul energy allows for specific and unique ways of experimenting with the nature of existence, involution and evolution. It allows spirits to experience existence as thoughts, emotional energy, electromagnetism, atoms, waves, particles, biological energy, chemicals, molecules, fire, gasses, liquids and solid minerals. Aum is placed into a specialized soul which is made just for its mission. It has many components that other souls don't have, and lacks many components that other souls have.

Aum becomes more aware of its fifth-dimensional blue-ray body. The blue-ray body is layered within the violet and indigo bodies. Aum now has the complete head and throat of a humanoid being. The blue-ray body is made of all seven energy centers. Aum then becomes aware of its green, yellow, orange and red chakras which create the chest, torso, hips, legs and feet of its humanoid body. The lower four chakras are not activated in Aum as yet, so Aum is unable to use the body parts associated with them in any efficient way. Aum uses the soul. Practiced use of the soul energy allows Aum to become more familiar with the lower chakras. This will allow Aum, which is a non-physical spirit, to vibrate more and more in tune with the physical universe. A wise angel with intense and chaotic energy helps Aum. This angel is named Ustace-El. Ustace-El helps Aum to learn the use of the soul program. Aum practices being a soul for what would seem like millions of years in linear Earth time. Aum practices being gaseous and liquid, experiencing the denser but fluid physical substances of Source's essence.

At first, it's very difficult to hold, control, feel and learn movement and proper use of these new parts of its being. Becoming air and fire is extremely stimulating for Aum. Like a pilot learning the controls for a space shuttle, Aum studies and practices many aspects of being a soul. After a lot of practice, Aum is able to use awareness, thought, sound, movement, light, geometry, space and time to experience instances of a chosen reality. Aum learns to use thought to create fields of vibration within a chosen space for certain amounts of time in order to temporarily experience physical reality. Aum learns to work with waves and particles of atoms in order to hold single instances of a chosen reality in place with more and more control for longer and longer periods of linear time. Aum learns to orient its movement through space. Aum learns to use segments of time pulsations in order to experience the illusion of linear time. Aum creates longer and longer cycles of time within its chosen instances of reality. As complex and rich as these experiences are, there are many finer aspects of the soul that Aum is unable to experience at this point. The experiences of emotions and feelings are very, very faint and vague for Aum.

Ustace-El reveals to Aum a layout of the Soul Program. Aum's being contains a blueprint made of spiritual and semi-physical energy. Aum's blueprint is going to be used to experience many artificial incarnations into the physical world. Aum's awareness is set within a sphere of light and is surrounded by a seemingly infinite number of spheres. These spheres are laid out around Aum and contain a seemingly infinite number of artificial physical experiences on planet Akhen. Aum lives life as many plants and trees. Living as vegetation on a physical planet helps Aum learn how to spiral upward, striving towards the sunlight. Aum lives as many microscopic life-forms for millions of years, then as many different animals. This teaches Aum to master physical movement and control of body parts. It also teaches Aum about survival, and learning to use instincts as it is forced to make the most important choice in the moment. Aum learns to artificially fragment its soul into many parts and live as groups of animals such as wolves and cats. Aum also incarnates as whales and dolphins in order to practice advanced communication and some higher mental abilities within the physical world. As the separate mind and body of an animal in the physical world, each incarnation is experienced as lasting many years. As the soul, Aum experiences each incarnation as one scene in an apparently eternal movie. The experience of time and space is unique in the fifth dimension. There is no clear perception of past or future. There is only an indescribable and eternal sense of nowness. All experiences as every being, every situation, every thought, every choice, every reaction occurs now, now, now. There is no "this happened" or "that will happen."

From the point of view of the soul, the experience of the physical world is obviously an illusion. As the animal, the experiences are filled with simple and difficult mental challenges. As the soul, Aum simply observes and integrates the many lessons learned about the Self as a Creator. Aum's soul program holds the essence of all dimensions, but its primary connections and membranes are focused for experience on the fourth and third dimensions. The fifth dimension is home, the primary point of awareness. The fourth dimension contains the foundation; the blueprint for all that is experienced as the third-dimensional self-aware being. It also holds the essences of the second and first dimensions. Aum is aware of all its incarnations at once, and chooses to experience the one which is most needed in the now moment. Each experience is a holographic mental projection into an artificial field of reality on the planet within the mind and the soul of the individual. What is pictured in the mind is reflected "outside" in a field of space and energy that appears to be completely solid and moving linearly through seconds, hours, days and years of time.

Aum communicates with the other souls on the mental plane. All are living in their individual spheres of awareness. When souls communicate with each other as incarnated physical beings, they often use words and many non-verbal methods of communicating.

As souls, they always communicate through Concept Communication, which is also called Telepathy. Each soul creates unique personalities with their own strengths, weaknesses, quirks, and other features. Souls live with different body types, desires, interests, lifestyles, passions, goals, beliefs, definitions and motivations. They live within different cultures, ethnic groups and races. This variety allows souls to infinitely multiply the experience within the illusion of many selves in order to infinitely diversify The Creator's experience of The One Self. No matter how difficult the experience of separation gets for the incarnated being, from the view of the soul, it is always seen as an *illusion. Only the incarnated* mind and personality experiences the mental stress and perceives the experience as something being "wrong" that "shouldn't be happening." All information/experiences of each personality and mind are gathered and stored within the hard drive of the individual soul, the oversoul, the sovereign soul, the Solar Logos, the Galactic Logos, and The One.

After many incarnations, Ustace-El sees that Aum is ready to interact with the gods who are incarnated on the planetary sphere of Akhen. Each being on this planet lives within their own sphere of individual awareness. Within this awareness, they are The Creator of the entire planet, of everything that occurs, and of every other individual they interact with. Each fifth-dimensional being is aware of itself as the entire group of beings. Their connection to all others is obvious. Even with this sensitive connection to others, all things are experienced from a very individual perspective. Khenic beings can choose to live as individuals or as the social memory network. In this density, even the experience of the social memory network is created individually. The social memory network of Akhen is a Powerful, Poetic and Wise god called "Rājā Mārśala." Rājā Mārśala is a Master of Poetic Light Language. Whereas the souls of the social memory network Jabik on planet Julāhā is made of the entire planetary population, Rājā Mārśala is the combination of most Khenic souls, not all of them. This freedom of individuality and/or social memory network allows these fifth-dimensional souls to explore a very, very large variety of experiences within the beingness of The Creator as themselves.

By interacting with the incarnated gods of Akhen, Aum understands that achieving perfect mental clarity in creation is a challenge, and requires much practice. The primary goal for the beings here is to attain more and more wisdom, and to master the balance and unity of love and wisdom. They do this in their creations, their lessons, their response to challenges, and in their interactions with "others." They learn this balance in order to, more and more, learn the larger and finer details of creation as The Creator. This balance comes in many forms. Some Khenics are too rigid with wisdom. Others are too fluid with love and compassion. Although much work can be achieved with these imbalances, these souls must eventually achieve greater balance in order to progress towards the sixth-dimensional experience of Unity of love and wisdom.

The bodies of the incarnated Khenic beings are made of non-physical energy. They form their bodies by thought according to their desire. They can create a body, use it as desired, then disintegrate it and form another one. An individual may choose to create and live as many bodies. On the mental plane, there are many types of bodies available to live within.

All communication on Akhen is done telepathically. No words are spoken. Thoughts are sent in full to others through light signals. All communication is clear and honest. All experiences are created by the will of the mind. As a Khenic being evolves into higher vibrations of the fifth dimension, its body and environment is more and more under the control of its mind. The work of mental focus and the arrangement of the different components of creation allow these beings to create and dissolve their physical experiences as desired.

Entire planets are designed, changed, improved and dissolved within individual souls and group souls. Whatever is needed is thought of in the mind and manifested onto the planet immediately. Each being designs the entire planet as they desire. There's no need to even use the "outer" body and live on the surface of the planet. For fifth-dimensional beings on the positive spiritual path, there is value in socializing with others on the surface of the planet. Life on the surface of the planet is used for socializing, serving, studying, planning, playing, eating light, and many other activities.

Khenics use wisdom to face their own challenges as they serve beings in the lower dimensions. They use contemplation to learn more and more about The Creator as themselves. They analyze things, look inside, and learn more about the infinite portions of the Self. Through rigorous mental discipline, they refine their understanding of Self more and more. The exploration of The Creator as Self is an extremely exhilarating experience. These beings enter all sorts of new situations in order to further examine themselves. In service to others, they are faced with challenges that give them the chance to explore the vast world of the mind. As they serve and learn, they learn more details of exactly how Source creates. They achieve greater clarity of life and polish themselves as Creators through deep contemplation, introspection, right thinking, rational analysis, and clear, honest communication. These gods were once third-dimensional physical human beings. They know about survival. They have experienced levels of pain and stress that Aum can't imagine. The lessons learned from all their experiences in the lower dimensions give them the ability to properly find solutions as they serve beings on lower-dimensional planets. Love is the natural way and the only way for these beings, but they don't allow compassion and emotional attachments to cause misalignments and imbalances within themselves.

The beings of Rājā Mārśala are mainly focused on discipline, doing things the most efficient way, and helping all others to do the same. They do all of this while strictly adhering to the law of free will. When planet Akhen was a fourth-density planet, their focus was primarily on compassion and emotional love towards others. They learned many lessons as they served others with this intense compassion. They graduated from the fourth-dimensional experience as a social memory network, and are now experiencing reality through the eyes of wisdom. This was not an easy thing to achieve for the souls of Rājā Mārśala. When they first incarnated into the fifth-dimensional world, they were still full of that intense compassion. They were faced with a whole new operating system of the mind, body and spirit, as well as a whole new landscape of experience in the fifth dimension. It took great effort to serve others while learning the ways of wisdom. They were able to attain more wisdom by living on the inner mental planes, and diligently studying the ways of wisdom. Eventually, they became wiser and more full of light.

In the fifth-dimensional experience, wisdom offers an extremely freeing and fascinating experience of reality that compassion alone cannot offer. Being free from excessive compassion without balanced wisdom, these gods are able to see, learn, and master the ways of Source in a highly efficient and individual way. As they serve others, they attain more and more wisdom, and strive closer towards the sixth-dimensional experience of a unified and universal understanding of wisdom and love. This universal understanding of love and wisdom is one of the biggest "ah-ha" moments in the experience of an ascending soul. The unified sixth-dimensional world reveals way, way more about the self, other selves, and Source than the fourth-dimensional compassion and fifth-dimensional wisdom worlds reveal individually. The Khenics strive towards the attainment of this unified understanding. Their main teachers are those of Jabik, the social memory network of planet Julāhā.

Akhen has many beautiful cities and landscapes. Some beings

choose to live in houses, caves, mansions, pyramids and many other enclosed spaces. Although houses and clothes are not needed for survival, many of the beings still enjoy the experiences they had when their planet was third-dimensional. Since everything, including their bodies and homes, are made with the mind, they can always dissolve a body or environment at will and create another. All is experienced for the sake of the experience itself, for joy, bliss, teaching, and learning.

Many fifth-dimensional Arcturian souls come and go on Akhen as they please. Khenics live within different cultures and lifestyles, but all souls know of their connection to each other, the planet, galaxy, universe, and The One. On Akhen, newborns are raised in light. Many newborn fifth-dimensional souls incarnate here after graduating from another fourth-dimensional planet and choosing to come here. There are many other reasons souls choose to incarnate on Akhen. Children play and are schooled on lightwork, thoughts, and the ways of the mind. Teenagers chill, create, learn and party with thoughts and light. The Khenic teenagers enjoy social networking with their minds. Within the planetary social memory network, there are smaller groups of networks. They refer to themselves as soul crews or soul squads.

Aum hangs out with the teenagers and observes their trends, styles, customs, light designs, and their unique slang within the language of light. Adults and elders focus on mastering themselves, teaching the young ones, serving the beings on the physical planets, raising the vibration of the entire planet, and moving all towards graduation into the sixth dimension. They serve the physical planets by sending light signals to those planets. They use energy webs to project their consciousness wherever there is a calling for their service. Their bodies remain on the surface of the planet while they project themselves from the mental plane towards whatever location is desired. Sometimes, they send groups to many different worlds such as Earth in order to teach, inspire and guide individuals and societies. They answer the call of Prophets, Spiritual Masters, Awakening Ones, Starseeds, Scientists, Religious Leaders, Children, Politicians, worshippers, Inventors, Teachers, Musicians, Dancers, Artists, Speakers, Writers, Movie-Makers, Doctors, Engineers, Community Leaders, and Revolutionaries.   There are other fifth-dimensional planets where the gods are dedicated to the darkness. They are wise masters on the spiritual path who are negatively-oriented. Those fifth-dimensional beings use wisdom selfishly. Instead of evolving by providing service to others, they evolve by serving themselves only. This is done by enslaving, controlling and manipulating others in order to gain power over them. This gives them the light they need in order to consciously evolve towards Oneness. Their red, orange, and yellow energy centers are very bright and intense. Their green heart energy center is inactivated. It is an extremely difficult process to activate the blue throat center without first activating the green heart center. But it can be done. It requires an extreme amount of evil and dedication to discipline and knowing the Self. Negative beings work to keep lower-dimensional beings in the darkness, in ignorance, in fear and separation. They occupy their own planets, and do not enter positively-oriented planets such as Akhen.

On a planet like Earth, greed, anger, hatred, discrimination, intolerance, ignorance, and excessive fear can create terrible vibratory conditions, inviting negative beings. Throughout Earth's modern history, many positive and negative extraterrestrial beings have greatly influenced the way humans on Earth live. Contact with positive gods and extraterrestrials has aided in creation of many of the great religions, spiritual disciplines, sciences, art, and advancements in human evolution. Contact with negative gods and extraterrestrials have caused corruption of those very same religions and perversions of positive spiritual knowledge. Contact with negative beings has also resulted in the manipulation of scientific knowledge. This has created many major blind spots regarding metaphysical information in the mainstream scientific community. It has also created rigid systems of scientific dogma which has delayed major advancements.

Negative beings seek out and use any and every opportunity to distract, separate, scare, enslave, weaken, control and confuse the beings of Earth and other planets. Because of this, many positive advancements have been blocked, or have become distorted through lies, misinformation, advanced trickery, and fear tactics. Unlike positive beings such as Jabik and Rājā Mārśala, negative beings don't adhere to the law of free will. They intrude and infringe upon that law when they see a chance to do so. Positive beings in the fourth and third dimensions engage in large battles and wars with the negative forces. Fifth-dimensional gods such as those of Rājā Mārśala have enough wisdom and awareness of the big picture to not engage in any kind of battle. Negative fifth-dimensional beings also do not engage in battling positive forces.

Within the mental plane, Ustace-El helps Aum to lower its frequency of vibration. Aum vibrates closer with those younger and less-evolved Khenic beings. Aum spends some time with a large group of teenagers in a culture called the Trinikhens. Many Arcturian teenagers also hang out with the Trinikhens. These teens are raised in light and taught in the ways of wisdom. They are taught to live as The Creator of their own world while seeking Oneness in every aspect of life. In appearance, Trinikhens are much darker than the rest of the population. They look similar to Indians and Africans on Earth. They create unique and stylish thoughtforms, body types, light technologies, magical workings, games, dances and music. They also engage in fascinating sessions of divine love-making. All fantasies of "the perfect experience" are held within a field of infinite probabilities inside of every soul. The trinikhen teens use thoughts and feelings to create highly stimulating social and sexual experiences. They are skilled in party-promotion, and provide services of excitement, fun and joy for many civilizations in the galaxy. They throw interplanetary, interstellar, and inter-dimensional parties with beings from other planets and star systems. They enjoy road trips throughout the galaxy. In all of their experiences, the central focus is always on refining themselves to the purer and higher-vibratory love and light of The Source. As they provide their services, they are presented with challenges that help them to attain wisdom and expand in awareness.

Trinikhens love to dance and enjoy exotic, tribal drum beats mixed with blazing trumpets and the beautiful sounds of the instrument known as the steel pan. They create and attend concerts, comedy shows, light shows, and exploding star events. Beings from all over the galaxy come to experience holographic movies, plays and shows created by Trinikhens. Trinikhens are really good at creating and living out holographic dramatic stories, comedies, and documentaries for learning. Out of light and thought, they create and fully become living physical characters, caught up in dramatic situations. The fans flock to theaters of light to watch, participate, learn, and enjoy. Videogames are played holographically also. Thoughts, feelings, energy, matter, space and time are used to instantly play any game imaginable. With every creation, from thought to physical manifestation, they learn more about the nature of The Creator as Self. They do this individually and as groups. Since each being knows itself as Creator, each is its own universe. In their videogames, they fight through dimensions, teleport between locations, and throw physical planets at one another. They use black holes, space, time, fractals, focused thought and intense emotions as tools and weapons in their games. They race through the universe, through portals, planets, galaxies, dust, and asteroid fields. They play war games, become super heroes and villains. For study and service, they create new minerals, biological species, and new technologies/apps/programs of light. They use telepathy to share messages through holographic thought, text, audio, and video. Trending topics, hash tags, and memes are spread through direct thought. In all of their joyful experiences, they create, experience, analyze, learn, practice, stop, think, and calculate, over and over, as they better themselves more and more to the purity of the higher vibratory light and love of Source.

Living among the teenagers allows Aum to get a stronger sense of emotional energy. Aum is fascinated by the teenagers' ability to feel strong emotional desire. Suddenly, the original calling signal from Mr. Lightman's classroom is heard through the vibration of the sound "OM!" It vibrates and helps Aum to focus. Aum follows the sound of the signal. The signal leads Aum to another fifth-dimensional planet in the Ribak star system called Aten. The souls of Aten have just graduated from the fourth-dimensional experience. They have just evolved from the emotional level as an entire planet, a social memory network. They now have the ability to explore the fifth dimension as a social memory complex or as individuals. Aum visits a small community on the mental plane of Aten. There, it meets a soul that vibrates the sound, "Auh." Aum immediately knows that Auh is another aspect of its own soul. Auh knows that it is another aspect of Aum. The exact connection is unknown to them at this time. Auh is not incarnated onto the planetary surface of Aten either. It exists on the inner planes. Auh is also practicing the use of the soul program. Auh communicates to Aum that it also left the eighth dimension in order to explore these lower worlds. They share experiences and find a great deal of mental compatibility and vibrational harmony with each other.

Together, they explore the reality around them. They use thoughts to immediately create and experience whatever they want. They enjoy the simple things. They experience beauty in colors, designs, architecture, landscapes, vegetation, foods, geometry and music. They go from place to place, enjoying friendship, laughter, shows and games.

They interact with devachanic beings in many forms. They interact with many beings in the higher dimensions such as higher gods, archangels, ascended masters, lords, elemental beings, nature spirits, many kinds of celestial beings, and even some physical human beings who are visiting the mental plane while incarnated on physical third-dimensional planets. They communicate with beings who use many forms of light bodies. They also meet beings who have the humanoid form, but have evolved from trees, fish, insects, reptiles, mammals, birds, and countless other beautiful life forms. The joy of these experiences create the same Good stimulation as the rhythmic beats, the collective humming, the push and pull, and the changing geometric patterns did in the higher dimensions. Aum and Auh agree that this dimension is their favorite. They are free and able to go anywhere, do anything and be anyone simply by thinking it. They enjoy life as microscopic beings, plants, trees, animals, and intelligent beings of all kind. They live in perfect harmony and acceptance with beings of different points of views. They choose to live with many different points of views in order to gain new experiences and enjoy reality in every way they can. All gods live by the universal law of giving and receiving love to and from all other selves. All gods know that they are portions of One God, expressing The One Self in an infinite variety of ways.

Aum and Auh spend a lot of time on Aten, but always return to Akhen to hang out or to rest. When they return, they usually choose to hang out with the Trinikhens. While on Akhen, they enjoy a meal with Khenics, Atenians, and Arcturians. Aum and Auh resonate deeply with the Trinikhen vibe. They both adopt the physical features of the Trinikhens. They are also still deeply drawn to the emotional love that is felt by the incarnated beings. They are fascinated by the emotional connection that the Khenics, Atenians and Arcturians have for each other, and for the lower-dimensional beings they serve. Aum and Auh are puzzled at the fact that they can experience the togetherness, but can't feel the emotional bonding at all. They decide that they'd like to experience stronger emotional energy. The Khenic and Arcturian beings tell them about the nature of strong emotions. They communicate ideas of separation and irrational actions that emotional energy can cause. Aum and Auh are unable to vibrate deeply with the idea of separation. Even though they've lived in many ways and as many different kinds of beings, they've mostly been challenged by mental confusion, and have not been forced to endure fear and emotional pain. The teenagers don't want Aum and Auh to go. They tell the Arcturian and Khenic Elders about Aum and Auh's plan to go into the fourth dimension. They hope that the Elders will talk them out of going. The teenagers immediately see the thoughts of the Elders and see that they already know of Aum and Auh's destiny.

The Elders vibrate the energy of the calling signal that was sent out by Mr. Lightman and his students. They see that Aum and Auh have gathered enough experience within the higher densities, and are ready to go into the more physical densities. They vibrate the calling signal to Aum and Auh. The signal triggers an inner knowing within Aum and Auh. The Elders remind Aum and Auh that this inner knowing is the memory of their mission to be of great service in the lower dimensions. The Elders know that when Aum and Auh enter the fourth dimension, their conscious minds will forget more of the experiences gathered in the seventh, sixth and fifth dimensions. Those experiences will be held within what some call the Unconscious Mind. The Elders tell them that they will be sent to the inner plane/astral plane of the planet Amaru. Amaru is one of two planets in the Ribak system that vibrates at the fourth-density level. They tell Aum and Auh that they should be able to remain in contact with the beings in the lower mental planes, and if they raise their frequency, the higher mental planes. Aum and Auh give thanks and exchange energetic hugs with everyone. They go into a meditative state and enter a portal that connects to the planet Amaru.

They begin to vibrate at a slower frequency. The geometry of their souls begins to change. Their vibration of photons, atoms and molecules slow down significantly and syncs Aum and Auh to the fourth level of density. They are now able to explore the worlds of the fourth dimension. The energy of this **vibration is heavier and thicker. It is denser with matter and less dense of light.** The vibratory speed of light now reflects and radiates a Brilliant Green Color. They begin a slow energetic transfer into the astral plane of Amaru. This transfer is done slowly and delicately. A few beings of light are here to help them through this process.

The operating systems of their souls, minds, and bodies change. There is a rapid organization of new energies in their beingness. These energies create a blueprint that is unique to each soul. This blueprint will determine more specific themes of the kinds of experiences Aum and Auh may have in the lower dimensions. These themes are specific to the great mission given to them by the eighth-dimensional council. There is an energetic layout containing many components, including charts, plans, purposes, personality traits and challenging situations. These are just some of the many quantum elements that will be available for Aum and Auh to choose and experience as they live in the lower dimensions. Through duality, cause and effect, karma and dharma, these elements will be used to potentially learn and teach many lessons in the denser dimensions.

Their awareness of time changes significantly. Their awareness of the wider universal point of view becomes much more limited as they enter the deeper dualistic energies. Along with the torus and other basic shapes, the primary geometric design of Aum and Auh's souls is the Merkaba. They travel through a new portal and enter the astral plane of Amaru. The astral plane contains energies of the physical, mental and spiritual planes. Aum and Auh slowly awaken and find themselves covered in the vibration of strong emotional energy. The overwhelming feeling of compassion for all of creation brushes over them in waves. They become very, very confused.

They suddenly find themselves being automatically moved and shifted in an indefinable way. They experience themselves as every object, being, and event that can possibly exist at all possible times and in all possible locations. They can't even begin to grasp the idea of what is happening. They then start to flicker in and out of this reality at the speed of light. In their awareness, information is coming in from an innumerable amount of directions. They try hard to find some kind of reference point in order to have a clear experience. They feel themselves as the substance of emotional love. They are their own loving feelings, as well as the loving feelings of all beings in the universe. They are surrounded by many beautiful angelic beings. The angels send them light. This helps to loosen up the energy-flow in their astral bodies and bring clarity to their minds.

Their heart energy centers are activated. They become aware of their fourth-dimensional green-ray astral bodies. The green bodies are layered within the blue, indigo and violet bodies. The green ray bodies contain all seven chakras. They feel their awareness penetrate their humanoid chests, backs, shoulders, arms and hands. They feel the pulsating waves of emotional love as they enter the Heart of Ribak. The first thing they do is look out onto the physical surface of planet Amaru.

This planet is much more physical than the planets in the higher densities, but not as physical as third-density planets. Amaru is actually a planet that is fourth-fifth-density, meaning that portions of the planet vibrate strongly in both densities. It is transitioning into a fifth-density planet. From the third-density point of view, those who are incarnated in the fourth-density may be referred to as Awakened Human Beings. They occupy bodies that are made of much more light than physical third-dimensional bodies, but nowhere near as much light as fifth-density bodies. In appearance, these humans look similar to third-density humans on Earth.

Aum and Auh see that the time-space reality of the astral plane is where the thoughts, ideas, emotions, and feelings for the awakened humans are held. The inner planes are part of the metaphysical world which is explored in the study of quantum physics, string theory, anti-matter, dark energy, dark matter, and the unified field theory. The inner planes are also the field where many historical, psychic, religious, and mythical events occur. These occurrences are mostly hidden from the majority of humans on third-dimensional planets. These occurrences usually affect third-dimensional beings in mysterious, vague, immeasurable and improvable ways. The awakened humans of fourth density are very in tune with the inner planes.

At this density, the physical world is more fluid, energetic, and gooey. The physical material of the world responds to the thoughts, feelings, and intentions of the awakened humans. It is common knowledge in this dimension that what is thought of and felt in your mental time-space inner world creates your experience on the physical space-time outer world. When Amaru was a third-dimensional planet, most people did not experience the inner planes consciously and with full clarity. Like third-dimensional humans on Earth, they only experienced the astral world this deeply during certain experiences such as dreams, trances, high creativity, high excitement, astral travel, out-of-body experiences, fearful and traumatic events, and other psychic experiences. Now, the inner world can be explored and experienced deeply with ease and clarity. All awakened humans can see the thoughts, feelings, attitudes and vibrations of all others. Virtually nothing can be hidden. This makes for a more honest and peaceful life for all. Christ-consciousness, togetherness, harmony, brotherhood, and sisterhood are the norm on this planet.

Aum and Auh see that on the inner planes, there are angels and many other kinds of beings. There's a class of angels which have no free will, and operate in a strictly "mechanical" manner according to universal purpose. Some angels are known as gods to people on third-dimensional planets. Beings on the inner planes can change form at will. Aum and Auh are also able to do this. Through mental focus and intense feeling, anything that can be imagined can be experienced within one's own soul center. The astral beings teach and guide the awakened humans on the surface of the planet. They also learn from them. The beings in this world communicate telepathically. Angels work with light to serve the awakened humans on Amaru in many ways. On the mental plane, there are intelligent beings who live in many different forms. There are hybrids and mixtures of humans and other mammals, insects, fish, reptiles, birds, felines, and amphibians. There are deeper inner regions of the astral plane which are occupied by beings that have been created by humans through myths and stories. Characters from books, spoken tales, movies, videogames and television shows live in these regions of the astral plane. They interact with the imagination and intentions of the awakened humans.

Aum and Auh realize something very different about themselves in this dualistic world. They suddenly realize that unlike in the fifth dimension where their bodies were androgynous, in this dimension, they experience existence primarily as one gender. Aum is male, and Auh is female. Both of them still use the darker-skinned Trinikhen body type.

In this world, there is a greater sense of general uncertainty and confusion. Amaru is a positive fourth-dimensional planet. There is no evil or wickedness. Aum and Auh are currently vibrating in the higher sub-planes/sub-layers of the astral plane. Life is perfect. They feel a whole lot more uncertainty than they did in the fifth dimension, but everything is Good.

As they explore their dualistic nature, they see that both genders are perfectly equal, but work in very different ways. The genders also compliment each other perfectly in many ways. Both genders contain the energies and qualities of the opposite. They are always able to take the form of the other gender when desired, but for the most part, they live as only one.

Aum and Auh enjoy this world. They use specific thoughts and emotions to create intense feelings. If a thought is charged with enough feeling, it becomes a direct and solidified experience here and now. The subatomic particles and the spirits of the elements perform their service by interacting with the minds of the self-aware beings in the fourth dimension. When a self-aware being looks at a tree, the beings of the atomic and mineral kingdoms spring into service by becoming the energy which creates the illusion of the solid tree. Aum and Auh only need to focus on the thought and feeling of doing something and they're immediately doing it. The intense feeling of any thought creates an environment within the awareness of the soul. Within their own center, they see, hear, smell, taste and touch whatever their heart desires.

On the astral plane, time is very fluid, and is influenced by the mind of the individual. Time moves as a circular/cyclical energy. It seems to swirl around in a slippery circle, seeming to loop itself around over and over. All of these statements generally depend on the relative perspective of an individual observer. All past experiences of all events in the history of Amaru can be observed and interacted with here and now in the astral plane. The ability to observe all possible futures is exhilarating. How the future will play out exactly in the physical world cannot always be clear, but all *possible and probable* futures can be clearly seen and interacted with. Again, the experience of time relates only to the individual soul who is creating, witnessing and observing an experience. Each soul is able to rewind, pause, fast forward, and slow down the world around them during their chosen manifested experiences. This is useful for fun, service, studying, teaching, learning, meditating and magical work.

Aum and Auh are able to exist in many locations and timelines at once. The atoms, molecules and elemental beings support all thoughts, feelings and intentions in a neutral way. Although they have a basic awareness, they have no self-awareness, no free will, and no agendas. They are neutral and provide their service according to their nature.

Aum and Auh observe the awakened humans who are incarnated in the physical bodies on the surface of the planet. Also visible are the elemental spirits which exist as air, fire, water, and the minerals of Amaru. On earth, the elemental spirits of air are commonly called Sylphs. They create the elements of air such as oxygen. The elemental spirits of fire are called Salamanders. The water elementals are called Undines. They live within the liquids of the planet. Gnomes are the elemental spirits who create the minerals, soil, crystals and rocks of the planet. Together, they create an exalted and glorious semi-physical environment that radiates beauty in every way. The elemental spirits help to give life to all animal and human life by creating energy of the air, fire, water and minerals that make up their bodies. The elemental spirits also create the energy of the trees, plants, seas, rivers, oceans, deserts, the sky, and the world underneath the surface of the planet. The elemental beings help to create the weather conditions of the planet. The sylphs, undines, salamanders and gnomes interact with the brain chemistry, energy fields, and auras of the Amarucans.

The bodies of the enlightened humans on Amaru look similar to the bodies of humans on Earth. The primary difference is in the average height. These beings are much taller than the third-density humans on Earth. The beings of 𝐘𝐀𝐇𝐖𝐄𝐇 personally created and modified the genetic coding for third-dimensional Amarucans just as they did for third-dimensional humans on Earth. Although their fourth-dimensional bodies appear similar to their third-dimensional bodies, when you look inside, there are many differences. This fourth-density body is made of a whole lot more light and electricity than physical flesh. It's easy to see that the organs are made of energy and the spirits of the elements. The atomic structure and the chemical genetic make-up of the fourth-density bodies are very different than they were in the third-dimensional bodies. The DNA and chromosomes are of highly evolved and awakened human beings. The evolution from third-density to fourth-density bodies occurs as consciousness aligns strongly to the energies of universal love and compassion. Love and compassion are the primary energies which brings divine revelations to third-dimensional humans. The divine revelations allow human beings to gain greater Understanding of the Self, of other Selves, of the environment, and of The One. This understanding is nowhere near complete.

These people are much more aware of Truth now than when they were third-dimensional beings. They are physically and mentally enlightened. There is much more spiritual and electromagnetic light running through the energy centers, nadis and organs of their bodies. The chemicals and elements of their bodies interact with a thick, spiritual plasma-like substance which creates a very fine layer of biological cells, blood, inner organs, veins and skin. These biological organs are lighter, refined, *redeemed,* and more subtle than they were when this population and planet was third-dimensional. As the humans raised their consciousness through universal love and compassion, the living, conscious planet also rose in vibration and evolved from third to fourth dimensional. Fourth-density bodies are less dense with light than fifth-density bodies, but much more dense with light than third-dimensional bodies.

Through focus of thought and intensity of feeling, telepathy, flight, teleportation, telekinesis, remote viewing, clairvoyance, precognition, and many other higher psychic abilities are a part of daily living. Spiritual light is used to learn, grow, serve and play. Life is so much more harmonious now that these people truly Know and Understand that their reality is a holographic projection of their own consciousness.

As Aum and Auh explore this world, they enjoy the sweet, overwhelming experience of emotional love. As they get used to this dimension, they realize that manifesting experiences by thought is more difficult to do with the added ingredient of emotion. They find it hard to clearly create and experience reality without interruptions in thought. It's kind of difficult to balance their mental thought with emotional feeling. The experience of emotional feelings creates huge distortions in their perception of reality. Like a child learning to ride a bike, they enjoy trying to find the balance between the creative energies of love and wisdom, magnetism and geometry. They see how the inclusion of emotion colors their reality with a whole new layer of stimuli. The emotional energy works with the natural and neutral energies of light and darkness. Duality dramatically increases the experience of uncertainty. Uncertainty allows beings to better experience the contrast of light and dark. Emotionally, darkness is often experienced as fear. For those who are more evolved and mentally disciplined, darkness can be very useful in creating a clear contrast in perception. This can be used for studying, inner seeking, and serving others. Fear can also be used as a clear and non-stressful signal of misalignment with The Creator's central column within one's awareness. Once this misalignment is spotted, quick adjustments can be made, lessons can be learned, and greater harmony can be experienced.

On Amaru, the social memory complex is called "Ābhārī." Ābhārī is a very young social memory network. The Amarucans have only recently combined all of their knowledge, minds and souls to live as one entire planetary consciousness. They are just barely at the mark consciously where they can even be considered a social memory network. There are still elements within the population that are adjusting to other elements in order to produce greater harmony. Some would argue that Ābhārī is not a social memory complex as yet, but consciously, the root memories of the social planetary mind has been tapped into and brought out enough for the population to be considered a social memory network. It can be said that they are making final adjustments in achieving conscious planetary harmony.

As Aum and Auh continue their exploration of Amaru, an angel calls them to a school where students are prepared to go on a field trip. This is a trip through time. The purpose of the trip is to learn about Amaru's history, and their progress from an unenlightened planet of sleeping human beings to an enlightened planet of awakened humans. Aum and Auh go with the angel to the school. The teenage students do their best to tune their bodies, and then join their minds together with clear purpose and strong feeling. The teacher makes suggestions and gives guidance on proper tuning and fusing. The teacher is a portion of the god Rājā Mārśala. They serve by mentally projecting light to the astral plane of Amaru from the mental plane of Akhen. The light contains mental, emotional and visual information. Rājā Mārśala also teaches the students of Amaru ways to integrate wisdom with love. The students work with their chakras and the energy of the planet like a computer; with an operating system, programs, apps, browsers and bookmarks. They use body, mind, and spirit, along with the light spectrum of colors, and the tones of sound to surf through reality within their own energy centers. Each student uses intelligent energy and works with their own unique settings, applications and tools within their bodies and minds. Thoughts, feelings, words, actions, desires, beliefs, motivations, goals, and choices are among the tools used to experience, learn and evolve.

As these students receive service and learn from Rājā Mārśala, they give their own service by serving humans on the only third-dimensional planet in the Ribak system. They also serve humans on Earth who are on their path to awakening. Each chakra and organ plays its role in storing, processing, analyzing, receiving, and releasing information. Learning is done by using the inner technology of their beings, and sometimes, outer physical technology. Like humans on Earth, Amarucans are very skilled in engineering physical gadgets, inventions and advanced technological devices. Much of this outer technology was used in order to form social networks, and to eventually form the social memory network. Some choose not to use any outer technology at all. They prefer to discipline their own personality only by exercising their own mental faculties.

They also use many magical workings to aid themselves in evolution. In fourth density, magic is a part of everyone's daily life. There are many different types of mental/spiritual browsers, devices, and apps. As Amaru transitioned from a third to fourth dimensional planet, the ability to communicate mentally was learned for the sake of surviving quakes and floods. As the fourth-density green-ray energy became stable upon Amaru, telepathy became the main way of communication. The trials and errors, and the lives lost due to failures led to the development of certain mental skills and details that are unique and exclusive to Amaru. This was until they shared it with open, like-minded beings on other planets. Amarucans keep their bodies pure in order to allow the purer love and light of spirit to flow clearly through their bodies and minds. They regularly heal, balance, purify, and tune themselves to the higher, purer light. They use body postures, breathing techniques, and other disciplines that are similar to the Hindu, Buddhist, African, Egyptian and Native American techniques done on Earth.

In the school, Aum and Auh observe as the students tune and focus their consciousness for the trip. The students sit in their physical bodies and tune into the time-space inner world. They all meet up on the astral plane in their astral bodies. They are joined by other students in schools and other locations around the planet. Aum and Auh take a look at the way of life on present-day Amaru. All atoms, minerals, plants, animals, and humans work in harmony. The planet and all its inhabitants live as one organism. All parts support all other parts. The exchange of energy between the environment and all inhabitants are well-balanced. There is no need or desire for any being to eat the flesh of another. Humans, animals, elementals, and vegetation are all in sync so that all food is ripe, ready, and prepared in a way that is custom-made for the experience of the individual who seeks to eat. Before food is eaten, Amarucans give heartfelt praise to What they once referred to as "The Infinite One" or "The All." As they do this, they send waves of love to the beingness of the food itself. The energy of the eaten food merges with the energy of the soul who eats it. All food contains light and information from the sun, galaxy and universe. There are no diseases on Amaru. Many aspects of life on Amaru are similar to life on Earth. There are different cultures and communities across the planet. There are different religious practices, political organizations, business corporations, and media outlets. All differences are due to personal taste and are not done in the nature of dog-eat-dog competition. Within the different sections, all individuals, organizations, and conscious social networks work in harmony for the purpose of evolving together as a planet. There are different cultures on Amaru that live by different customs. Everyone lives in open acceptance of all others' ways of life. This is an unnecessary statement to actually express on Amaru because there is no need to say that one is in open acceptance of all others. Everyone sees and knows all others as other portions of the One Self, so all are accepted by all as "my other self." When Amaru was a third-dimensional planet, this started as a philosophy of "Love thy neighbor as thyself." As fear and darkness were cleansed by love and light, it became second-nature for all to be loving of all others. The fact that all beings are one is no longer a lesson that has to be taught in order to achieve peace. The connection to others as one is felt in the same way one being feels its arm as a part of itself. There are still disagreements, but they are usually resolved quickly. This is due to the ability to see and adjust all energies within the illusion of separation.

There were a very small amount of people who graduated from third-dimensional Amaru through the negative and selfish spiritual path. When they died in their third-dimensional life, their soul traveled and incarnated upon a negative fourth-density planet in another star system. On that planet, the entire population evolves by the ways of Service to Self only. They fight wars and create empires to enslave, control, and rule over each other. On that planet, the individual cultures, religions factions, political parties, businesses and social groups argue and fight for greater dominance at the expense of the others. Every aspect of society is based on the "us vs. them" mentality. Aum and Auh receive a dark feeling as they and the students scan the energies of that planet.

When they place their attention back on Amaru, they learn that all plants, trees, animals and humans are perfectly balanced in population numbers. As a third-density planet, Amaru suffered from overpopulation, which caused many problems.

Aum and Auh see a group of small children bathing in a river. The children use their minds to direct the undines, the elemental spirits of water. The children laugh and play as the living water spirals around them, splashes them, lifts them up, and plays peek-a-boo with them. Aum and Auh see how imagination works directly with the spirits of the elements. Although flight and teleportation are a daily part of life, many Amarucans choose to drive stylish cars, ride on trains, and fly in airplanes. This is done completely by choice by those who enjoyed these methods of travel on third-dimensional Amaru. Many other activities that are no longer a necessity for survival are used for fun, joy, learning and teaching others.

Auh, Aum, and the students observe many of the political, religious, and social changes which occurred as Amaru transitioned from a third-density planet to a fourth-density planet. Many systems within the societies were torn down and then rebuilt in the ways of compassion and universal love. The energy of teenagers led to many great changes on Amaru.

The feminine energy and the women of the planet also played a central role in planetary evolution towards enlightenment. As the magnetic feminine energy flowed throughout the planet, it caused a great deal of environmental and social disturbance. The disturbances were not due to the returning feminine energy itself. They were due to the domination, ruling, and abuse of the masculine energy in the previous ten thousand years. The feminine energy was met with energetic resistance within the energy fields of the planet and the male-dominated cultures. Gender roles and sexual identity became more fluid within societies as this went on.

As many ideas and beliefs were clearly proven to be incorrect, many mainstream Scientists, scientific deniers, atheists, and religious fundamentalists who were too rigid in their perspectives had no choice but to let go of their overly-fixed ideas about the nature of reality. Each new generation found it much easier to integrate new updates and incoming Revelations. They adjusted well to changing ideas and living in new ways. It was an extremely painful change for many individuals who invested most of their identity with overly rigid scientific, religious, social and political viewpoints. As new information was revealed, it became very clear that many of the most foundational and strongly held beliefs were simply wrong. This caused a great deal of anguish, depression, nervous breakdowns, psychotic episodes and suicides. Towards the end of the 3D Amaru cycle, teenagers used technological and mental social networks to revolt and start social movements against political, social, religious and business systems which promoted selfishness, unfairness, elitism and discrimination. They fought against ideas and influences that were seen as destructive or as something that slowed down planetary conscious evolution. As the decades went on, planetary consciousness was raised more and more. The young ones didn't have to use force as much to create change. Compassion and Understanding was used more to accept some qualities of the old ways while creating new positive religious and spiritual understandings, political policies, social customs, economic empowerment for all, and temporary economic assistance and training for the many who needed help to sustain themselves. Eventually the use of physical currency was done away with completely as the deeper energetic currency became more visible and better understood. Currently on Amaru, marriages are formed on the level of the soul, and are made official by the spirit according to harmonizing energies. There are no government papers. There is no force by religious dogma. Most couples stay together for entire incarnations because they are perfectly in sync with each other's energy centers. All thoughts, feelings and desires can be seen by all others, so the ability to perfectly harmonize with your "soul mate" is simple. Any desire to separate is easily understood and accepted since there are always a balanced number of compatible partners. Many Amarucans change partners repeatedly in a spiritually harmonic and mature fashion. People are able to easily harmonize with the energetic needs of their partners. Rigid rules that force conformity and strict behaviors are no longer in place as they were on 3D Amaru. Wild passionate bliss and joy can be balanced by the development and proper use of wisdom and discipline. Since all energy is visible, behaviors are not usually judged as right or wrong. Focus is put on the ability to see disharmony within the energy and to correct it.

Families come in many forms on Amaru. Some families consist of a household with a mother, father, and children. Some families consist of multiple married couples and their children living together. Some groups of Elders live together in their own dwellings. Some families are made of all females or all males living on their own. Some families are made of multiple single parents raising their children together. There are travelers who don't live with any one family unit. They travel from place-to-place. Many households welcome other selves who are travelers and are passing through their location. A traveler may stay with a group of other selves for one night, or a few months before moving on to their next location. Children are raised by their parents, their community and the planet.

The currency on Amaru involves a combination of energetic and material value. All people contribute to society through their service, talents and passions. Energetic currency flows evenly between all on the planet. There was a time in fourth-density Amaru when some individuals had a lot more than others. This was never seen as a bad thing. Through understanding of the whole and compassion for all, the economic imbalances naturally evened out. No one is ever forced to live in poverty, and no one who generates more currency than others is ever forced to share it with others. The act of sharing is as natural as the act of breathing on fourth-density Amaru.

Politics is a part of Amarucan life that is understood in a universal context. All political actions are carried out with compassion for all as one. As new policies are made and put into effect, the ability to see the needs of all within the region makes the work of politicians much easier than it was on 3D Amaru. There are always disagreements, but the ability to see imbalances in energies allows for fast resolutions. The understanding and compassionate use of *Politics* greatly help to *Organize* Amarucan life in a way that is fair and balanced for all.

Education is also understood and expressed with compassion on Amaru. Imagination, music, dance, art, laughter, creativity and sexual energy are all used to teach and learn about the self, others, and the nature of Source. Most teachers on the planet are Amarucan. There are also portions of Jabik and Rājā Mārśala who teach classes and guide individuals. Many of the teachers from this dimension are Elders. The Elders are well-respected, valued and cherished by younger people. Education focuses on understanding the self, understanding all other selves, and understanding the planetary, solar, galactic and universal environment. One primary focus of education that was difficult for many was the literal understanding of knowing all others as your self. This was taught as the most basic idea of Unity; the nature of The Infinite One. This was learned quickly by some, and took much longer for others. Also at the center of education on Amaru is the mastery of fruitfully using thoughts, feelings, words, actions, beliefs, desires, and choices.

Spirituality and sexuality go hand-in-hand on Amaru. Understanding, conserving, and transmuting sexual energy is a fundamental way of seeking greater conscious Oneness with The Creator and evolving on Amaru. On 3D Amaru, the sexual energy was extremely strong, but was misunderstood, feared, and demonized by many organized religions. The joy and bliss of sexual enjoyment was often accompanied by guilt and shame. This repression of sexual energy caused a great deal of damage to social consciousness and the planetary environment. Sexual repression caused ignorance, darkness, rigidness, violation of others and perversions. Ignorance of The Creator's love, light, and power within sexual energy caused blockages in individuals, in the planetary energy, and slowed down conscious evolution in many ways. As the fourth-density energy slowly stabilized on the planet, third-density Amarucans were more free to explore and experiment sexually without the painful mental restrictions experienced previously. As the vision and understanding of etheric light grew, it became obvious to all that sexual activity transferred a great deal of metaphysical energy between sexual partners in fundamental ways. This helped many to go within and explore themselves as creators. Couples came to know the Self, each other, and the universe through their sexual experiences. It became widely known that the conservation and use of electromagnetic and electrochemical male and female energies could be used for conscious evolution. This knowledge was used by late third-density Amarucan couples and individuals to tap into intelligent infinity and to come to know their own inner light. The inner light which was activated by cultivating sexual energy allowed Amarucans to use the intelligent energy of the universe which creates all things. This was used to learn, heal, serve, and grow; all in the seeking to better know The One Which they are. Many in the population didn't use stored sexual energy to activate and expand their inner light. They did it through compassionate behavior, intense bliss and joy, and creating great works which help many others. Some activated their inner light through extremely high-quantity and high-quality service to others. Others activated their inner light through advanced spiritual/mental/physical disciplines and techniques. High excitement and high creativity were explored in the astral plane. This helped many late 3D Amarucans to make huge leaps in mental/emotional discipline through detailed and subtle exploration of body, mind and spirit in self and other selves. That led to much conscious expansion and knowledge about the power of thought, feeling, and creation through the power of The Word. Some couples used spiritual sexual practices to continuously practice the balancing of love and wisdom. The clarity of thought, intensity of feeling, and the infinite variety of selection, forms, themes, styles and flavors taught late 3D Amarucans many lessons about creation on many layers of their being and of the universe. The purity and joy of love and light through sexuality brought forth huge advancements in healthcare, medicine, inventions, art, and music. It also guided many social revolutions in a more positive direction. Many used advanced pranayama breath control techniques, asanas/yoga postures to evolve consciously.   Currently on Amaru, Sexual meditations are common. Couples are able to make passionate love when they are miles apart. Solitary sexual practices are used by many to explore the biological, mental and spiritual nature of the self, other selves, the inner universe, and The Origin. This has led to many scientific discoveries that contributed to greater knowledge of the planet, solar system, and the universe. Some choose to be celibate through their own free will. This is used for personal reasons and has many benefits for the individual who seeks in this way. Everyone accepts and understands each other's ways of evolving and seeking The Source. No one feels like they're doing the wrong thing. And no one feels like they're missing out on anything they don't want to participate in. All is done in balance with a matured level of Understanding.

Music is another fundamental energy which is used for Amarucan conscious evolution. The scientific, spiritual and playful understanding of vibration, tones, and rhythmic sound were used for evolving from a

3D to a 4D planet. In the final decades of third-density Amaru, one of the many uses for music was to entrain the hemispheres of the brain. This was used to gain greater clarity and awareness of body and mind in the space-time physical body and the time-space astral body. This led many to better Know Themselves by exploring the more subtle/finer aspects of behavior, thoughts, feelings, relationships, reactions and psychic empowerment. This also helped to discover many metaphysical functions and relationships of all parts of the body and mind. Through music, many truths were realized about time, consciousness, compassion, energy, matter, space-time, and time-space. Healing, levitation, telepathy, advanced mental discipline, and heightened emotional intelligence were also learned through the use of sound. As it is on Earth, there are many genres of music on Amaru. The experience of complex rhythms, beats, and musical instruments generated great beauty, playfulness and *Vital Energy* which greatly raised personal and planetary vibration to the stabilizing fourth-dimensional light. As consciousness evolved, the general experience of sound became a lot more colorful and flavorful.

Currently on 4D Amaru, music is understood and used metaphysically. In singing, chanting, rocking out, rhythmic poetry and hip-hop, the word *flow* takes on a cosmic understanding. Musicians have a wider range of sound frequencies, consciousness, energy, time and space to deliver performances of a truly divine nature. With conscious energy being better understood, musicians are now able to express themselves by placing subtle aspects of their consciousness into specific portions of their music. The musicians, as well as all artists, empower themselves and others by artistically radiating more refined energies of love and light through their art. Fans are able to use the love and light for knowledge, power, to tap into intelligent infinity, and to provide service through the experience of divine ecstasy.

Of course, dancing goes hand-in-hand with music. Aside from divine enjoyment, dancing is used to move biological, electromagnetic and electrochemical energies throughout and around the body, the aura, the chakras, and through the environment. Dancing is also used to spin, heal, balance, build, and use the energy centers of the body. Amarucan dance groups like to form conscious social networks where hundreds of thousands of individuals form themselves into a large humanoid body which is made of all their individual bodies. Each individual performs their moves individually and collectively to create spectacular choreography. Dancing is used to ground the purer essence of love and light into the planet. The study of sacred geometric patterns through dancing has led to many scientific discoveries and monumental expansion in consciousness on Amaru. Many lessons about oneness and understanding are learned as dancers learn to mentally, emotionally, and physically move as one. Dancing group souls move much like flocks of birds or schools of fish.

Having almost identical genes to humans on Earth, it's no surprise that Amarucan dances are similar to many African, indigenous, Atlantean, Lemurian, Shamanic, Hindu, Buddhist, Egyptian, Hebrew and Middle-Eastern dances. Many American dances such as the twist, the jitterbug, and the cha-cha are used to charge and tune the energy centers of the body. Dances such as the electric slide and country line-dancing are used to enhance conscious blending among multiple souls. Hip-hop dances such as the cat daddy, the Dougie, the Shmoney dance, the walk-it-out, the two-step, nae-nae, cabbage patch, and the running man also have their parallels on Amaru. Jamaican dances such as the butterfly, the bogle, the wacky dip, the weddy-weddy, and the out-and-bad are also performed on Amaru. These dances aid in the study of mathematics and sacred geometry within physical, mental and emotional rhythmic patterns. This allows for many breakthroughs in technology, energetic healing, and social unity. Some dancers used dancing to discover and express their deeper/higher identity as a soul and as a personality. The movements and feelings strengthen inflowing and out-flowing universal energies, which intensifies the spiraling geometric light which flows through the aura and chakras of the dancer. This is used for teaching, learning and healing. Similar patterns flow into Singers, Violinists, Pianists, Drummers, Inventors,

Scientists, Painters, Sculptures, Gardeners, Interior Decorators, Healers, Actors, Directors, Videogame Designers, Programmers, Authors and other individuals during creative activities.

Laughter is also a central part of Amarucan conscious evolution. Some of the benefits of laughter were known to Amarucans while they were still a third-dimensional planet. Stand-up comedy, comedy plays, shows, and movies are all used for divine playfulness and further knowledge of self. Laughter and play helps Amarucans to align and tune their minds and hearts to the awareness of Unity and The Creator's central column of pure energy. This produces a great deal of learning without trying to learn at all. Spontaneous, juvenile pranks, games, fun, and laughter guides the population to knowledge about the playful nature The One. The joy of feeling so good and gaining powerful insight brings out a natural feeling of wanting to help all others feel good. This helps many people to better use their personal talents and passions. By following their excitement, Amarucans tune themselves and gather highly useful knowledge for whatever their needs are.

They then offer this knowledge to all who are seeking and open to their message. Amarucans know that all souls are unique in their purposes and their ways of seeking. Therefore, no belief or piece of knowledge is ever forced on anyone who is not seeking it.

Sports continue to be a primary form of enjoyment on Amaru. Soccer, cricket, rugby, basketball, football, baseball, and golf are now played on large colorful fields of swirling energy. Players direct the ball or object mentally as well as physically. The simultaneous use of physical and mental fields makes it impossible to have a boring game.

Aum, Auh, and the students observe how mental holographic social networking revolutionized Amarucan communications and interactions. Many business meetings, social and spiritual gatherings, weddings and parties are experienced through mental and emotional merging of energies. Mental projection parties are used to have fun and to work through many challenges. The more Amarucans practice togetherness with mental/emotional balance, the better they're able to project their combined thoughts. Much service is done through mental projections of ideas, symbols, and images. Shared mental work is often mixed with physical exercise, yoga, meditation, breath-work, swimming, dance, laughter, art, and sports. Many activities that were previously done just for fun are now also used for energetic tuning to higher consciousness.

The increase of compassion on the planet changed the way business was conducted on Amaru. The dog-eat-dog competitive drive to dominate over others has turned into an atmosphere of cooperation, creation, service, and friendly competition. Those who consider themselves to be business women and men understand that all businesses can be designed to compassionately support all other businesses in some way. Everything fits and everything has its place. When service is given, an equal energetic value is always received.

As Rājā Mārśala teaches, Aum, Auh, and the students see how these many individual parts of the planetary society contributed to the advancement of science and spiritual knowledge. The scientific search to understand reality through seeking The Source became merged with the spiritual search to know the Universal Self. Many of the greatest advancements on Amaru came through scientific experimentation and inner seeking. One of the simplest ways to attain higher knowledge is to experience silence. For Amarucans, the ability to go into the silence of the mind/soul is considered to be one of the most cherished gifts from The Source.

The newer generations of Scientists used physical technology along with the divine technology of their own inner being to gain insight. By looking within, Amarucans discovered many treasures. By exploring themselves, they found more and more specific and profound uses for the pineal gland in the center of their brains. They found the so-called nothingness, the empty awareness, the black hole, the void. They found the sound, the light, and the star, Ribak. They found The Word, The Galactic Logos, The Co-Creator, the Living Being of the Milky Way galaxy. This being is an offspring and a representative of **The Infinite One**, and is The One which created all stars in the Milky Way. Each star is a co-creator, a Solar Logos, an offspring and a representative of The Galactic Logos. The solar co-creators created planets and life-forms, including self-aware beings who are also co-creators.

As Amaru became a completely fourth-density planet, Amarucans realized, and are continuing to realize the oneness of it all. They realized that they are The One Creator experiencing One Self as The Galactic Logos, the stars, planets and humans. The Galactic Logos fragmented and limited Its awareness until fragments of itself fell asleep. The sleep occurs in the third-dimension while living as human beings. Awakening to fourth-density is Salvation. The awakening comes through sufficient Compassion, Understanding, and service to others.

The pineal gland, in balanced use with all other glands/chakras, allows Amarucans to break through the many veils of the holographic illusion of physicality. During the 3D to 4D transition, inner knowledge of etheric light, antimatter, plasma, time-space, and the astral & devachanic planes gave way to monumental Revelations. Proof of the existence of angels, demons and nature spirits also lead to life-altering insight. The study of DNA became a metaphysical study which was connected to religious and spiritual life. As more Amarucans were born into the 4D layer of the planet, the 4D layer was slowly grounded into the 3D layer, and the 3D layer was slowly exalted up into the higher light of the 4D layer. As this occurred, people looked deeper inside of themselves for answers. During the transition, there were some negatively-oriented individuals who used these great Revelations for self-service, control and domination. This prolonged the suffering and darkness on the 3D planet. At the very end of the 3D cycle, the old tricks of the negative ones were widely known, and less people fell for them. The old games of separation and pitting one group against the other proved to be useless against a population who came to know their oneness. In the end, the population of Amaru, like Earth, was positively-oriented.

During the transition, Amarucans learned to communicate with their 5D soul and 6D Higher Self by using The Kundalini Fire within, and also by learning the language of symbols, catalyst and meaningful coincidences. When it was widely accepted that there are other aspects of themselves in higher dimensions, it became popular for Amarucans to contact the Soul and the Higher Self for guidance, protection, and many other services. Excitement, joy, and many disciplines were also used to open communication with the soul and the Higher Self. The information gained was used to learn, teach, give, receive, and expand. Soon, the pyramid within the self was discovered and Amarucans learned to consciously use this pyramid power. The inner world contained The Inner Scriptures and the details of The Revelations. The understanding and use of natural DMT, melatonin, gravity, light, sound, water, space, time, toroidal fields, sacred geometry, thought, feeling, and intention to create within became a part of daily life on Amaru. They began to learn that linear space and time are illusions, and that, in reality, all that exists is one eternal moment. Many people discovered their light body. The toroidal fields of spiritual-electromagnetic energy within the heart allowed for universal connections from heart to heart, to heart to heart until all knew all others as one. The ability to levitate, fly, teleport, heal, see probable futures, and mentally move objects became popular and used for the good of all.

As they explore the planet's history, Aum, Auh, and the students see that by going within, some Amarucans learned to completely detach themselves from emotional pain. They learned about the emotional veil which is layered upon the third and fourth dimensional fields of energy. This emotional veil creates thicker filters and limitations of perception which prevent beings from having the fuller, clearer awareness of oneness. It's much easier to know oneness in the fifth dimension. In the middle and lower-fourth dimension, the fuller experience of oneness is clouded by thick waves of emotional energy. Some Amarucans, as well as some Earth humans learned to see past the emotional veil and achieve oneness while living in the third and fourth dimension. The emotional veil can be lifted as Universal Love & Understanding is gained, as challenges are faced, lessons are learned, and enough wisdom is developed.

The students learn that there are specific filters/distortions in the perception of all beings within all dimensions. The distortions allow The One to experience One Self with different levels of awareness and from an infinite number of points of views. The Infinite One is experiencing and interacting with One Self in order to learn more about Its own nature. By using movement, light, darkness, manyness and linear space-time, The One is able to slow things down and interact with every portion of The One Self in an infinite number of ways. New experiences are had, new points of views are formed, and new lessons about The One Self are learned. Before the separation and illusion, these lessons and viewpoints were not experienced and expressed by The Infinite One in these ways. This is because Source is Infinite, is One, is no "where" in space, and no "when" in time. Without the illusion of finity and manyness, All That Is cannot be expressed and observed. It all exists in a timeless, infinite state, but is not expressed in any specific way that can be experienced by The One. It is by dividing One Self, creating cycles of time, creating expanded points of location in space, limiting One's awareness of infinity, and becoming "many others," The One is able to forget the big picture for a while and experience life within Its expressed Self. The Infinite One lives as galaxies, stars, planets, minerals, animals, angels, humans, and all other spirits in order to temporarily dis-member, forget, and then re-member The One Self. Without the limited point of view, the linear time, the expanded space, without the forgetting, the confusion and uncertainty, without the colors, sounds, interactions, beauty, joys and sorrows, there are no surprises, no twists, no fascination, no wonder and much less appreciation of The Oneness and The Allness of being The One Infinite Creator.

The students receive many revelations from these teachings. Aum and Auh are filled with wonder from these revelations. The beings of Rājā Mārśala receive a very large amount of higher light energy for their service to the Amarucan students.

Rājā Mārśala goes on to show that all co-creators are placed in a state of uncertainty as to the full nature of their reality. For third-dimensional beings, the uncertainty can be considered to be in the extreme. The uncertainty, along with the need to work with others in challenging situations, gives all 3D beings a primary divine gift from Source. This divine gift is known as Free Will. Without uncertainty, all is known, so all beings think, feel and behave with total compassion and perfect wisdom at all times. Under these conditions, lessons are learned, but those lessons are very, very few when compared to the amount and quality of the lessons learned when beings are faced with great challenges, and are faced with the opportunity to choose selfish or compassionate behaviors. Through uncertainty and free will, beings are allowed to love, fear, help, hurt, reject or depend on each other as they attempt to survive, evolve, learn, create, enjoy life, and seek truth.

These kinds of challenges allow The One to experience and appreciate some of the most profound and cherished lessons about The One Self. The beings who choose to incarnate in the most difficult physical planets receive the greatest opportunities to learn lessons. They provide an extremely valuable service to The One. The process of going from ignorance and darkness to compassion, wisdom, then universal unity is always a unique journey in each solar system, each planet, each community, and each individual spirit. The struggle of physical, emotional and mental pain in the lower dimensions makes the blissful love, light and life in the higher dimensions much, much more appreciated. The third-dimensional world is used to ground and integrate all that has been experienced in the highest dimensions into the physical dimension, while exalting the physical dimension up to the purest love and light of the highest dimensions. The up-flowing/down-flowing, in-pouring/outpouring of all energies interact in an innumerable variety of ways on many, many layers within the densities.

Rājā Mārśala gives the students a simplified example of how social memory networks are created. The students see how individual atoms fuse themselves together to form molecules and elements. They see how molecules and elements combine to form chemicals. As each individual and each group combine, they reach a higher, more complex level of awareness. The students know that all of these things are The

Infinite One. They see how individual atoms, elements, molecules and chemicals merge to reach higher levels of awareness, creating biological cells, microscopic life, and the plant kingdom. Biological cells reached higher levels of awareness by merging and creating animal bodies. This allowed souls to experience life as second-density group-aware beings. Biological cells then allowed for even higher levels of awareness by fusing together to create the third-dimensional human body and brain. This gave souls the ability to experience individuality and third-density self-awareness. With self-awareness, each human has the ability to recognize their soul, to feel compassion for others, and to reach the highest levels of conscious awareness while in the third-dimensional body. On a third-dimensional planet, the ability to merge many minds into one is virtually impossible due to the inability to see and feel the movement of energy within and all around.

When Amaru became a fourth-dimensional planet, as they expressed more and more compassion and togetherness with each other, it became obvious that, just like the atoms, molecules, chemicals, elements and biological cells, they were able to fuse their minds together to form mental/soular social networks in order to gain even more awareness. As many individuals learned how to come together and experience reality as one, the power to literally move mountains and dramatically improve the world was better understood. The social memory network was built slowly as each individual and each community learned, served, strived towards wisdom, and evolved in their compassion for each other, and their understanding of the nature of reality. As this process went on, all of the different portions of knowledge that was used by each to evolve were integrated more and more into the consciousness of the social network of the population. As this occurred, the most fundamental memories of the planetary group mind were revealed more and more. When all individuals had accepted all others and their ways of living and seeking, they remembered their oneness. They remembered the deepest planetary memories which were forgotten in the third dimension. This group mentality is not the limiting and negative mentality of slavishly conforming to dogma or anyone's "right way." This group mentality comes from the nature of unity, from universal compassion in the population, and the acceptance of all others as other versions of yourself.

This revealed the information needed for all to know all as one. Individuals, communities, countries, and regions with different ways of evolving were able to put the pieces together and seek Oneness in unity as one mind in a way that benefited all equally. This seeking by the all of The One as one allowed the entire population of Amaru to accept and radiate the purer love and light of Source. As the collective mind grew in awareness, the deepest memories from the deepest roots of the planetary mind spiraled upwards into the planetary consciousness like a *Grateful Shining Serpent*. They reached higher levels of vibratory frequency, and the social network of Amaru became a social memory network which was called Ābhārī. Ābhārī is considered to be the most innovative, creative, and well-respected being in the Ribak system. As a social memory network, Ābhārī is still very young, and trying to hold themselves together and evolve in harmony. Their harmony is far from perfect. As a social memory network, they are a very delicate being. Sometimes they are way too aggressive in their approach to a challenge or to their service. Other times, they're very gentle; sometimes to the point of being too soft. They are highly creative, impressing higher-dimensional beings with their skills, style and approach to life.

Aum and Auh continue to travel with the students through the 3D to 4D transition of Amaru. They see that the end of the 3D cycle was frightening. It was almost as bad as Earth's final 3D cycle. The path from hell to heaven seemed impossible. It took a lot of time, and many traumatic challenges to bring about change. There were rapid environmental, social, political, and spiritual changes. There was a long period where electronic technology was unavailable to most people on the planet. The loss of technology caused a great deal of depression and shock to those who depended on it heavily for daily living. Things got very dark. The indigenous cultures who were in communication with the environment and the planet herself became leaders and teachers for outside communities who needed their knowledge. Their knowledge of oneness with the living planet helped to prevent many deaths. They freely passed their knowledge on to those in the previously technologically advanced cultures. Out of necessity, those in the so-called first-world regions of the planet learned how to connect their bodies to the planetary body. The younger generations found it much easier to flow and learn to communicate with nature.

Without the electrical technology, they were forced to go within and explore their inner selves more often. They learned to rely heavily on vivid imagination, strong focus, deep concentration, and the power of thought. This was done for survival and to relieve boredom. As more people learned to do this, a clearer connection between the outer physical plane and inner astral plane was made. During this time, there were many spontaneous creations of new beliefs, values and definitions of themselves and what they considered reality to be. Many of the ancient beliefs, values and definitions were re-energized and became a part of daily life.

Many of the old beliefs which stalled evolution faded away. The older beliefs that aided evolution were integrated with the new ways of life. The integration was not a smooth one. Many religious traditionalists held onto old beliefs that no longer served the population well. They saw the darkness and destruction on the planet as their God expressing anger, and judging; murdering those who were evil. Younger generations angrily rebelled against the idea of a jealous, vengeful male-only God who rules through fear and demands worship through force under the threat of annihilation and eternal damnation. Some of the religious traditionalists respected the old beliefs, but realized the negativity, and were able to accept a new view of the nature of The Creator. Other religious traditionalists could not let go of the idea of an angry and fear-based God. They called the young ones evil and considered them to be a lost and immoral generation who rejected the knowledge of the one they considered their true God. They warned the young ones of the dangers of turning away from thousands of years of traditional fundamental religious beliefs.

The younger ones embraced the basic attitudes and behavior of The Christ and the Buddha, who also walked upon Amaru in the third-dimension. The younger ones later saw that their angry rebellion against the old ways caused them energetic blockages and slowed down their spiritual progress. They later learned to forgive, accept, and integrate the useful lessons of the older generations. Some of them actually began to listen carefully to the religious traditionalists with open minds and hearts. This led to the younger ones adding an ingredient in their seeking that was lacking. The missing ingredient was strong devotion and worship of The One. Many of the younger ones avoided the devotional aspects of conscious evolution. They didn't consciously choose to reject the ideas of devotion and worship. It was more of a cautionary behavior since all of their knowledge of worship and devotion involved a god that demanded it under severe threats. Through meditation, compassion, wisdom, discernment and devotion, the young ones learned to further integrate the older ideas that personally felt right to them, and respectfully reject the ideas and beliefs that didn't feel right. This single act of compassion and openness to the older ways brought in a tremendous amount of light into the planetary sphere. This also created much more energetic opportunities across the planet for beings such as Jabik and Rājā Mārśala to communicate with third-dimensional Amarucans through channeling/syncing, automatic writing, symbols, synchronicity, nature, and dreams.

The higher-dimensional teachers taught 3D Amarucans details about what is required for salvation and resurrection into fourth density. Many were shocked to learn that salvation had more to do with the quality and quantity of compassion and service to others than it had to do with a particular religion, holy book, or god. They learned that salvation and resurrection into the higher dimension depended on an individual's level of genuine compassion, service to others, forgiveness of disharmony, and understanding of the Self & reality.

Salvation depended on that same old lesson that the greatest spiritual teachers have always taught throughout Amaruian history — Love each other. Amaruians learned that those who died in the third dimension either graduated 3D and reincarnated on 4D Amaru or did not graduate 3D and reincarnated on another 3D planet. On the other 3D planet, 3D repeaters faced similar challenges as they faced on 3D Amaru because they had not learned the necessary lessons required. Those who graduated to 4D Amaru live a life that is about a million times more harmonious and peaceful than any 3D planet. There are challenges in all dimensions, but the idea of intense stress and extreme suffering no longer exists on a positive 4D planet. Those who graduated from 3D Amaru to 4D Amaru felt an intense amount of compassion for all who were still in 3D. They took on the duty of serving them and helping them to graduate. From the 4D Amaruian body, they were able to see the metaphysical energies behind all thoughts, actions, situations and matter. 4D Amaruians saw that, to graduate from 3D to 4D, an individual had to attract enough of The Original Love/Light of Source into their mind and body. This is done in many ways. In the third dimension, this light was primarily attained through compassionate thoughts, behavior, service, and also through a much deeper Understanding of the Self and reality. Opening the heart chakra in compassion was central for graduation. This is what welcomed the most Light into the energy field of the individual.

Many 3D religious people preached harshly about others being unsaved while truly believing they were saved. In most cases, this was not the truth. From the perspective of the fourth dimension, it was obvious that most people who condemned others were not attracting the light which was necessary for graduation into 4D. Some of them truly believed they would graduate because they knew every chapter and verse in their chosen holy book. Many remembered all of the stories and interpretations of these holy books according to their particular system of teaching. Many had nearly-perfect attendance when it came to religious services, yet they had very little compassion for others and understanding of reality. They were able to deceive and convince others that they were saved, but they could not deceive the exact workings of The Light. Many of these individuals knew that they were being hypocritical by preaching one thing and thinking/feeling another. Knowing this, they still convinced themselves that they were the "good people" and that those who did not follow their god, belief system, or holy book were the "bad people." From the fourth dimension, it was clear to see that this mismatch only reduced their light and, for some, caused much confusion for their souls after death. Many individuals were reincarnated onto a different 3D planet where they lived with individuals who needed to re-learn similar lessons. Many of them were able to graduate into 4D Amaru because they changed their ways after being taught by 4D Amaruians who guided them through certain challenges or spoke to them in dreams. Many people who were meek, unlearned, and had little understanding graduated to 4D Amaru because of their freely-given love, their compassion, and their desire to truly help others. 4D Amaruians felt such an intense amount of love and compassion for even the most negative 3D individual. They did not judge at all due to their ability to see the precise energetic information which caused such negative behavior.

As the 3D Amaruian planet approached its final century, it blended more and more with the light of fourth-dimensional Amaru. Things went from bad to worse, and then got much better. It took a long time for many people to become tolerant, then fully accepting of those who were very different from them. Many only learned to accept others after being forced to spend time and depend on them for survival. Others who were more positively-oriented learned to tolerate, then accept others because they were able to spend time together and have in-depth conversations. Oneness slowly became known, not only as a belief and a philosophy, but as a scientific fact, an inner knowing, as the way things actually are, always have been, and always will be.

It became scientific fact on 3D Amaru that all there is Is One Source, The Infinite, existing as every atom, element, chemical, mineral, plant, animal, human, angel, planet, star, galaxy, and universe. Even after this was known, it was not accepted into the heart by many. Many of those who accepted oneness/unity as true did so in mind only.

It took them a long time to actually think, feel, speak and act from this knowing through the heart. Others who felt this oneness in their hearts were able to forgive those who enslaved and controlled them. When compassion and forgiveness were displayed by some people during their most difficult challenges, many others who didn't believe the science behind oneness became convinced that there was something to it. This lead to more scientific proof and more detailed explanations of the qualities of oneness. As more people accepted oneness as truth, it still took a long time for many to actually realize that other people are literally other versions of themselves living as one consciousness.

At that time, the awakening ones on 3D Amaru continued to learn the power of their bodies and minds. They soon learned to see, accept, and use the visible, tangible golden-white light that was pouring into their pineal glands. They practiced going within more and more. They spent much time together, sharing, serving others and enjoying life. Many also spent a great deal of time alone and away from the distractions of the world. For many 3D Amaruians, learning how to meditate was an extremely frustrating process. Learning to enter the silent inner space was very difficult to do while dealing with the extremely stressful situations in the world around them.

Rājā Mārśala continues the trip through the 3D to 4D transition on Amaru. The students see that things got much worse before they got better at the end of 3D Amaru. As the fourth-dimensional light came into the third-dimensional planet, there was a great deal of resistance and disturbance on the 3D planetary sphere. This was due to the high level of darkness on the planet; the disharmonious vibration of the people, and their reluctance to accept the higher light in their bodies, minds and behaviors. The students observe as floods, quakes, tsunamis, tornados, hurricanes and volcanoes wipe out hundreds of thousands of people at a time. They see how the many tragedies forced people of different races, cultures, lifestyles, regions and religions to work together and depend on each other for the sake of survival. Even though many were intolerant or hateful towards the other, they eventually learned to trust each other and work together. As the years went on, their children were raised together as friends with less knowledge or care for the hatred their parents had for each other during easier times. Religious, cultural, and racial knowledge was shared casually in conversations, but were usually not adapted by others. They just learned to respect each other's ways and learned to see that others were sincere in their customs and their interactions with The Infinite. They learned to see each other as people just like themselves, and no longer saw them as "those people."

The students of Rājā Mārśala have never seen such details of how bad things actually were on the third-dimensional planet. They feel for the 3D humans on Amaru as they watch death and destruction occurring all around them here and now. Their empathy swells. All of the students feel a stronger desire to help people on planets that are currently third-dimensional. They think about their own lives in the fourth density being more about creativity and service and not at all about survival.

Rājā Mārśala teaches them that some 4D planets do engage in thought wars with negative 4D planets. The students feel gratitude for their own challenges, disagreements, mental confusions and other disharmonious experiences. These experiences are so much easier to deal with and learn from compared to the stressful experiences of their 3D ancestors. Aum and Auh are touched by this as their own compassion for third-dimensional beings increase. They finally feel the stronger pull of fear and pain through the suffering of others. Their empathy surrounds them and the students with loving light energy. Aum, Auh, and the students are all thankful for their inner light and their ability to find answers from within. They didn't even realize that this knowledge was something to be so thankful for. To see a world without such peace and knowledge brings the greatest appreciation for Oneness.

The Amaruian students return to the present space-time location in their school, changed forever. They've received an extraordinary amount of light energy. They give thanks to Rājā Mārśala. Rājā Mārśala tells them to give all praises to The Creator, then bids them farewell. Aum and Auh thank Rājā Mārśala and the angel who called them along for the trip.

The angel directs them to an Arcturian ship that is going on a tour of the galaxy. They meet the Arcturian crew of the ship. These Arcturians are fourth-density physical awakened human beings with appearance and genetics similar to Amaruian and Earth humans. Aum and Auh join them in the ship. This ship is made of semi-physical material. For Amaruians, a ship like this, one made of outer technology, is rarely used for travel to other planets and star systems. These ships are mostly used for tourism, and for those who simply desire the experience of traveling in such a ship. Amaruians primarily travel using thought. They do this by projecting their consciousness to the desired location. They use the hologram of the space ship only to cover their lightbodies as they travel.

The Arcturians turn on the ship's invisibility force field. They do this to avoid being seen by people on the only third-dimensional planet in the Ribak system. People on that planet have not yet discovered life beyond their own sphere. The Amaruians, Khenics and those of Julāhā assist them when they see opportunities. They help them to evolve at their own pace without infringing on their free will.

An energetic force field in the shape of a torus surrounds the ship. The ship takes off and flies out of Amaru into outer space. The vibration of the toroidal field around the ship speeds up. The ship doesn't propel itself at all. It simply moves through space within the stabilized toroidal force field. The vibration of the field speeds up until it reaches the speed of light. Light speed is then doubled again and again until they reach their desired location. There are Arcturian and Amaruian tourists on the ship. There are also angels and other astral beings who learn from, teach, or just enjoy the company of the beings aboard.

The Arcturians laugh, play and tell jokes. When they begin to see the highlights of the tour, they observe. Everyone enjoys the beauty of star clusters, colorful nebulae, pulsars, asteroid fields, dwarf stars, red giants, and supernovas. There are two tour guides who give information about what is being seen. They laugh and make the trip very enjoyable. Aum and Auh are stunned by the beauty of a glowing purple planet spinning on its side and shooting spiraling red dust out of its center. All appreciate the beauty of this. An elderly Arcturian couple reminds everyone to give praise to The One Creator for their experience of this beauty. The other passengers do this. This appreciation brings more of the higher-dimensional light into the energy field of the entire ship, and increases the vibratory frequency of all the beings within it. This increase in vibrational speed is felt by all immediately. It also provides greater protection from negative forces who may wish to harm or seize control of the ship for their selfish purposes.

As they go on, they see colorful patterns of dust and planets rotating around each other. They visit a few star systems and planets. The tour guides and passengers learn a lot about this small region of the galaxy.

As they go on, they come into our solar system. They pass by the planetary sphere of Pluto. They pass a few other planets, then they come to Earth. The tour guides explain the great experiment that is being conducted on planet Earth. They explain that the Earth is currently transitioning from the third to the fourth density level. They explain that beings from far distances in the universe and much higher dimensions are watching, and are extremely excited to observe and participate in the transition of Earth. They explain that this 3D to 4D shift on Earth is unique. It is unlike the shift of any other planet before it. This is due to a combination of different circumstances — the inter-dimensional wars for control of the people, positive and negative extraterrestrial interferences, genetic alterations, the extreme level of darkness and ignorance, and also the many extraterrestrial and multi-dimensional beings who have incarnated onto Earth at this time to serve. The tour guides give a simple explanation about the actions upon the Earth humans by The Ones of ЯAHWEH and The Ones of Ra which altered the history of the people on the Earth in very profound ways. The positive information from 𐤉𐤄𐤅𐤄 and Ra were perverted, edited, deleted, changed and molded by negative higher-dimensional entities. The information was also perverted and distributed by the Politicians, Councils Royalty, and Religious leaders who held worldly authority over the "official" texts and knowledge given to the people. Auh gets a strong feeling in her heart. She can't explain it. She feels a strong magnetic emotional pull towards Earth. Aum sees a flashing light as he looks at the Earth. He tells Auh. Auh tells him about the feeling she's having.

They decide to go into the astral plane of Earth. As they're about to go, they receive a telepathic message from a nearby ship. This ship is a semi-physical fourth-density ship which is cloaked, and is stationed near the moon. The ship contains beings from the Sirius, Pleiades, and Arcturus star systems. They are The S.P.A Alliance. There are also three Elders from Sirius, Arcturus and Alcyone, the brightest of seven stars in the Pleiades system. The Elders are from much higher dimensions, and are here to supervise Aum and Auh's process. They are nameless, but can be called the S.P.A. Elders.

There are other fourth-density ships flying around the Earth and near the moon. Many of the ships are piloted by positive, service-to-others fourth-density beings working in service to Earth and to Oneness. Many are negatively-oriented beings with their own selfish agendas. The positive beings remain mostly invisible to human eyes and radar, though there are times they allow themselves to be seen for various reasons. This is occurring more often as time goes on. They send light, teach and communicate with many of the awakening ones of Earth. The negative groups are allowed to interfere with the Earth population due to the free will of the people, and their strong calling for negativity. The negative ones would take over completely if they are allowed, but must work within certain limits due to the work of Senior Guardians, protective firewall systems, and other protections which have been placed on Earth. Positive groups work with an extremely high respect for the free will of humanity, and only serve within the boundaries of adherence to the law of free will. When they're not sure if their service would violate that law, they consult the greater council. Often, they have to watch tragedies and painful events take place without interfering.

The Sirians send the original calling signal from Mr. Lightman's classroom. This is what Aum is seeing and Auh is feeling. It is received by Aum and Auh as a subconscious message, reminding them of their agreement to go to Earth on a special mission. Due to the limitations in consciousness as they traveled from dimension to dimension, they have forgotten their purpose for even being here. Aum and Auh both feel tired for the first time. This is from their many geometric and conscious changes as they traveled through the dimensions. They are given comfort and love by the Sirians, and they take some time to rest and heal their astral bodies. Afterwards, they head into the Earth's ionosphere and vibrate within the highest layers of the inner planes of Earth.

There are many kinds of beautiful and enlightened beings here. Their beauty and diversity are stunning to Aum and Auh. The elementals, animal spirits, and other nature spirits on this planet are much more diverse than those on the inner planes of Amaru. The beings in this region are all positively-oriented. Many are visiting here just to learn a few specific lessons before moving onto another world. Others are here in dedication to serving humanity in many different ways.

Aum and Auh explore this world. They then mix into the emotional energy of the humans who are physically incarnated on the surface of planet Earth. They experience the highest feelings of emotional love, compassion, joy, beauty and laughter felt by humanity as a whole. Since they are in time-space, they are able to travel through the entire history of Earth as they desire and experience the positive emotional energy of humanity. They interact with humans who are dreaming and astral projecting their consciousness through this world. Some of the humans here have mastered the practice of lucid dreaming. They are more balanced and in control of their astral bodies and their dream experiences than the majority of people who are dreaming.

Aum and Auh watch as beings of light assist humans who are in transition after their physical death. The light beings help individuals who have died peacefully in their sleep. They help them to get accustomed to using their time-space astral bodies, to navigate the astral plane, to explore and experience their desires, and then to go through the lifetime review process before incarnating again into an appropriate space-time environment. Many newly-departed souls meet with the religious figures they have known during their lifetime. Many get to experience nirvana, heaven, divine ecstasy. Some individuals require a great deal of mental healing after physical death. Some are thrown into the lowest layers of the astral plane where they experience the state known as hell. Individuals who have been shot dead or killed suddenly usually experience much more confusion than those who departed in a more peaceful way. Some departed souls are unable to accept their physical death and wish to remain in the physical world. They yearn for physical sensations again and are not ready to move through the process of acceptance, lifetime review, healing, and reincarnation. Some remain on the astral plane for a very, very long time before moving on. The angels and light beings who are there to assist them have understanding, compassion, and a great deal of patience when dealing with individuals who are not ready to move on. Eventually, all souls complete the transition process.

Aum and Auh come into contact with other humans who are daydreaming, in deep thought, deep prayer, and meditating. Some are creating music, playing instruments, singing, rapping, dancing, and experiencing other forms of art. Some are having positive near-death experiences. Many are experiencing the deep love of pure being through sexual enjoyment. On the astral plane, there are many beings arriving and leaving alone and in groups. There are self-aware beings in the form of every kind of plant, fish, bird, insect, reptile, amphibian, and mammal. Aum and Auh enter the brighter layers of the *Imagination Fields* of Earth. Here, there are many characters from humanity's greatest myths, folklore, religions, spoken tales, books, movies and television shows. Aum and Auh are welcomed into the

circles of some of the indigenous and tribal people of Earth. They
travel through the heart of humanity to share and enjoy feelings of
delicious, satisfying, passionate divine beauty. They experience erotic
innocence. They experience compassionate unconditional love between
humans. They experience the energy of healing, helping, teaching,
balancing, family, friendship, sisterhood and brotherhood. They
especially enjoy playing with toddlers and adolescent children as they
observe, learn, laugh and play. They enjoy the purer energies of
daycare facilities, as well as kindergarten and preschool classes. They
enjoy children's laughter, innocent confusion and learning experiences.
Aum and Auh then travel and dwell with people who are telling stories
and the people who are listening. They travel within the imagination
fields, observing fragments of different perspectives of the
experience as the story is being told. They are only drawn to the light
of those who are welcoming of them. They love to be around those who
are consciously tuning themselves to having a greater awareness of
Oneness. They enjoy the emotional fields of tribal initiations, dances
and rites of passages. They enjoy the energy within the astral fields
of churches, mosques, temples and other structures where people
gather in love, devotion and worship of The Creator. They enjoy
interfaith churches where people of different religions and beliefs
mix and mingle. They dwell with those who are reading words from
Ancient Kemetic texts. The energy of Indigenous tribes and the
energy of Egypt are especially delicious to Aum and Auh. They're
similar to the energy of the Trinikhens on planet Akhen. Aum and Auh
dwell with humans who are reading Sumerian, Mesopotamian, African
and other Indigenous sacred texts. They dwell with those who are
reading passages from The Upanishads, The Vedas, The Egyptian Book
of The Dead, The Tao Te Ching, The Tripitaka, The Torah, The Bible,
The Ohaspe Bible, and The Quran. Aum and Auh have intense astral
encounters with the positive gods, angels, and humans who are the
subjects of these texts. Aum and Auh share the positive emotions
radiating from the individuals who read these texts. They don't
experience any of the confusion, ignorance, negativity and lower

emotions of the readers. Aum and Auh also enjoy the company of those who seek The Source in non-spiritual ways. Some of them are Scientists, researchers, and others who are experimenting and learning more about the nature of reality. Many are studying quantum physics, string theory, the unified field, the human brain and heart, and the nature of consciousness.

Aum and Auh dwell with humans who are using the aid of first and second-density beings through the use of mind-altering chemicals and plant substances. The lower-dimensional entities help many disciplined humans to alter there state of mind and body, and to increase awareness and use of spirit. Aum and Auh only vibrate with those who are responsibly using these substances for increased knowledge of self, spiritual guidance, balance, healing, service to others, or to increase their awareness of Oneness.

Aum and Auh then explore the loving emotional energy of Earth's history. They experience the love of people in Africa, Atlantis, Lemuria, India, Asia, Australia, Europe, The Middle East, on various Islands, as well as Central, South and North America. They experience Earth during its glorious Edenic state. They see the Great Works of Akhenaten, and his attempt to spread a higher standard of knowledge of Oneness. They see Moses on the mountain and Yeshua in the Garden of Gethsemane. They see and feel Martin Luther King's "I Have a Dream" speech. They feel the emotional energy of the extreme hope and extreme pain experienced by Dr. King and those who listened to his speech. They feel Yeshua's loving sacrifice of himself, and the intense emotional anguish he endured.

The feeling of such negativity is new to Aum and Auh. As they feel the joys and pains of humanity, they experience the deep compassion they felt while exploring Amaruian history. They stand on battle fields during the many holy wars. As the holy warriors kill each other, Aum and Auh feel the energy of misguided devotion to The Creator, as well as the energy of hatred for the enemy. Aum and Auh become overwhelmed with compassion and a deep desire to make the suffering stop, to make things better.

They return to present-day Earth. They see many angels who are performing their service by distributing quantities of light to serve, guide and protect the incarnated humans. The angels are skilled in knowing when to distribute light, how much light is needed, and when not to distribute light. The angels in the higher astral planes are much more advanced in their understanding of light and of their own beingness as light. They are more neutral in their service. Aum and Auh continue to vibrate their light out to those incarnated humans who reach out to The Universe for help of some kind in their time of need.

Their vibration of love gives comfort to many people. They help a mother in India to move through the grieving process after losing her daughter to starvation. They give comfort to a man in Sudan who lost his wife to aids. They comfort a female social worker in Texas who has a terminal illness and can't afford healthcare. Their comfort gives the woman enough peace to find a solution to her problem in an unexpected way. They offer comfort to a single father of two in Greece who just lost his job. They vibrate near a group of children in Iran after a suicide bombing kills seven people. They help to protect the mind/body of a woman in Chicago who is having a violent seizure after she's just seen a stray bullet tear through the smull of a toddler. More and more humans unknowingly come to Aum and Auh for some kind of help and comfort. Their heart chakras expand as they open and extend themselves in service to humanity. As they assist the humans, they see, feel and mix in with the lower emotional energies of planet Earth.

They come into the middle astral plane. They continue to send waves of love to the incarnated humans. They send them loving thoughts, feelings, and some of their own light. They feel the emotional energy of more and more people passing through them. The fearful energy slows down the speed at which their entire being vibrates. As they dwell in the middle layers of the astral plane, it becomes a little more challenging to focus creation with clear thought and feeling. It's not as easy to receive clear thoughts, and to choose the perfect one out of many to experience. It's not as easy to manage the wave of emotions and to experience only the feelings they wish to experience. The astral environment is now thicker and denser. Their whole experience changes as emotion becomes a thicker barrier which further skews their perception of reality. The thicker waves of emotion lessen their ability to be reasonable and think rationally. Aum and Auh feel this, but their hearts are so open that they are only concerned with helping others in some way. They offer themselves totally in love with very little wisdom. They continue to come into contact with many who are in utter despair and are desperate for a miracle.

As they help, they don't realize that their geometry is changing and they are vibrating slower and slower. Being so inexperienced, being so full of compassion, and lacking enough wisdom, they assist all at their own expense. They slowly fall into the lower layers of the astral plane. They continue to open themselves to many human beings. The amount of fear, negativity, and despair becomes overwhelming. It's too much to handle. They themselves now begin to think negative thoughts and experience fearful feelings. They decide to head back into the higher layers of awareness. They try, but the negative energy is sticky, restrictive, and flowing in the opposite direction. A negative astral being sends them a psychic attack.

The being sends a negative thought that says, "you're not going back." Being inexperienced and confused, Aum and Auh choose to receive the thought and give it feeling. The shock of having an undesirable thought confuses them even more and brings in the feeling of terror. this level of fear throws them far out of alignment with the creator's central column of pure energy. the lacm of enough wisdom and experience meeps them in this state of high mental and emotional imbalance. the lower astral plane is a bad neighborhood for those who are so undisciplined, inexperienced, and imbalanced. this layer of vibration holds the negative emotional energy for all beings on the earth. aum and auh feel more specific negative feelings from the humans on earth. the intense emotion of fear allows them to experience feelings of elitism, anger, jealousy, discrimination, prejudice, bigotry, judgment, hatred, vengeance, resentment, greed, self-righteousness, arrogance, laziness and despair. they try to pull away, but their own fearful feelings continue to magnetically attract more and more negativity. the more fear they attract, the more they give out. the more fear they give out, the more they attract. all of this negativity is only a manifestation of their own choice of vibration. within their own beings, there exists the centered, aligned, peaceful eternal state where they can instantly feel oneness. this peaceful state always exists within all beings no matter what they are experiencing. aum and auh have the choice and the chance to relax, to realign themselves within their center of being, and immediately experience the higher vibrational light and love. they would quickly rise into the higher astral layers with the other beings of light and love. The angels, light beings and others in the higher astral planes see this happening. They prepare to help, but the Elders above let them know that this is a part of Aum and Auh's call to service. As eighth-dimensional spirits, they made this very agreement with the great council. They have given themselves in service to The All, and it is their honor and duty to aid planet Earth. Their great mission was to come into the consciousness of humanity and aid the awakening ones in the beginning of the year 2017.

as aum and auh move through the astral field of negative emotional energy, they come into contact with negative astral beings. these beings are angelic also, but have chosen to evolve through the ways of the darkness by serving themselves only. like everything else in existence, they are also the creator experiencing the one self, and they are also seeing their source. this way of seeing is one of the infinite ways the one experiences and comes to know the one self. it is considered to be the negative spiritual path. as a negatively-oriented being evolves, it comes to know itself more and more as creator. but instead of sharing their love and light to help others evolve, these beings love themselves only, and use their light to dominate, enslave, misguide, weapen, and keep others in the darkness. by doing this to extreme degrees, they may evolve through the densities towards total oneness. this path is a legitimate spiritual path, but comes with an inherent imbalance in the being, lacking activation of an entire energy center, the heart. third and fourth-density humans who choose the negative path may enjoy temporary power over others, while always being owned, enslaved, mentally-imprisoned, and always owing a heavy depth to higher-ranking and higher-dimensional negative beings. they are also guaranteed repeated painful karmic returns in energy. at some point, all negativity which is sent out by any being must be paid for with a return of that negativity to that being. this goes for all positive beings who radiate negativity towards others as well. all beings evolve by activating and balancing their seven energy centers. positively-oriented beings seem to activate their red/root, orange/sacral and yellow/solar plexus centers first, and then seem to activate the heart through genuine compassion and service to others. negatively-oriented beings activate the root, sacral and solar plexus centers, and skip the heart, rejecting compassion and universal love. this doesn't stop them from seeing further. they skip the heart and seem activation of the throat and single eye centers. this creates a terrible imbalance in their beingness as they seem like positive beings, they seem to strengthen their awareness of oneness. not as the unity of all, but as a special chosen group or as an absolute authority who everyone else must obey. without the activated heart, they become extremely intelligent, but instead of radiating their knowledge to others, they use their intelligence to enslave and rule over others. this is exemplified by the ones known as the "illuminati" on earth. they sought and used the power of the creator's light to keep others in darkness.   Positive entities such as Yeshua, The Christ, and Siddhartha Gautama, The Buddha, used the power of the activated single eye along with the activated heart. This was done in order to share the light with all others and to come to know themselves as being one with The All - The All being Love/Light/Unity seemingly separate parts of creation.

Negative beings serve multiple purposes within the universe. These purposes can be clearly seen through the mature eyes of Love/Wisdom/Unity. They provide humans with the chance to honestly choose between the positive and negative paths in their seeking. From a higher point of view, this is seen to enrich the law of free will. Negative beings help humans to see contrast between the positive and negative paths in every choice, every moment. From a higher point of view, it can be seen that negative beings provide another purpose: they provide challenges for physical human beings, giving them the potential to learn, serve, grow and evolve. Negative beings serve as The Adversary within the duality of light/dark fourth and third dimensional energies. Within the geometric, mathematical and energetic layers of existence, there are natural energetic occurrences of imbalance and misalignment. These are all neutral energies, just like gravity. In the higher essence, they have nothing to do with right or wrong, good or evil. In the lower vibrations of the original essence, the lower astral beings and higher negatively-oriented beings are the self-aware personification of these neutral, natural energies. In the fourth and third dimensions, these natural energies manifest as darkness, stress, suffering, elitism, anger and evil. Within the grand scheme of the beingness of The One, negative beings provide a service by answering the call for darkness within each individual being. In the eyes of Unity, they help humans to better face their own darkness and Find Their Own Light. They provide obstacles and resistance which challenge humans to think, analyze, learn more, help others, and give love to each other. Many of these obstacles are not used by humans to learn and grow. By their free will, they react in anger or sorrow. From the third-dimensional point of view, negative beings are not seen as providing a service in the universe. A small amount of individuals, advanced masters, adepts and those who have activated and crystallized their higher energy centers are able to truly see Unity in the actions of these negative beings. These people are able to accept the positive and negative events which occur in their lives because they observe them through the eyes of Unity. Negative beings are not totally aware of their greater role in the universe. They are not consciously choosing to aid humans or to serve their greater purpose within the universe. They do what they do because they are simply greedy, evil, and selfish for the sake of greed, evil, and selfishness. The way a third-dimensional human being deals with a negative being depends on their own level of mind/body/spirit evolution.

This is why Love, Forgiveness, and a healthy diet are so important for humans. Love serves as the ultimate protection against any interaction with negative beings. Genuine forgiveness forces these negative beings to let go and leave the presence of a human being. When they see that they have no more sway over the mind or body, they retreat, or move on to another target. Negative beings are able to evolve on the negative path through the third, fourth, fifth, and very early sixth dimension. In the middle layers of the sixth dimension, all negative beings must become positive or they will be forced to begin the evolutionary process again from the third dimension. To vibrate in the higher sixth dimension requires unity of all energy centers, including the heart. No negative being ever chooses to remain negative and start over. They must take full responsibility and pay for their actions. All beings must choose to vibrate with unconditional love in order to proceed into greater and greater awareness of Oneness. No negativity ever enters the higher united essence of The One.

aum and auh are horrified by the thoughts, feelings and deeds of these lower astral entities. these beings use clever tricks to fool and harm the incarnated humans on earth. some of them attach themselves to human minds in order to feel the many sensations of physicality.

not all of the beings who are doing this are negative. there are many positive beings who have lost their physical bodies through death. they are not ready to let go of physical existence and seem to regain the stimulation of the physical world.

the negative beings are only able to attach themselves to humans who are vibrating on low and imbalanced frequencies. they seem humans who are vibrating feelings of elitism, self-righteousness, greed, selfishness, jealousy, hatred, intolerance, fear, depression, laziness and anger. they enjoy interfering with the bodies, thoughts, feelings and actions of humans who ingest and release thoughts, emotions, foods, minerals and chemicals that are overly toxic to the physical body. negative astral beings have less influence over humans who are vibrating at higher frequencies of love. they also have less influence over those who take care of their bodies and eat a cleaner diet. if an individual keeps their body clean and healthy, but has a toxic mind, a negative being may seize on that. individuals who are positive and loving in their thoughts and feelings have the greatest protection against negative beings, but a toxic diet may still open the body to potential negative influences. negative astral entities choose to live in environments where there are a lot of negative emotions. they influence individuals towards self-righteousness, arrogance, deceiving, scamming, controlling, enslaving, killing, stealing, discriminating, and violating others.

many negative astral beings work directly with those humans on earth known as the illuminati. together, they've created large mental programs, mental memes, psychological prisons, and social systems which keep the majority of humans ignorant of their true selves, of the higher dimensions, and of the nature of unity/love/light. for thousands of years, they've created confusion and separation among humans by manipulating positive spiritual information. they've changed and edited vital information, giving just enough truth to keep the people satisfied. these truths are layered with many lies, diversions, trickery, smokes and mirrors. these tricks are easy to spot. they always include very wise and uplifting teachings which help the believer to feel a connection to something greater. this is mixed with teachings that involve controlling people's thoughts and actions, forcing conformity, repression of natural emotions and behaviors, strict behavioral requirements, and creating the idea that "our group is the right group." the "us against them" mentality is usually the ultimate red flag which indicates manipulation of positive information by negative entities. many very positively-oriented individuals fall into this behavior, often as a result of being wronged by an oppressor or a larger group. understandably, they respond in self-defense, but end up carrying the low-vibrational energy of resentment and vengeful thinking for a long time.

negative astral beings also work with negative fifth-dimensional beings and negative physical fourth-dimensional extraterrestrials. together, with the negative elite humans on earth, they all work to evolve themselves through control and self-service. many negative fifth-density souls work with negative fourth-density souls by controlling them. the negative fourth-density souls and astral beings control and dominate the negative elite humans on earth. each looks out for them self or their own group only. they use each other only for what can be gained in order to evolve the self. the more advanced negative beings are extremely wise, but not loving towards others. they usually present themselves to humans as having the absolute truth. they laugh as many humans end up arguing and fighting for their oppressors. they laugh as they get humans to continue playing their main game of separation, separation, separation. the power of these beings over humanity lies in their ability to convince humans to separate themselves in many ways. instead of enjoying the differences and variety of creation, they fight against the idea of "different." negative beings tempt humans towards separation through race, culture, ethnicity, nationality, gender, sexual orientation, economic inequality, social status, lifestyle choices, social and political issues, and the most successful of all, religious absolutism and elitism. they use the minds and hearts of humans as weapons against themselves in order to keep them locked into a very limited and low-vibrational experience of reality. one of their most ingenious and effective weapons against humanity were the ideas of "the chosen people," "the true religion" and "the holy war." throughout the past 3,600 years, they have used the poisonous energetic brew of ignorance and arrogance which have influence many well-intentioned, good-hearted humans to distrust, murder, terrorize, discriminate and argue against each other over which group deserves the creator's glory and which group does not. some of these humans are led to believe that if they join a certain social, religious or political group, or tame a certain point of view on a topic, the creator will favor them over others. Although the idea of the chosen people can come with many positive qualities such as a strong sense of family, community, comfort, protection, togetherness, and like-minded individuals, the negative qualities such as elitist exclusion of others create an imbalance which mimics the negative spiritual path due to division and separation of souls rather than unity.

There are many ways for human entities to protect themselves against negative astral beings. There are sound vibrations, mental and physical disciplines, healthy behaviors, foods, minerals, rituals, first-density entities such as crystals, and advanced magical workings which can, when used properly, create energetic barriers between a human being and negative astral beings. The greatest known protection against negative beings of any kind is the radiation of genuine love, compassion, gratitude, and the strong conscious awareness of the presence of The Creator within. if a positive, high-vibrating individual, leader, prophet, messenger, master, healer, psychic, or servant of any mind opens themself enough to lower vibrational thoughts/feelings/actions/foods, they may also open themselves up to negative astral beings who desire to influence them in some way. these negative astral beings have absolutely no power over the free will of any human being. they may be persistent in their goal to influence an individual, especially if that individual holds the potential to provide a great positive service to the world. when they see that there is no possibility of controlling or influencing an individual at a particular space/time, they usually leave, and may seem another who vibrates closer to their lower frequencies.

negative astral beings come in many forms. one of the most popular ways negative astral beings influence humans is through the offering of temptations. they attempt to guide many well-intentioned individuals away

from their genuinely positive service by offering easy
money, power, many followers, and wide-spread attention
with no genuine exchange of value. there are many
trickster beings who pose as positive beings and pretend
to be of service. these beings can usually be spotted
very quickly by individuals who have an open heart and
the ability to differentiate the attributes of positive
and negative universal service. negative astral beings
influence humans to misuse and abuse love, light,
information, sex, money, power, goods, chemicals,
information, food, politics, organizations, social
movements, and many other natural neutral portions of
the human experience. by guiding human entities away
from their own center, negative astral entities can
cause confusion, ignorance, greed, hatred,
discrimination, irrationality, and insanity.

    aum and auh are horrified at the grossness of all
this. they try to find comfort in each other, but now,
for the first time, they see and feel the other as being
completely separate. suddenly, they feel something
familiar. it's a vague signal which brings in a vague
feeling. they tune into the signal and receive the
information associated with it.

mareem: they hate me. i want to go home. i wish i never
have to come to school.

vincent: see, bro? i told you! that's why i can't stand
those minds of people! dammit!

They see the astral bodies of Mr. Lightman and his seven students.
They don't see their physical bodies or the physical classroom in the
same way physical humans do. They tune into the calling signal that
they've been following throughout their descent. They experience the
signal as feelings of hope, compassion, sadness and confusion given off
by Mr. Lightman and his students. Aum and Auh struggle to hold onto
the positive energy of Mr. Lightman. He comforts them.

As they tune themselves to his energy field, they feel a greater
connection to the higher astral layers. Their astral bodies are
damaged. They are tired and in a great deal of emotional pain. They
vibrate at a very slow rate of frequency. There are angels observing
their struggle. The S.P.A. Elders let the angels know that everything is
in divine order, and that this is how Aum and Auh's call to service was
programmed to be experienced in the astral plane.

Above the Earth, the S.P.A. Alliance place protective golden spheres around the astral bodies of Aum and Auh. The golden spheres gently attune their souls and minds to the light of the physical world. Inside the spheres, Aum and Auh's consciousness are tuned into a new vibrational layer of Source's essence. The souls slowly extend a portion of there light into the vibration of the third level of density. They enter third-density Earth and vibrate to a new tune. The new tune creates- the breathtaking physical Golden-Yellow Light of The Sun.

The spheres containing Aum and Auh's souls hover in the lower layers of Earth's ionosphere. The geometric makeup of their souls transforms to match the more dense vibration. They lay in the fetal position as the spheres provide healing. The Arcturians want to teleport Aum and Auh to one of their underwater bases on Earth. They decide it would be safer to fly the spheres into the base instead due to their delicate state. The spheres are flown down into the Atlantic Ocean and transported to a hidden underwater base. In the base, there are more physical extraterrestrial humans from Arcturus, the Pleiades, and Sirius. They are young Scientists who are in training, learning to work with the Earth and humanity. They arrived on Earth on December 22nd, 2016. They work with many other extraterrestrial, angelic, devachanic and celestial beings. The S.P.A. Scientists have come to know and love the humans of Earth in a very personal way. They speak telepathically, but sometimes choose to use native Earth languages. The spheres holding the souls of Aum and Auh float into the base. The Scientists use Arcturian cloning technology to design special genetic codes for two physical Arcturian human bodies. This is approved and supervised by the great council. This connects Aum and Auh to the second density level where the essence radiates a bright orange color. The genetic codes for Aum are given in service by a Nameless Pupil of Master ᵞᴼᴰ ᴴᴱᴴ ᔕᴴᴵᴺ ᵛᴬᵁ ᴴᴱᴴ. The genes for Auh are given in service by The One known as Ra. The codes hover in an energy field in the center of the room. The field forms two sets of double-helix DNA strands. They form two single celled organisms. The spheres holding the souls of Aum and Auh float over and merge with the organisms. The DNA strands begin to spiral inside the cell.

The single-celled organisms are placed into hexagonal-shaped **crystals. Aum and Auh are now grounded into the first level of density where the**

Creator's essence radiates a bright red color. The crystals hold a specialized magnetic feminine energy. The Scientists are instructed by the S.P.A. sky crew to beam the hexagonal crystals into Mr. Lightman's classroom. As Mr. Lightman and the students talk, the crystals are silently materialized on the floor in the closet. They shoot energy upward to create two magnetic fields of energy. The fields form magnetic energy outlines for two tall extraterrestrial humanoid Arcturian bodies. The hexagonal crystals then shoot atomic, elemental, molecular, chemical and mineral Earth energies up into the heart centers of the energy bodies. In the ship above the Earth, the S.P.A. Alliance work with two other crystals. Each crystal is in the shape of two counter-rotating star tetrahedrons. The star tetrahedrons hold a specialized electric masculine energy. One crystal holds the energy of a lightbody for Auh. The other holds a lightbody for Aum. The star tetrahedrons materialize in the closet near the ceiling, high above the hexagonal crystals which spin near the floor. They spin and shoot light energy down into the heart centers of the tall Arcturian energy bodies. The down-flowing electric light energy meets with the up-flowing magnetic energy in the heart center of the bodies. The atoms, elements, molecules, minerals, and chemicals intelligently interact with the electromagnetic love/light. The golden spheres containing the souls and astral bodies of Aum and Auh appear in the closet. The souls appear like tiny points of condensed etheric light. They are placed into the middle of the brains of the energy bodies. The souls then create a connection from the brain to the thymus, which is located on the chest above the heart center. These different energies and energy centers interact intelligently to continue the process. The Scientists keep the tetrahedral and hexagonal crystals projecting their energies into the energy body outlines in the classroom.

Just as the process is about to be completed, the souls of Aum and Auh disconnect from the process and instantly enter a black hole at the core of the Earth. The Scientists are shocked and assume that something went terribly wrong. They are assured by the Elders that all is in divine order. They are relieved to know that they did nothing wrong. They know of the many mistakes made throughout the history of Earth by naive positively-oriented extraterrestrials who were not prepared for the unique difficulties of working with the humans on this planet. The souls of Aum and Auh enter the lower layer of the first level of density. From this state, it can be seen that there are many more levels below and above the eight levels they've been focused in. This current level is a void. They move into a state of artificial inter-dimensional processing. The souls are held in the loving embrace of The Heavenly Father and The Divine Mother. And Look! Located here is the information stored for all the worlds above and below, but nothing is expressed in any specific way. All potential experiences, thoughts, feelings, energy, matter, objects, places, times, beings, and events seem to be held here. This is the void of nothingness and the plenum of All That Is. The souls of Aum and Auh spiral out of the void as the rhythmic musical beats within The Logos, The Word of The One Creator.

The rhythmic beats blaze as the souls spiral through the Central Sun of the Milky Way galaxy. Through the rhythm and beauty of the sound, the souls become spiraling light and beautiful geometric shapes dancing with intelligence within the Galactic Central Sun. They continue the dance as holographic fractal patterns, eventually becoming the sacred shape known on Earth as the flower of life, which transforms into many other geometric shapes, including the fruit of life and Metatron's cube. They dance and shift with the rhythm as Metatron's cube fragments into five more geometric shapes which are sixth-density etheric designs for the forms of the physical geometric shapes known as the platonic solids. Within the Central Sun, Aum and Auh continue the energetic dance as a unified field of all organized universal information, collective awareness, and all space, time, energy and matter. They continue the dance towards the outer layers of the Galactic Sun as the non-physical anti-material formless holographic information for the projection of physical material form. They pulsate and resonate outwards as subatomic particles, dark energy, dark matter, electromagnetism and gravity. They become finer, more complex intelligent sixth-density geometric patterns. They vibrate as the many arrangements of energy which governs the behavior of all subatomic particles in this Galaxy.

Aum and Auh are now the zero point of existence. They are the basic quanta of all potential physical phenomena. They are the complex cosmic mathematical equations which relate to the physical spatial dimensions, basic geometry and sacred geometry which are energetic offspring of sound, motion, the blazing rhythmic beats, the intelligent light energy of all things, and The Original Thought of The Infinite One. Aum and Auh are One and All with the infinite and eternal process of Creator, Creating and Creation. As Infinity, Thought, Awareness, Unity, Movement, Magnetism, Sound, Light, Geometry, Intelligent Energy, Ether, Spirit, Soul, and The Unified Field of All That Is, they thrust forth, projecting the illusion outward as Ether, Air, Fire, Water, and Solid Matter. They dance, dance, dance in the etheric essence which is now vibrating to a new tune which syncs them to a new layer of existence. In this layer, the essence sings forth a beautiful tone which returns them to the Dazzling, Spectacular, Heavenly, Awe-inspiring Golden Light of the physical universe. Aum and Auh exist as the plasma, atoms, molecules, chemicals, gasses, liquids, and minerals that create the hologram for apparent physicality.

They 5 begin to pulse 1 between the fifth 5 and first 1 dimensions. They are able to have certain sensations within their soul/minds. In every moment, there are an infinite number of things for Aum and Auh to see, feel, know and be. With no control and no point of reference, they are automatically moved through the dance. They feel themselves pulse across this region of the galaxy as empty space, dust, and all material objects. From their state of being, it seems that they are nothing and everything at the same time. The Holy Spirit gives them a blessing, comfort, and assurance that all is well. They know that they are Chosen Messengers, working on behalf of the Totality. The Logos of the Milky Way and The Logos of Andromeda supply Aum and Auh with their shared essences, and gives downloads of special information that will help them during their mission on Earth. Aum and Auh are then teleported to Sirius, The Pleiades, Orion, Ribak and Arcturus. Many positive individuals and social memory networks within those civilizations are aware of what Aum and Auh are about to experience. Many project their light and offer their assistance for this grand event that will take place on planet Earth. On one of the ships in the Arcturus system, there are two third-dimensional human Christ-Conscious Arcturian women. These women are virgins from the only third-dimensional planet in the Ribak system. On their home planet, there is a lot of conflict. They are both among the highest-vibrating individuals on that planet. Both express Christ-Consciousness in a way that is highly unusual for third-dimensional people in such negative situations. Both women have dedicated their lives to serving the poor and disenfranchised on their planet. The governments of that planet know of extraterrestrial life, but have not revealed such information to the people. The leaders have not been told about these two women being taken aboard an Arcturian ship. They were chosen by the Arcturians and have agreed to supply the souls of Aum and Auh with their unfertilized eggs. Aum and Auh are implanted with genetic light codes containing the information of the eggs. Aum receives the egg of the woman known as Hēri'ēṭ. Auh receives the egg of Rozah. Both are then SHOT at light speed to the Sun.

As souls who are attached to codes of biological life, they get pulled into the gravitational grip of the Sun. Each one revolves around the sun 72 times in opposite directions. They do the same around Pluto, Neptune, Uranus, Chiron, Saturn, Jupiter, Mars, Venus and Mercury. Each planet gives specific information to Aum and Auh. This information relates to the accurate portions of astrological, mystical, magical and mythical teachings given throughout human history. Auh and Aum are then thrown to the Moon of Earth. The

Moon gives them a complex of energies which is the foundation for all the potential experiences they'll have on Earth. As they enter the Earth's ionosphere, they are welcomed by many beings on the astral plane. The elemental beings of air known as Sylphs create a beautifully choreographed routine of blowing wind across regions and continents. Aum and Auh are blown across the Earth through this choreographed design. The power of The Christ is shared as Auh is taken to the metaphysical energy field which was left on the grounds where Yehoshua, the Nazarene, walked, taught and left his essence. Aum is blown to the grounds where The Buddha, Siddhartha Gautama, taught his wisdom and left his essence. Both sweep through Egypt and receive the essence of Heru. They are then blown over to North America, The United States, New York City, into Manhattan, down the busy streets, through the window, and into the closet of Mr. Lightman's classroom.

In the closet, the souls merge their violet, indigo, blue, and green-ray bodies with the cloned electromagnetic energy bodies. The Indigo bodies of Aum and Auh use all of the genetic information from Hēri'ēṭ, Rozah, Ra, and the Nameless Pupil of master YOD HEH SHIN VAU HEH. This begins a slow materialization of two physical Arcturian bodies. There are primary portions of their souls which take their posts in the brains and thymuses of the bodies. The star tetrahedron crystals spin at the ceiling, shooting beams of indigo light down into the hearts, while the hexagon crystals shoot red beams containing atoms, minerals, molecules, and chemicals up into the hearts. The crystals create two large spiraling strands of energy around the spines of the bodies. The up and down movement of energies create heat, and begins to form seven primary condensed centers of energy in the head, throat, heart, pancreatic, naval, genital areas, and the legs of the energy bodies. There are also smaller secondary centers of condensed energy throughout the bodies. There are also energy centers above and below the bodies.

The physical biological bodies are formed as countless invisible spiraling double-helix DNA strands form thousands of tiny channels which grow out of the heart and spread throughout all portions of the energy bodies. The spiraling strands help to form trillions of cells within the bodies. The electromagnetic energy spins strongest around the heart center. The spiritual light thrusts itself into the material Earth elements of the energy bodies. The Earth elements remain open as they receive and accept the thrusting spiritual light. Within every cell, the crystal hexagons and star tetrahedrons shoot the spiritual and physical energies back and forth between the physical and metaphysical elements of the bodies. The Blue, Red and Yellow Light Energy is pumped into the receptive Primal Brown Mother Earth Material. This Macro/Micro Intercourse distributes PRANA, KA, SPIRIT through the energy bodies and pumps blood through the physical bodies. The Brown Mother Earth Energy secretes a large amount of MELANIN into the physical bodies as the final organ, the skin is being formed. Their bodies resemble the bodies of the Native Trinikhens which Aum and Auh enjoyed on planet Akhen. The beings in the sky crew, in the underwater bases, and the Elders Radiate Love/Light with tremendous Joy and Appreciation of the completed process and the Divine Glow Up, as the dark green skin of the physical bodies Shines and Radiates a Stunningly Beautiful Reflection of The One Infinite Creator in physical human form. The bodies become denser and denser, until they solidify in the more physical fourth-density state. They are able to be seen by human eyes. The male body is thirteen-feet tall. The female body is eleven-feet tall. They are both fourth-density extraterrestrial human beings with blueish-green skin. The male body is a little darker than the female. These bodies are similar to the bodies of the awakened human beings on Amaru. These bodies are perfect and beautiful, but have no self-awareness. The spiritual and material energy continue going back and forth, in and out, pushing and pulling inside every physical cell. They continue until there is a perfect balance between the two energies. The Divine Mother opens her sacred space within every cell of the bodies. The Heavenly Father breathes vitality into the sacred space. The Arcturian bodies begin to breathe.

The souls of Aum and Auh settle into the bodies. The soul essence spirals through every strand of DNA and settles into the pineal gland and the other glands of the endocrine system. They awaken and become self-conscious of themselves as fourth-density beings. They have knowledge and memory of their experiences as they descended through the dimensions.

In the underwater base, the young Scientists give thanks to The One, and join their hearts in love and appreciation for a mission accomplished. This celebration turns to confusion as their computers show a drastic change in the beingness of Aum and Auh. In the classroom, Aum and Auh suddenly lose their memories of the involution through the dimensions. Their bodies lose some of their solidity and become lighter. They begin to float uncontrollably. The Scientists in the underwater base quickly create a cloaking device around their bodies, making them invisible to human eyes. The bodies float outside of the classroom into the hallway. Through their will, Aum and Auh float back into the classroom, above the heads of the students. They seem to be vibrating between dimensions. Their bodies suddenly become much shorter. The S.P.A. Scientists and sky crew are still confused as to what went wrong. Once again, the Elders let them know that this is all a part of Aum and Auh's service. The Elders give thanks to the young Scientists. Their work is complete for now.

In the classroom, Aum and Auh are still not grounded in the physical world. As they learn to control their will, they realize that if they concentrate, they can become more balanced. Aum realizes that it may be possible to slow his rate of vibration down. This would sync the vibrational rate of his body to the vibrational rate of the material world. Auh attempts to do this also. Aum knocks Mr. Lightman's plastic cup onto the floor.

MR. LIGHTMAN: Oh, my sweetness!

EARL: Aye! Quit playin'!

VINCENT: I'm dead @ "Oh, my sweetness!"

EARL: You did that?!

MR. LIGHTMAN: Me? The cup just jumped off the desk.

VINCENT: Probably from hearing all that love noise coming outta your mouth.

NADIA: I saw it. The cup just, like, flew itself off!

EARL: Quit playin'!

Mr. Lightman sees Vincent looking at him.

VINCENT: "Oh, my sweetness?" That's how you express surprise?

EARL: "Oh, my sweetness" is wild. That's outta control.

Aum and Auh can only perceive bits and pieces of what is happening on the physical layer of the classroom. They feel as if they are in two bodies - one non-physical and one semi-physical. They feel the heavy pull of what seems to be a third body which is completely physical. They struggle in mind and spirit to align the perceived multiple bodies. They struggle to get into alignment with the energy fields, tubes and points of the physical world. The energies of time and matter are difficult to work with. The eternal now moment doesn't seem to exist anymore. The fluid movement and relativity within cycles of time doesn't seem to be available either. Interaction with matter also seems to be out of direct mental control. They look into the aspect of time called the past. Matter seems as if it isn't vibrating at all. The energy which makes up the matter seems frozen. The material seems fixed, solid, and unchangeable. Aum and Auh feel stuffy, stuck, limited. They look into the aspect of time called the future. There, matter is flowing, fluid, wiggly, uncertain, and doesn't exist in any particular way.

In this state, the original essence of Source is dualistic in every way. For every one thing, there is an opposite. It takes Aum and Auh a while to balance the new laws of time, space, energy and matter. For beings who have incarnated into matter and opened their eyes to the higher light, the physical world is enjoyed as a heavenly place with many advantages that are not available in the higher dimensions. For beings who are confused, who are too focused on the physical matter, and who are unaware of the higher light, this dimension can be a miserable place to be. For Aum and Auh, the newness, uncertainty and weirdness of it all creates restrictions, fear and confusion. These experiences could just as easily create excitement, openness and freedom, but their thoughts and confusion tune them to the limiting aspects of the experience. It's a suffocating experience. They can't consciously create segments of time as souls do on the spiritual plane. They don't experience the eternal nowness as they did on the mental plane. And they can't experience the fluidity of time as they did on the astral plane. Everything seems slow, solid, and limiting. The limited perceptions make them ignorant of the fact that the original essence of Source is exactly the same in the third dimension as it was in all the higher dimensions.

Time and space seem to be aggressively pushing them in one direction. They perceive the energy bodies of the children sitting in the room. As his mind and brain try to adjust, Aum floats over to where Vincent sits. The movement causes interference in his and Vincent's experience of time.

VINCENT: "Oh, my sweetness." That's funny! I won't forget that one. I wish I had my phone. I wish there was a rewind button in life. Button in life. Button in life. Button in life. Button in life.

SCOOTER: Why are you repeating yourself?

VINCENT: I didn't repeat myself.

EARL: Yeah, that sounded kinda freaky.

VINCENT: "Oh, my sweetness." What does that mean?

Mr. Lightman shakes his head.

MR. LIGHTMAN: I think I tried to say, "Oh, my goodness" or "sweet Jesus." I guess I tried to say both at the same time.

SCOOTER: Okay, guys. What just happened?

DIN: It was a ghost or something. Or …

KAREEM: A sign from God. What did I do? What did I forget to do?

VINCENT: The guy said, "Oh, my sweetness." I — I just can't look at you the same anymore.

BINDIA: It was nothing! Everybody calm down.

SCOOTER: You can pretend it didn't happen. I know what I saw.

BINDIA: Are you actually taking this seriously?!

A piece of chalk levitates off of the chalkboard and CRASHES into the door!

EARL: Saw it! Saw it! Saw it! Saw — Yall! I saw it! It — it ...

Kareem trembles and mumbles to himself uncontrollably.

KAREEM: Allah! I didn't pray this morning. Allah, I am sorry. I missed my prayer because Mother stayed up late last night, because Aliyah had diarrhea, because she ate the wrong ice cream, because I brought the wrong kind, because I didn't want to go into the store with the dog in front of it. It looked like it bites, but I don't know. Those dogs ... Mother told her to not eat it, but she would not listen. I would've prayed if I woke up early. Now I am not ready for ...

He gets onto his knees.

KAREEM: Please, God! Come back tomorrow! I will be ready! BINDIA: Stop it!

Kareem stops babbling but continues to breathe heavily. He stands up, then sits in his seat, panting.

BINDIA: It's not … It was the wind or something.

VINCENT: Did you just say the wind? Really? The wind? The cup just flew off of the table and the chalk smashed into the door and you say it's the

wind?! The wwww-ind?! Could you be any more delusional?! Are you in a
cheap horror movie?! The wind?! Wow. How could ... Really?! Really,
Bindia?! Seriously?! The wind?!
Nadia turns to Vincent in a rage.
NADIA: VINCENT! SHUT ... UP! OH, MY GOODNESS! Do you ever
listen to yourself?! Do you know how you sound?!
VINCENT: Kind of a smooth, manly tone with a hint of —
NADIA: Shut up! Bindia, you know that was not the wind!
MR. LIGHTMAN: Guys. Calm down.
Mr. Lightman closes his eyes.
Kareem holds his chest and leans on his desk.
MR. LIGHTMAN: Kareem, relax.
VINCENT: What are you doing? This gotta be a prank.
Aum and Auh use their mental willpower to shift their bodies more and
more into alignment with the physical world. They experience themselves
becoming more and more solid. They become fully rooted into their
physical bodies. Orientation and movement in space becomes stable. The
perception of time flows smoothly from past to present to future in a
seemingly straight line. Now they can clearly see, hear, touch, taste and
smell physical matter. Most of the strands of their DNA have been
deactivated. This is why they have lost many of their higher-dimensional
perceptions and abilities. They have lost the conscious memories of their
expanded Self. They have lost their feeling of connection with the beings in
the higher dimensions. All higher-dimensional memories and information
are stored deep in their subconscious mind. They both feel lonely and
afraid. They've completely lost their feeling of connection to their soul
family, the stars Ribak and Arcturus, the angels, extraterrestrials, and The
Infinite One. They both use their limited psychic abilities to absorb
information from the environment. They receive information from the
mental and emotional fields of the students in the classroom. First, they tap
into the religious beliefs of the children. They feel the great reverence,
devotion, respect, love and worship of The Creator which the religious
beliefs offer. These feelings give Aum and Auh some vital energy. These
feelings are powerful, but the organized belief systems feel extremely
limiting compared to the feeling of oneness they once knew. They begin to
feel the fear, guilt, elitism, unworthiness, control, competition, domination,
and arrogance of many of the religious belief systems. They receive the
horrible vibration which presents The Creator as a jealous, angry, irrational

and murderous tyrant who is "up there somewhere", separated from them and looking down in harsh judgment. Overall, the energy of the religious belief systems gives them comfort, but they still feel a great emptiness within their awareness.

They send out a call for more light. Mr. Lightman continues to sit at his desk with his eyes closed. On the level of soul, he offers his light to Aum and Auh. They immediately begin to download information from his mind. He gives his understanding of the English language, and some basic information about Earth and humanity. Auh receives more of Mr. Lightman's sense of humor, creativity, intuition, feelings, and the feminine heart-centered love of his being. Aum receives more of Mr. Lightman's ability to think logically and analyze experiences. Aum receives more of the masculine, mind-based wisdom of his being. Aum and Auh exhale as they feel a great deal of relief. They feel appreciation for Mr. Lightman's expanded and more unified Christ-Conscious perception of the Earth and humanity. They experience the energy of humanity's more positive qualities. Now they can perceive more of the Higher Light. The large influx of light allows their DNA to mutate quickly and activate more of their higher senses, which includes telepathic communication. The mutated DNA also gives them a more conscious access to the sacred essences which they picked up in Egypt, India and Nazareth. Even with this, they are still only vibrating at the beginning stages of fourth-density awareness.

Kareem takes his seat and is finally calm. Aum and Auh stand up in the back of the classroom. The Elders instruct the Scientists in the underwater base to release the cloaking field around the bodies of Aum and Auh. At the corner of his eye, Kareem notices a figure behind him. He turns around and sees his reflection in the shiny black eyes of Aum. The bizarre sight of the otherworldly being sends his nervous system into shock and he blacks out. His muscles go limp and he slumps forward onto his desk. The Pleiadian Elder comes to Kareem's aid. He offers protection for Kareem's body and mind. The others turn around and see The Arcturians. Vincent glances at them quickly then looks away and shakes his head. He mouths, "Prank." The others get a good look at the smooth and unusually fast movement of Aum and Auh's body parts. It's immediately obvious that they are not Earth humans wearing costumes. Bindia SHRIEKS and Nadia SCREAMS! EARL: OH, HEY-LL NAW!
Everyone besides Vincent dashes towards the door in a panic. Scooter and Din take turns fussing and trying to open it but it's locked. Earl pulls Nadia

and kicks the doorknob. He then turns to face the Arcturians. He shields Nadia.

Vincent sits in his seat shaking his head and smiling at the others. Din and Scooter pick up textbooks. Din tries to break the doorknob with his. Scooter swings his as a weapon to hold Auh and Auh back. Earl shields Nadia.

EARL: Back up! Aye! Back! … Up!

Aum and Auh don't move. Earl bangs on the door. Then clenches his fists for a fight, then clasps his hands for prayer. He raises his fists again, then jumps backwards. He's confused, ready to fight, ready to panic.

EARL: Please don't hurt us! We're ... good ... people!

Aum uses telepathy to communicate. His lips don't move. He transmits clear thoughts through signals of light. The students hear his voice in their minds, but to them it still seems like its coming from a distance. They perceive it as a young boy's voice, with what can be considered a general West-African accent. When Aum and Auh speak to each other, there is no voice. Instead, they communicate thoughts and ideas directly from mind to mind. The children stay close together and move along the wall. Mr. Lightman is still sitting at his desk with his eyes closed.

AUM: We come in peace.

VINCENT: (Smirking) How original.

EARL: Stay back! I ain't playin'!

BINDIA: What is ... Is this really happening?!

Din fiddles with the doorknob.

AUM: We have no intention of harming you.

Earl pulls and turns the doorknob with all his strength!

AUM: We mean you no harm.

EARL: Nah, y'all probably got ... lasers or something!

The children hear Auh's voice as a young girl, speaking with what can be considered a general Americanized accent.

AUH: We don't have any weapons.

Earl shouts as he pounds on the doorknob with a textbook!

EARL: Nah, but you could ... do some Jedi mind tricks and ... make us ... think ourselves to death or something!

He pounds on the door.

EARL: Open the door! THEY 'BOUT TO TAKE US OOOOUUUT!

The fearful energy from the students goes into Auh's aura. She falls to her knees in pain. She sits on the floor.

AUM: What's the matter?
AUH: Hurt.
Aum turns to the children.
AUM: What is that response?
He closes his eyes.
AUM: Opposites. Fearful. Separated. Elitism. Ignorant. Static.
Vincent gets a good look at Aum and Auh. He looks at their flesh and the movement of their facial features. He starts to believe that they really are extraterrestrials. He stands up and backs away. VINCENT: Oh ... What is ... *happening* right now?
EARL: Come!

Earl pulls Nadia towards the window. He climbs onto the window sill and throws the plant out of the way. He sticks his foot out through the window and tries to kick the protection bar outside. He loses his balance and falls off the window sill onto the floor. Auh bursts into laughter.
AUH: Ah-ha ha ha ha!
SCOOTER: It's laughing.
VINCENT: What is going on in my life right now?
Vincent looks around the room, searching for a hidden camera.
As Auh laughs, her energy immediately shifts from pain and fear to pleasure and love.
AUM: What is that response?
AUH: Ha ha ha!
AUM: Laughter. Love. Connected. Equality, cooperation, unity, harmony. Understanding. Flowing.
As Auh sits on the floor laughing, Aum feels the light and love that is flowing through her body. Auh wants to see Earl fall again. She mentally tries to recycle the experience in time.
AUH: It ... can't ... again.
AUM: No. The cycle of time is experienced much slower.
Auh puts her hands on her hips.
AUH: That's kind of stupid. So, time just drags us along without our control? That's crap! I feel so locked in. Who lives like this?
The children look at each other, surprised at the way she speaks.
Auh then experiences the memory of Earl falling.
AUH: Bwah ha ha ha ha haaaaa!
AUM: Imagination. Memory. Recollection. It seems as though we do have access to what has been experienced ... earlier. Earlier. Later.

AUH: What's a later?

AUM: We can think of possibilities which may be experienced later. And we can remember what has been experienced earlier.

Auh watches Earl fall in her mind again. She laughs hysterically.

AUH: He fell! He — He couldn't even fit through the window! Then, BAM! He dropped flat on his head!

Aum closes his eyes and remembers Earl's fall.

AUM: Gravity. Space. Time. Electromagnetism. Waves. Particles.

Without knowing how, Aum taps into the collective mind of humanity and the Earth. He feels the presence of others.

AUM: Even deeper. Even higher, many entities: Angels, Ascended Masters, Christed ones, Guardians.

Kareem slowly regains consciousness. As Auh laughs, Earl gets a good look at her eyes. All of a sudden, he approaches her and helps her to her feet. The others are surprised.

NADIA: What are you doing?!

The energy from Auh's deep belly laugh enters the auras of the children. They feel the Christ-Conscious nature of the Arcturian soul. This allows them to relax as they feel the special connection between the beings of Earth and Arcturus. The positive energy is overwhelming. Kareem opens his eyes and looks at what's going on. As the energy radiates throughout the classroom, he feels safe.

NADIA: What happened to Mr. Lightman?

Aum and Auh assure the children that he's okay. They then explain who they are and how they got here. They let the children know that they want to return to the eighth dimension. The children let them know that there's nothing that they can do to help them.

BINDIA: I wanna get outta this place, too.

AUH: I can see why. All these restraints. What a rip-off. How do you get anything done here? The time … The bodies ... can't change. It's claustrophobic. How are we gonna get home?

AUM: I do not know.

Mr. Lightman takes a deep breath. He invokes and embodies his Atma. He then communicates a message from Aum and Auh's eighth-dimensional Self. Mr. Lightman feels a point of pressure on the top-back of his head. As this is adjusted, he speaks in a soft tone.

MR. LIGHTMAN: I….Am…Kabir. (Pause) Children.

AUM: Father, it is you!

AUH: I feel him.

EARL: Hold up! Lightman got alien kids?!

VINCENT: That would explain a lot.

AUM: May you please open a portal so that we may return home?

MR. LIGHTMAN: We shall assist you in your return home, but We will not open a portal for you. You must do that for yourself.

AUH: What? Can't you just say it and take us back? Zip-zip! We're home! I mean, come on. You got all kinds of powers up there.

MR. LIGHTMAN: We see that you have discovered Terrestrial humor. It pleases us to see you in third-level form.

AUH: Why do we feel you as a father and not a mother?

MR. LIGHTMAN: That is due to your third-dimensional perception of reality, and because we are speaking through a male instrument.

SCOOTER: He's speaking through Mr. Lightman. This is so cool!

VINCENT: This is so ... fake. Something's not right.

AUM: So, how shall we return home?

MR. LIGHTMAN: In order to open the portal to return home, you must use the knowledge that is available to you from the Earth, from her inhabitants, and from her vast database of information. This knowledge is available to all of you, within your hearts and minds.

Auh walks over to Mr. Lightman and whispers into his ear.

AUH: But, Father, you really don't understand. These humans are out of sync with everything. They dwell on fear and separation ... a lot ... on purpose. Who does that?! I don't wanna deal with them.

MR. LIGHTMAN: These events offer you an opportunity to experience the forgetting and the separation. And then to regain awareness and evolve in your knowledge of who and what you are. You will assist the young Terrestrial human beings to evolve and come into the knowledge of who and what they are. If this can be done, you will all evolve consciously to a higher Understanding. That is why you chose to incarnate into the physical world.

AUH: Chose? We chose to come here? Here?!

MR. LIGHTMAN: Search within and you will see this to be true.

VINCENT: Okay, see that ... that was from *Star Wars*.

MR. LIGHTMAN: This planet and her inhabitants are experiencing a major transition in conscious evolution. You will do your part to aid them in this process. You will use knowledge from the ancient Scientists, teachers, and spiritual traditions to do this. You will all need to open your hearts and minds. Doing so will allow you to access the deeper Revelations.

VINCENT: Oh, not the heart. Close back the heart. Hold on, what is really happening right now. Am I the only one who —

BINDIA: Shh.

VINCENT: Really? No "shh." This is time to talk! Look around!

MR. LIGHTMAN: These Revelations will give you the chance to raise your awareness and access what has been called the fourth-density level of awareness.

SCOOTER: Fourth density level?

MR. LIGHTMAN: These terms and these states of awareness will be personally known by you all if you choose to listen and learn. This will require knowledge of Oneness, balanced in wisdom and love.

BINDIA: This depends on our love? Ha! You guys are never getting home. And I don't wanna get mixed up in this.

EARL: I'm kinda with Bindia on this.

MR. LIGHTMAN: This is the only way that a portal, as you call this opening, may be accessed. And this is the only way the Terrestrial humans may ascend to the state of awareness which is needed to live on the fourth-density planet which they call Earth 5.0.

EARL: Say what, now?

VINCENT: Prank! Fake!

MR. LIGHTMAN: Once the portal is opened, Aum and Auh may use it to return to the eighth level, or to incarnate on any fourth, or possibly fifth-level planet. The Terrestrial humans will use it to move into a slightly higher-vibrational Earth before moving into the vibration of Earth 5.0.

SCOOTER: Yeaahh, Buddy!

DIN: Earth 5.0 is real?!

Vincent smirks at the others as they celebrate.

VINCENT: Really? Y'all gonna fall for this? I gotta see this.

MR. LIGHTMAN: We have provided you with a ship in which you may travel around the Earth.

SCOOTER: Around the Earth?

AUH: Why do we have to travel?

MR. LIGHTMAN: You will need to generate a tremendous amount of energy in order to access the portal. You will then use your inner knowledge to complete the movement between densities. This inner knowledge will require learning the necessary lessons. Many will guide you towards your destiny. But it will depend on you all to complete the process yourselves.

SCOOTER: This is awesome! I'm ready to go!

KAREEM: It will be perfect!

VINCENT: You're going along with this? Who is behind this?

MR. LIGHTMAN: Your ship awaits you on the playing grounds. There is a cloaking feature which makes it invisible to other humans at this moment. We have also arranged for you all to be cloaked as you exit the schooling structure.

SCOOTER: We're invisible?

AUM: I still do not understand how we will generate this energy.

MR. LIGHTMAN: You will know when you need to know.

VINCENT: I knew he was gonna say something like that!

EARL: Wow! You want a doggy biscuit?

MR. LIGHTMAN: From this point on, there shall be no directions from us to you through spoken words. You will be guided by the shared light and love between yourselves. You will be provided with symbols, clues, and harmonious events as you are guided to your goal. It is up to you individually and collectively to progress with sufficient alignment and balance. You will also need to maintain a high enough state of conscious vibration so that you may be able to tune in, notice, and comprehend the subtle messages.

SCOOTER: Alignment.

VINCENT: What language is he talking?

AUH: What if we can't open the portal? We'll be stuck here?

MR. LIGHTMAN: That is correct. Remember that you will have to maintain a high rate of vibration in your bodies, hearts and minds in order to feel a connection that is strong enough to continually receive the most useful messages.

SCOOTER: Vibration.

VINCENT: See? Fake! All mysterious with signs and messages that we have to figure out. Whoever set this up, just know that this feels like a cheesy movie, or a badly-written novel.

EARL: It's like a video game. Just let it ride. Have fun with it.

MR. LIGHTMAN: That is an appropriate way to approach what is to come.

AUH: Is it really possible that we might not make it back home?

MR. LIGHTMAN: From your perspective, there are many different possible outcomes which may come to pass within the third-dimensional reality. Another thing that must be made clear is that the free will of the Terrestrial humans must not be infringed upon in any way. Children of Earth, you will learn a great deal about yourselves and your world. It is up to you as individuals to accept or reject the information given. As a general practice, accept what resonates or vibrates with your feelings. Accept what works through practice and testing. Question what does not feel right to you. If the answers are not sufficient, you may either seek further information, or reject the information completely.

SCOOTER: Why would he say that?

VINCENT: Wait, wait. Let's slow this down for a minute. What's really going on right now?

SCOOTER: What do you mean?

Vincent shakes his head at Scooter.

AUM: What is the tremendous energy you speak of?

SCOOTER: Yeah. That's what I wanna know.

MR. LIGHTMAN: That is what you are here to learn.

VINCENT: I bet it's love. Huh, Mr. Lightman? Love is the way?

MR. LIGHTMAN: We leave you now …

AUM: Is there any clue at all that can help us to know where to start?

MR. LIGHTMAN: The suggestion we may give is one that will assist you in every moment: Seek The Infinite One within yourself. See The Infinite One in each other, in the Earth, and within the entire process. It is possible for this to be grasped immediately. But it is likely that grasping this knowing will take great deal of your time. The experience of oneness allows for more clarity and vision of the bigger picture. This is the greatest clue we may offer. Go to the ship and you shall discover the next step. Enjoy your progress in the Love and Light of The One Creator. Adonai Vasu Borragus.

VINCENT: (Deep voice) And may the force be with you!

Scooter and Earl laugh.

SCOOTER: Imagine!

VINCENT: The guy kinda looks like you, Earl.

SCOOTER: Oh, wow. Whoa, you could be brothers.

EARL: Ohh…mi-Lrrd! Brother from another planet.

NADIA: So when he said, "The Infinite One," he meant God, right?

AUH: Yes, he did, Nadia. We may use the term, "Creator" more. But you may say, "Universe," "Source," "The One," or "Oneness" if you're not religious. Or say "God" if you're more religious. When we speak of The Creator or The Infinite One, we're speaking of All of Existence without the illusion of the separated parts. Uhh, we'll explain that soon, I guess.

Mr. Lightman sits with his eyes closed.

NADIA: Is Mr. Lightman gonna be okay?
AUH: He is okay, darling.
BINDIA: I'm not going.
AUH: We're gonna need you, Bindia.
BINDIA: That's too bad. You guys are crazy for going. I'm not.
AUM: Very well, then. Children, lead us to the playing grounds.
Bindia goes over to Mr. Lightman as the others walk out of the room. She taps him on the shoulder and calls his name.

3

EXPANSION OF AWARENESS

**KNOW THYSELF
LIFTING THE VEIL
STAGES OF ASCENSION
CONSCIOUS EVOLUTION
MIND/BODY/SPIRIT HEALING
SPIRITUAL ENLIGHTENMENT
FOURTH-DENSITY SALVATION
SEEING THE BIGGER PICTURE
WE ARE READY TO KNOW MORE
SEE THE PRISON BARS OF YOUR MIND
RISE ABOVE THE "MAINSTREAM" STATE OF MIND**

As they walk through the halls and out of the school, no one sees them. When they get to the playground, they see a seven-story-high ship that is shaped like a cylinder and seems to be made of a weird silver material. As they approach the ship, Aum and Auh get a good look at the younger fifth-grade students as they play tag on the playground. They feel their hearts beating faster and harder as they take in the beauty of simply watching the children of Earth play. The electromagnetic energy from the beating hearts of the joyful children causes Aum to drop to one knee. He feels a tingling in his frontal lobe. He feels intense joy and receives a large dose of intelligent energy. As this occurs, a group of beings belonging to the social memory network Jabik transmits an important message to Aum. He doesn't receive the exact message, but his overall thinking becomes clearer. He's better able to think rationally and analyze the challenges they face. Auh receives more intelligent energy also which enhances her intuition. A door slides open and they all enter the ship. Jabik continues to vibrate with them in the ship.

EARL: Yooohhh! Look!

They're standing in a room which is on level one of seven. A bright red light shines throughout the room. There are twenty-two glowing red pillars which reach up from the floor and penetrates the ceiling. When everyone gets inside, Auh presses a button that causes a hexagon-shaped portion of the floor to rise up like an elevator. As they rise, a bright spiraling white light rotates around them. Earl closes his eyes tightly.

EARL: Oh-mi-Lrrd! Come on, man! You tryin'a blind me?!

They all marvel at the beauty of the lights. They arrive on level two which is lit by an orange light. This level contains a complex arrangement of sacred crystals, lasers, other highly-technical equipment, and markings of mathematic equations and Egyptian hieroglyphics. The children can't get enough of how cool this is. For the first time in many years, they actually experience beauty without thinking about taking pictures with their phones. None of them even realize as yet that they don't have their phones with them. Auh presses a button and they travel up again to the third level which is lit by a golden-yellow light.

AUH: This is it.

DIN: Whoa!

The walls around the room are shiny and are adorned with crystals. The crystals reflect the golden-yellow light. This room is much bigger than the lower two. They see seven chairs which are made of little fluffy spheres. The seven chairs surround a cube-shaped table. Two triangular pilot's chairs are a little ahead in the front of the room. A control panel and a circular yellow screen are in front of the pilot's chairs. The screen is attached to a long pole which holds six smaller circular screens arranged vertically. The first screen is red and is closest to the floor. The second is orange, followed by the large yellow one. The ones above are green, blue, indigo, and the seventh is violet and white. The violet screen contains an image of the other six colored circles, each within the other. The indigo circle is on the outside and the red circle is inside all of the others. The fourth vertical screen is the brightest. It projects its green light onto the back wall of the room. On the back wall, it displays a twirling tunnel of green light with little green bubbles which randomly pop in and out of sight. Those patterns change repeatedly, displaying dazzling geometric designs. For about ten minutes, the children explore the ship with wonder and excitement. Eventually, they sit down. Aum and Auh get into the pilot's chairs and prepare to take off.

AUH: Wait.

Auh presses a button that opens the entrance door on level one.

Back in the classroom, Bindia tries to talk to Mr. Lightman. He opens his eyes and speaks to her in his normal voice.

MR. LIGHTMAN: You should head home now.

After thinking of the boring routine waiting for her at home, she runs out of the classroom, out of the school and into the ship. Auh brings her up to the third level.

BINDIA: Don't say anything! I just wanna see what this is all about.

She looks around and then sits down. The Arcturians use their inherent memory to prepare the complex controls for flight. The ship has many upgrades which would allow them to operate it with thought alone. For now, they use the physical controls.

Vincent puts his arms up and makes a gesture to stop.

VINCENT: Okay, am I gonna be the one to say it?

SCOOTER: Say what?

VINCENT: Scooter, you ... Come on. Aliens? We're on a spaceship going to another planet to live? Is that the situation we're in right now? And we're all just okay with it? Really? Really?

NADIA: You don't think this is real?

EARL: They're right here. You saw them just pop outta nowhere in the class with your own eyes.

VINCENT: Whatever the explanation is, y'all know this isn't real.

EARL: I'm a skeptic, too, bro. But I know what I saw.

Vincent pauses for a while. He squints his eyes, looks at the others, and then nods. He looks around at them and continues to nod.

VINCENT: Okay. Okay.

EARL: What?

VINCENT: Nah, nothing. I'll play along.

EARL: What you talkin' about?

NADIA: It's real!

VINCENT: It's real?

NADIA: This is exciting. It's fun.

VINCENT: It is fun! I'll give them that.

KAREEM: It is real.

VINCENT: Okay, so I'll play along! It's so funny to see you guys fall for this.

EARL: Fall for what?!

VINCENT: Are you serious? Earl, are you serious? Where are the cameras?

KAREEM: You think this is a show? Or a prank like on the internet?

VINCENT: Obviously! There are people doing all sorts of big pranks everyday for TV and online. It's a prank, or an experiment, or something. Maybe our parents set it up.

NADIA: Boy, you are beyond paranoid.

VINCENT: Okay. I'll be the one who's gonna be able to say, "I knew it all along." The viewers are gonna say, "Vincent was the only one who knew. He said it from the beginning. Look how manly and confident he is."

EARL: What?

VINCENT: That's ... just something they'll notice.

Vincent turns to a make-believe camera and winks.

BINDIA: Don't ruin this for me. If it's fake, we'll find out.

EARL: If this is fake, how come nobody on the playground saw us?

VINCENT: They're extras. They're a part of it, too!

The ship turns on and vibrates. The engine roars! The noise is deafening at first, then suddenly, silence. The third yellow screen on the pole lights up and displays a view of the front, back, left, right, top and bottom of the ship. A swirling vortex of white light spirals around the ship. The vibration of the room gets more intense.

VINCENT: Wait. How —

The ship suddenly SHOOTS UP into the Earth's atmosphere, and in less than a second, it's flying horizontally through the clouds.

Vincent let's out an EAR-PIERCING, HIGH-PITCHED SCREAM!

VINCENT: Iiiiiiiiiiihhhhhhhh! Ih! Ih! Ih!

The others laugh hysterically. Earl falls on the floor.

VINCENT: (Panicking!) We're getting abducted by freaking aliens! They're gonna do weird experiments to our butts! I can't even look at those things on TV or in movies! They're freaky-looking! Look! Look! They give me goose bumps. And they're real! They're real! Look! Look! How is this real?! Prank! It's a — I mean it's *not* a prank! It's ... We're gonna die! Kill them first! What about our families? Take me home! Mom! Oh, my God!

The others keep laughing and pointing at Vincent.

BINDIA: We're going to another planet with the same family.

EARL: You might see your moms and pops.

VINCENT: I ... gotta piss! Where's the bathroom?

BINDIA: Too late.

A wet spot appears on Vincent's pants. He turns away from the others and runs to the corner.

AUH: Your urine can be converted into drinking water and returned to your

body.
NADIA: Eww!
VINCENT: I'm not drinking pee! I need to use the bathroom.
AUH: You already did.
The need to use the bathroom goes away. The urine on his pants dries up.
VINCENT: What just happened?!
AUH: I saved you from a lot of embarrassment.
EARL: Did you piss yourself, bro?!
VINCENT: No!
Earl laughs.
VINCENT: We're really going to Earth 5.0?!
EARL: Yeah, change the subject from your piss-a-pants turkey self.
Nadia laughs.
NADIA: Piss-a-bed turkey!
Earl and Nadia laugh.
EARL: Inside joke.
NADIA: Our cousin use to pee his bed.
VINCENT: We're going to Earth 5.0 for real? Wait what is going on? Okay. Okay. It's real. I'll accept it ... for now. I mean ... Something's going on. I could deal with that. Okay. Okay. Okay.
SCOOTER: You said you wanna leave the planet! You're leaving it!
VINCENT: I don't know what to believe right now.
NADIA: Earth 5.0. It's gonna be perfect!
VINCENT: How is this possible? Aliens are real? We're really flying right now? Can we see outside?
AUH: You'll see.
VINCENT: This is ⌊it! I'm gonna be a king on Earth 5.0. Aside from the freaky aliens, this is dope. I mean, I did kinda believe it when I first saw them. And I do wanna get out of this crazy world.

He thinks of the many possibilities of experiences on Earth 5.0. For the next few minutes, they all do. They marvel at the chance to live a life without the problems they spoke of in detention.
VINCENT: So, it's that serious? Things are so bad that we're actually willing to leave the planet?
NADIA: Shoot. I know it is for me. All these women getting all kinds of surgeries and stuff to fix their faces and their bodies. I'm not rich. I can't just get rid of my ugly face like that. Leaving this planet ... to go to one where I'll be beautiful is not that much worse than having somebody cut

your face open and change up the parts. Or suck stuff out your stomach. It
is that serious for me!

EARL: Tell 'em girl!

Earl hits his sister on her back playfully. He pushes her shoulder.

EARL: Tell 'em!

NADIA: Stohhp-uh! I hate when you do that!

EARL: I hate when you talk like you really ugly.

NADIA: Shut up! You hit me hard!

EARL: Sorry. I mean the bad is all mine. Lightman said that earlier. "The
bad is all mine."

KAREEM: What will happen to Mr. Lightman?

BINDIA: He started talking like normal before I left.

SCOOTER: Really? What did he say?

BINDIA: He told me to go home.

SCOOTER: I meant about this whole thing.

BINDIA: Nothing.

SCOOTER: What was that all about? This is all happening so fast.

VINCENT: So fast? Why is it happening at all? Lightman's probably gonna
try to tell people what happened to us. Then they'll lock him up and put
him on some powerful medications. Old man Lightman. Muttering to
himself for the rest of his life in a mental institution.

SCOOTER: They spoke through him. He has some kind of powers.

BINDIA: No. It's called channeling. I heard my grandmother's friend talk
about that before.

NADIA: That's demonic stuff, right?

BINDIA: No, it's not!

EARL: Speakin' of Lightman, you went in on him hard for that "oh, my
sweetness."

VINCENT: Yeah! Who says that?!

Earl and scooter begin to snicker.

VINCENT: What?

They try to stifle their laughter.

SCOOTER: You shouldn't talk about how anybody reacts.

VINCENT: What? When I screamed?

Earl and Scooter burst out laughing.

VINCENT: Nah, that was completely different!

SCOOTER: He said "Iiiiiihhhhhhhhh!"

Nadia laughs really hard.

SCOOTER: What kind of a sound is "Ih?" What's "Ih?"
VINCENT: I didn't say —
Scooter nods his head.
SCOOTER: Yeah.
VINCENT: No, I —
SCOOTER: You did.
VINCENT: I said —
EARL: You said "Ih", bruh.
VINCENT: It sounded like —
EARL: Just take the "L."
VINCENT: No, 'cause —
EARL: Take the "L."
BINDIA: What is an "L" anyway?
EARL: A loss.
VINCENT: I bet Nadia's the only one who heard me right. She —
NADIA: I heard "Ih!"
She bursts out laughing again!
NADIA: I'm weak!
VINCENT: So? I don't usually make sounds like that.
EARL: You did that time.
He looks around for support from the others, then gives up.
VINCENT: Okay, but it still wasn't worse than, "Oh, my sweetness."
SCOOTER: Yes it was.
EARL: Way worse.
BINDIA: It was sad.
NADIA: For a man.
BINDIA: Really sad.
NADIA: Especially —
VINCENT: Aye! How?! Okay! Yeah! Okay! Aright, I screamed like a girl! I get how funny it's gonna be now! Especially because I would be the one going in on anybody else who did it! But it was me! It's funny! We got it! But can you spare me the stupid jokes?!
EARL AND SCOOTER: NOOHHHHH!!!!!!
EARL: You said, "Ih!" I never heard that sound before from somebody who was scared. "Ih." That's gonna stay fresh for a coupl'a weeks. Everybody at school on Earth 5.0 gotta hear about it.
NADIA: Boy, your lazy self is not going to school on Earth 5.0.
EARL: I won't have to, but I will. School is where I have the most fun. The

work is gonna be easy now 'cause that's what I want. On Earth 5.0, you get what you want, right?

SCOOTER: I don't think that's exactly how it works.

VINCENT: Like you know exactly how it works.

EARL: Well, I'ma deal with that when I get there.

Earl looks at Scooter.

EARL and SCOOTER: Iiihhhh!

They continue to laugh. Vincent shakes his head.

EARL: Oh, my sweetness, he said "Ih!" Hold the "L," Bruh.

Earl hands him an imaginary "L." He takes it and puts it in his pocket.

As they fly through the Earth's atmosphere, they enjoy the ride. They discuss the idea of leaving their problems on this Earth.

EARL: No hard work!

NADIA: I *know* I'm gonna look good. All girls are beautiful on my Earth 5.0. We won't have to fight about looks. We don't have to feel bad or get jealous. It's like heaven. I'm gonna be foine.

EARL: You already foine!

NADIA: I wanna look like Ciara. No, Megan Goode. That's the *right* look. It doesn't matter. I just want to have light skin and have a human nose instead of ... this thing.

The ship flies out of the atmosphere and into outer space.

AUM: Now is the time. We must learn how to generate this powerful energy in order to open that portal.

AUH: Well, what is the strongest energy we know of?

VINCENT: An exploding star.

SCOOTER: Money! Joking. I think it is an exploding star.

NADIA: Love.

KAREEM: Yeah. Love for God.

EARL: The Sun!

AUM: Your star. Hmm.

Aum thinks about that for a while.

AUM: Let us fly to the Sun.

Earl jumps up and yells in everyone's faces.

EARL: Booyakasha! I got it right!

NADIA: You spit on me!

VINCENT: I said a star!

EARL: You said "exploding star." I said the Sun. Told you!

VINCENT: Congratulations. You want a doggy biscuit?

EARL: You got one? (Dancing) 'Cause of me we're headed to Earth 5.0 now!

SCOOTER: Through the sun?

VINCENT: Flying into the Sun. Well, what could go wrong there?

They fly towards the Sun for few minutes. As they get closer, the automatic control system takes over the ship and slows it down.

AUM: Something is wrong.

EARL: No, it's not!

The lights in the room begin to blink.

AUM: Oh, no.

Kareem's eyes widen.

VINCENT: You can't say, "Oh, no."

SCOOTER: Wait, were in space?

EARL: Oh!

On the yellow screen, they see a huge wave of fire being shot at them from the Sun.

SCOOTER: Solar flare! Cool!

VINCENT: Not cool! What the hell is wrong with you?!

Nadia stands up and puts her hands together. She steps backwards away from the others and prays.

AUM: Turn it around!

AUH: What if this is the energy for the portal?

VINCENT: "What if?!" You don't "what if" in this situation!

AUM: If it is the energy, we would need to harness it.

SCOOTER: Isn't there something on the ship to do that with?

VINCENT: This is not the time to be figuring something like that out! A butt load of fire is coming right at us! And these are supposed to be superior beings? How could y'all be so clueless on something like this? We could die!

The ship automatically turns around and heads towards Earth.

AUM: What was the purpose of that?

Auh closes her eyes and tries to quiet her mind.

AUH: Shhh.

The children quiet down. Auh takes a deep breath. The area at the upper-back of her head pulses slowly. Her entire skull pulses slowly. She feels a tingling in her frontal lobe.

AUH: Our answer is not the Sun.

AUM: But that is the strongest energy I can think of.

EARL: Hold up, now. *I* thought of it! It was *me*!

Aum and Auh look at Earl and remain silent. They stare at him. EARL: What?

He feels weird watching their big eyes piercing through his. He walks backwards slowly and bumps into the cubed table. His pick falls out of his hair. The pick falls onto the table, then falls to the floor. Earl hears a familiar hip-hop beat in the rhythm of the pick hitting the table and floor. He bops left-to-right and starts rapping. EARL: Teach me how to Dougie. Teach me, teach me how to Dougie.

He performs The Dougie, a popular hip-hop dance. His shoulders and arms lead his body left-to-right. He goes lower, then higher. He continues and gives the dance his unique flavor. He feels the hype and Tha Goodness of the dance. There's high excitement with every move as his mind slips into the state he calls *The Zone*. His excitement mixes with the left-right swirling motion of his body to create a certain geometric field of subtle energy around his body. The energy radiates the sixth-density living light energy throughout the ship. Auh gets a really good feeling from this energy. Aum feels it also but doesn't notice it enough to choose to use it in any practical way.

AUH: What is that?!

AUM: Pardon?

AUH: It's coming from Earl.

EARL: It's the Dougie. You want me to teach you how to Dougie?

VINCENT: If it was 2011.

AUH: I want you to teach me how to create that feeling.

Auh gets up and begins to dance the Dougie.

EARL: Ahhhh, she bussin' it!

The others look on and laugh at her little body as she gets down.

VINCENT: Her head, though!

EARL: Get it! Get it! Get it!

Nadia isn't paying Auh any attention. She's standing near the back wall. She looks at the spiraling green light as it is projected onto the wall from the green screen. She observes the twirling tunnel and the bubbles of energy popping in and out of sight. The beauty of the twirling tunnel holds her attention. The movement of the brilliant green plasma-like bubbles is dazzling. She tilts her head and falls in love with the beauty.

NADIA: (Whispering) So pretty.

Auh stops dancing with Earl and goes over to Nadia. She also becomes

caught up in the beauty of the green light's effects.
AUH: Wow! So pretty!
 A group of beings from the fourth-density social memory network Ābhārī enter the energy field of the ship. They have followed Jabik and Rājā Mārśala from the Ribak star system. All have projected their consciousness here from their home planets of Julāhā, Akhen and Amaru. Ābhārī sees a great opportunity to be of service. They transmit lots of love and a very useful message through the living light and the fun and joy produced by the dancing and the appreciation of beauty. Rājā Mārśala has a much more fundamental message for everyone on the ship. Together Ābhārī and Rājā Mārśala help Aum to see the electromagnetic energy which is pulsing outwards from the hearts of Earl, Nadia and Auh. He looks at Earl dancing and sees the field of energy. He closes his eyes and tries to analyze and rationally understand what's happening. As the ship approaches Earth, the walls all around the room become transparent, allowing everyone to see into outer space. There are dozens of other spacecrafts flying towards and away from the Earth. Almost all of them are invisible to the eyes of humans on Earth and their radar systems.
VINCENT: Yoooooo!
EARL: Dooohhhhhpe!
DIN: Whoa!
SCOOTER: Oh, my God!
NADIA: Would you stop saying that?!
AUM: There are many civilizations working in service to the Earth and her inhabitants.
Nadia lays her eyes on the Earth, glowing and floating in front of them. The beauty gives her goose bumps.
NADIA: Oh, my goodness! Oh, my goodness! Look, you guys!
EARL: That's waaaavvvvyyyy!
NADIA: It's so pretty!
Auh closes her eyes. She uses her attention to feel around her brain and mind. She scans the organs of her body. She gets a greater awareness of the subtle energies of her chakras. Through the pulses in her heart, she uses her feelings to send a signal to the heart of Earth. The Earth receives her energy and transmits a portion of light which contains an important message for everyone.
AUH: The Earth is called "Gaia" or "Terra" by many Terrestrial and

211

extraterrestrial beings. It is a living biological being just like you all.

NADIA: What do you mean "living?"

SCOOTER: It's a planet. It's a big rock. And trees and water.

AUH: She is a soul. And she has a physical body. You are only aware of her physical body. You are a part of her physical body.

KAREEM: It's alive?

EARL: You serious?

AUH: It's a living organism.

They get a wider view of the Earth. It's breathtaking!

DIN: Whooaa!

SCOOTER: Dude! That's our planet right there!

VINCENT: It's like, right there!

SCOOTER: Not some globe in class!

VINCENT: Or a picture on the internet!

SCOOTER: Or Google Earth.

EARL: Nah, Google Earth is poppin'.

SCOOTER: Not like this!

EARL: This is waaaavvvvvyyyy! Gaia, I love ya, babay!

Bindia's eyes are fixed on India. That's where her family is from. Although she's never been there or felt any closeness to it before, seeing it from outside of the Earth builds up a strong sentimental feeling inside. She tries hard to ignore the sentimental feelings and just enjoy the view. She suppresses the deeper emotional feelings.

AUH: The Earth is one living being. Her body works much like yours. She takes care of her body by constantly balancing the regions within the whole. Balance is fundamental. Volcanoes, earthquakes, rivers, lakes, oceans, fires, rain, and hurricanes are some of her body parts and functions. All of these things have their place and plays their roles in achieving and maintaining balance. She is currently very, very imbalanced.

SCOOTER: Rivers and lakes. Like the bloodstream. Or like veins. AUH: Right!

VINCENT: I got that, too. I was gonna say it first.

AUH: All of the gasses, liquids and minerals in your bodies such as sulfur, water, iron, magnesium, zinc, and calcium come from the body of the Earth. You are made in the image of The Creator and of the substance of the Earth.

NADIA: (Whispering in wonder) "And Jehovah went on to form the man out of dust."

AUH: You are mineral, liquid, gaseous, electric, magnetic, self aware, angelic, etheric and God-like beings.

VINCENT: God-like?

AUH: The Earth's body receives the elements from your star, the Sun. This all began many billions of your years ago. Your bodies are literally made of the stars.

SCOOTER: Epic!

EARL: If she got all these body functions, does she, um ...

Vincent and Scooter look at Earl.

EARL, VINCENT & SCOOTER: Fart?

AUH: It's all connected. When she coughs or sneezes, you feel it. When her body gets sick and polluted, you feel it. She also feels it when many of your human bodies and minds are sick and polluted.

BINDIA: She must be really sick. She must have some really bad diarrhea. Since she's full of humans.

VINCENT: Ahh, I see what you did there.

Bindia nods her head while ignoring Vincent.

VINCENT: 'Cause humans are ...

BINDIA: Uh-huh.

VINCENT: We're full of ...

BINDIA: Yeah.

VINCENT: Ha! I get it!

BINDIA: (Aggravated) I know!

VINCENT: You're so grumpy, you don't even think your own jokes are funny.

EARL: She was not jokin'.

They all laugh and clown around for a while, but can't take their eyes off of the Earth.

SCOOTER: It's aliiiiive!

AUH: She *is* alive. And you are her living cells.

SCOOTER: Cells. That makes sense. Why does that make sense? BINDIA: So, she *is* sick, then. Because most of her cells are diseased and cancerous viruses.

VINCENT: Good lord, you are dark! I mean, I feel the same way about people, but ... come on, now.

SCOOTER: This is the most epicest of all epic things ever!

They continue to look at the planet and the glow of the atmosphere.

VINCENT: Every single thing we ever knew is right inside of that.

213

BINDIA: From up here it's so nice, though.

KAREEM: ALLAH, Your Creation *Is* Good. It *Is* Very Good.

Kareem gets onto the floor and begins a prayer of deep appreciation for the Earth. After a while, Nadia joins him in prayer. Their worship, reverence and adoration for The Creator strengthen the vibrational patterns of the energy within and around the ship. The energy from everyone's excitement fills the room with a strong field of loving energy. The vibrating field of love radiates in all directions. The field contains a grid which is used by souls to receive and transmit information between the lower and higher dimensions. This grid is one of many larger and smaller grids. The grid is part of an interplanetary network of inter-dimensional computer systems. This network is connected to all self-aware beings in this solar system. The network is connected to planetary, interplanetary, interstellar, intergalactic, and universal networks. The bodies, minds and spirits of everyone on the ship have their individual grids and systems which are perfectly compatible to all of the larger grids and systems. Within all grids are points of focused light where information for sentient experience are received and transmitted. Those with sufficient awareness, proper vision, access, and understanding of these metaphysical energies are able to send information to the ship and the beings inside. Information can be sent through signals of high-frequency light by angels and extraterrestrial beings. Those of Jabik, Rājā Mārśala and Ābhārī use these grids to serve the children and Aum and Auh.

The intense love and light energy in the room gives Aum, Auh, and the children more access to metaphysical information, which can also be called Higher-Light information. This information is neutral. It can be ignored, misunderstood or misused. It can be properly used for positive and negative work. Aum, Auh and the children sense the energy in different ways. Aum and Auh are aware of so much more, but also have many blind spots in their perception of exactly what is going on and how this all works.

AUM: This energy is incredible. It is coming from your hearts. When the boy moved to the sound, it generated that same energy.

EARL: Name's Earl, dude.

AUM: When the girl viewed the energy projection, it also generated this energy.

EARL: Nadia.

AUM: When —
EARL: Sister's name is Nadia. Not "the girl."
AUM: When they enjoyed the beauty of the planet, the energy was also very strong.
EARL: We don't just call you "little weird blue thing."
AUM: Even the boy's poor attempt to be humorous causes a flow of this energy.
SCOOTER: "Poor attempt!" Buuuuuurrrrrrn!
VINCENT: Got Em! He shut you down!
Vincent and Scooter point and laugh at Earl.
AUM: The laughter, the music, the appreciation of beauty, the worship, the prayer, the feeling of unity, of togetherness, of being one, causes the energy to increase in vibrational strength. This is the strongest energy there is. This is the only energy there is — the Unity of Love and Light. For beings like all of us, it can be experienced in many ways. When we are strongly tuned into it, it is experienced as the realization of the here-and-now literal presence of Our Highest and Deepest Source. That experience has been called Nirvana, Heaven, divine ecstasy, and spiritual enlightenment. It is the realization of Infinite Oneness. And that is our key to opening the portal. Love/Light is the strongest energy.
NADIA: I have goose bumps!
VINCENT: I said "love" in the classroom. It was sarcastic, but I was right.
NADIA: I said "love" too.
VINCENT: Well, I said it first, so …

As the ship enters Earth's atmosphere, the walls of the room become solid again, and they can no longer see outside. Nadia sees her reflection on the shiny wall. The sight of her cheeks and lips immediately changes the feeling in her heart. She goes from joy to disappointment. She fakes a smile. Aum notices the shift in energy immediately. Auh does also.
AUH: It's a little less now.
AUM: This energy does not last long enough to open the portal. It needs to be intensified and sustained. We must somehow generate, focus, and guide enough of this energy in order to open the portal.
AUH: How?
AUM: I do not know.
SCOOTER: Can't you ask your alien friends? They're flying all around. Send a text.
AUH: This is a challenge we will face ourselves.

VINCENT: MY PHONE!

NADIA: Oh!

Earl drops to the floor and lies on his back!

EARL: That's not fair! That's not fair! That's not fair! Life is wrong!

They all realize the tragedy of not having their phones for this adventure. They wine about it for a few minutes.

AUH: Even if you had your phones, you would not be able to use them for images, videos or social media.

VINCENT: Oh, come on!

EARL: She shut *you* down!

VINCENT: You want your phone, too! She shut all of us down!

EARL: How we gonna get through this without our phones, though?

AUM: Let us focus our minds upon the generation of this energy.

EARL: That's impossible.

NADIA: Nothing is impossible.

EARL: It's impossible to me.

NADIA: God has the answer to everything.

Earl closes his eyes and prays.

EARL: God, can you please make our phones magically appear?

NADIA: I'm talking about the mission, idiot!

AUH: Mission.

SCOOTER: Are there aliens on the other planets in our solar system?

AUM: Many of the self-aware beings who live on other planets in this galaxy are also humanoid in appearance, and look very similar to you guys. Many look like us. There are many, many different races of beings in the galaxy. Many vibrate at your level of consciousness, but do not take the human form. There are many variations of beings who vibrate at your level of consciousness.

SCOOTER: Huh?

AUM: Some evolve from plants, felines, canines, reptiles ...

VINCENT: So, like, *Star Wars* and *Star Trek* are real?

AUH: Many extraterrestrial beings are physical people vibrating at your level of awareness. Others are less physical and have higher levels of awareness. Others are completely non-physical and have much higher levels of awareness. There are beings living on many planets throughout this galaxy.

SCOOTER: How? There's just toxic gas and stuff. No food or water. I know that you have to have water, at least, for life to exist.

216

AUM: At higher levels of awareness, entities may live in forms and environments that are very different from the ways of which Terrestrial humans are familiar with. They're bodies vibrate at much, much higher frequencies of light.

SCOOTER: Vibrate? Frequencies of light? Awareness?

AUM: The planets they inhabit vibrate at higher frequencies of light. Most humans on Earth are unaware of conscious beings existing beyond the chemical and gaseous levels of these planets.

VINCENT: Did you say that you guys are human?

EARL: Y'all don't look human to me.

AUM: From my memory, it seems that our appearance has been greatly altered. We were much taller than we are now, and had much more awareness. Perhaps this smaller sizing was done to set certain limitations within our awareness.

SCOOTER: Why?

AUM: I can guess that it is so that we would have the specific spiritual, mental and physical configurations which are needed for this experience. Aum is surprised that he knew that.

SCOOTER: There's so much we don't know. Dude, people live on other planets!

EARL: That's crazy!

SCOOTER: It's not crazy at all. If there were no people on other planets, that would be crazy.

NADIA: It feels kinda eerie.

BINDIA: Yeah, it's weird to think about.

SCOOTER: No, it feels wider. Wider. Like … broader.

AUM: What is important is that we now know that the energy of love must be used to open the portal. The next step is to come to know how to do this.

Suddenly, they hear the divine voice of an Angelic Being named Hathora. Hathora lives in the upper layers of Earth's astral plane. She is going through an intense training course that includes using complex light signals to simultaneously guide a large number of young humans on Earth. Her voice comes through speakers which are located inside of the fifth blue screen on the vertical pole. Her voice fills the room with a warm and comforting energy.

HATHORA: I am Hathora. Now that you know more about what you have called the strongest energy, and where it rests, it's time to sit in silence. Become still in order to know what you need to know. In stillness, you may allow your minds to open and your bodies to better attune to the frequency of the Earth. This will help you to communicate with the higher intelligence within yourselves. You can also communicate with the Earth. You only need minimal conscious contact with the Earth in order to receive guidance for the next phase of your quest.

AUH: Thank you, Hathora.

NADIA: Thank you! Her voice is so beautiful. Gives me chills!

VINCENT: A quest?! Really? A quest? That's what this is now? Huh? A quest? We're on a quest? She said "quest," right?

Nadia turns to Vincent.

NADIA: Why do you do that?!

VINCENT: What?

NADIA: Oh, my goodness!

HATHORA: It should bring great comfort for you to know that all information spoken on this ship is being recorded, and will be available for use as you put what is learned into practice. I will leave you now.

NADIA: Thank you!

SCOOTER: It's being recorded so we don't have to remember everything.

VINCENT: What? This seems like it's gonna be a lot of work.

EARL: For real. I thought it was gonna be quick.

Aum and Auh ask the children to be silent. They sit on the floor in the full lotus meditation position. They close their eyes and begin to take long, deep breaths. After a few deep breaths, they breathe normally. They are able to fall into the deep meditative state very quickly. This is because they don't have the third-dimensional human tendency to overthink and hold excessive mental information in their minds. Just as they are both about to take their awareness into deeper regions of their minds, Vincent interrupts.

VINCENT: We have to be quiet for long?

AUH: Shhh.

Din sits in the full lotus position near Aum and Auh. They breathe. He breathes. All three of them go into meditation. Vincent whispers and makes gestures asking how Din can fold his legs into that position. Earl whispers rap lyrics to himself and dances. Aum and Auh are interrupted again.

AUM: It would be best if everyone practiced stillness and silence of the mind.

The children sit Indian-style on the floor and try to meditate. They fuss, scratch, pick their noses, and shove each other around. It takes Aum and Auh a few minutes to settle their minds and enter the deeper regions. Their feelings of doubt slowly fall away as they breathe deeply. After a short while, they rest their awareness deep enough inside of their minds to observe their thoughts flowing one-by-one. This is a profound experience for both of them. They allow their thoughts to flow without paying them any attention, and without giving them any emotional responses. Aum is most fascinated by this experience. After seven minutes, they become more aware of subtler parts of themselves and the world around them. From deep in their own minds, they can feel the children fidgeting. They feel orbs and light beings on the inner planes on the outside of the ship. They feel the strong presence of Ābhārī and Rājā Mārśala, but somehow are not able to identify them. Being open to the Infinite Intelligence of All That Is, they intuitively move their awareness over the inner portions of their bodies and rest their awareness in the center of their chests — the heart space. They keep their awareness on their heart and sacred-heart centers. They both feel an intense burst of freedom. They get the feeling of being able to find all the answers they need. By now, the children are laying on the floor, lounging in their chairs, whispering in the corner, and walking around. Only Din is able to stay in meditation as long as Aum and Auh. Auh feels the Earth in her body. She feels the Earth *as* her body. Different body parts feel like they match up with different regions of the planet. Aum is able to explore the portions of mind. It is a large and complex world. Just as the different regions of the physical brain have their own look, shape, and function, the invisible metaphysical regions of the mind also have their distinct features. There is geography and there is geometry of the mind. Aum and Auh are able to consciously tap into the primary information database of the Earth. This database is known on Earth as the Akashic Records.

   Aum mostly thinks and analyses while Auh mostly uses her intuitive feelings to seek for answers. Jabik and the other two social memory networks don't send messages or interfere in any way. Instead, they allow Aum and Auh to receive intelligent energy and try to find their own answers. They gain more access to the lower and higher dimensions. There is still a whole lot that they don't see. There are still many blind spots. As they explore the vast regions of their bodies, of their minds, and of the Earth, Aum and Auh reach a new Level of Astonishment for the Creation. They know their divine nature. They feel exalted. Suddenly, Din SNEEZES!

KAREEM AND NADIA: Bless You!

Din sits with his eyes closed.

DIN: Thank you.

AUH: I Understand!

Auh quickly opens her eyes, runs to her pilot's chair and takes control of the ship. Aum stands up and goes to his pilot's chair also. Auh makes a sudden turn.

KAREEM: Whoa!

SCOOTER: What's going on?

BINDIA: She got the answers.

EARL: (Yelling) She ain't got the answers!

AUM: She does, actually.

Din is still meditating on the floor. He opens his eyes and smiles. Earl nudges Vincent.

EARL: Din … smiling.

Din stands up. Kareem walks over to him.

KAREEM: Did you do meditation before?

DIN: Yeah, when I was a little kid. My grandfather does it everyday.

KAREEM: I wish I knew how to do that.

They fly across the planet to North Africa and land in a desert in Sudan. It's after midnight here.

They exit the ship. It's dark. A large protective field of green light surrounds the area.

EARL: That is dope!

NADIA: Look at that!

BINDIA: This is scary.

AUH: No need to be afraid.

Auh asks the children to sit in a circle on the sandy floor. They are reluctant to sit, fearing bugs and snakes. Aum lets them know that no dangerous animals can enter the circle of green light. They sit in a circle and Auh stands in the center. She closes her eyes and looks up. She takes a deep breath.

AUH: I know it's there. I feel it. But I cannot see.

Aum steps into the circle near her.

AUM: What does Father want us to do?

As Aum steps a little closer. Auh takes hold of his hand. Their hearts beat quickly and come into sync through their hands and arms. This allows Aum to convert some of Auh's deepest feelings into words for clearer expression

220

and understanding. Neither of them knows exactly what they are looking for, but they have an inner knowing that they're doing the right thing. Everything feels right and strangely familiar. Even though Aum only sees a very small portion of what's going on, he tries his best to explain silently to himself. The children listen to his inner dialogue.

AUM: The Infinite One which you call God ... speaks to us from inside of ourselves and through All That Is. There is a great deal of information coming in and going out of our beings in every moment. We are receiving information from our expanded selves, our souls, many stars, planets, light beings, angels, and elemental beings. There are many more sending us useful ... information. There are streams of intelligent energy pouring into our bodies and our minds. There are streams of energy pouring out from our bodies and minds. There is so much more ... the moving parts ... the connectivity of all. It's fascinating, and overwhelming to try to understand. Every single movement, thought, experience, object ... involves inflowing and out-flowing streams of energy ... connected to the center of the galaxy, the Sun, the planet, higher-dimensional beings, plants, the minerals and cells of our bodies. This is ...

Aum is overwhelmed by the symphony of thought, energy, sounds and colors.

AUM: We are connected to each other in so many ways. We can communicate and connect to all others through our hearts. Everything we need to know is available inside. All knowledge that we receive is our own knowledge, and the universal knowledge of All That Is. All knowledge is available for the purpose of evolution of body, mind and soul. The primary purpose of all evolution is to move through the process of knowing the One Self with more and more and more levels of awareness.

VINCENT: What?

EARL: I have no idea.

NADIA: Listen, idiot!

AUM: I shall explain. I am ... seeing ...

Kareem and Nadia are the most attentive to this information. Din and Scooter are also paying close attention. Although Earl isn't paying close attention to the information, he is traveling through his mind, vividly visualizing what Aum is describing. Vincent is bored, but listening. He feels something touch his leg.

VINCENT: Yow! What's that!

He twists and turns, looking all around his body for bugs.

221

NADIA: (Whispers) Come on. Stop.

AUM: There are so many intelligent points of awareness in the galaxy. Sending answers. Desiring to help us. Not only now as a group, but at all times as individuals. Many are neutral, just moving things along for the purpose of universal evolution. Most have dedicated themselves to positive service to others. A smaller portion is not desirous of helping, but desirous of controlling ... and dominating and hurting.

Nadia's eyes widen with concern.

AUM: But we are currently protected — very, very well-protected from any negative forces. They pose no threat to us.

NADIA: (Whispers) Wow.

Aum and Auh continue taking deep breaths, trying not to get swept away by their emotions and astonishment.

AUM: There are many layers, many worlds, many kingdoms — one on top of the other. Or a bit more accurately, each within the other. Primary levels ... worlds existing within ... fields? ... of vibrating light. Each level contains living beings, laws, and unique organizations of many types of energies.

Scooter shakes his head, not understanding any of this.

AUM: Each level ... extends slightly into the one above and slightly into the one below. Levels ... Dimensions are layered — one within the next within the next. Our bodies and minds are layered within all of these layers. From the unexplainable energies, to the non-physical worlds, to the semi-physical worlds, to this physical world, The Infinite One lives as many ... interacting with each other within The One Self. The Self of All That Is lives as what appears to be separate points of attention ... all interacting with each other. That includes us. Every individual contains the seed of The Whole One ... and The Whole One contains all of the individuals. No matter how far out or how deep down we may seek, all is One and all is Infinite. Any experience of separation is part of an illusion. This grand illusion of separate ones is used for The Infinite One to experience and educate The One Self about every major and minor portion of The One Self. This is done by creating a fantasy of separation, and then having the separate portions interact with the other separate portions within the fantasy. Galaxies, stars, planets, elements, plants, animals, humans, angels of varying levels, and many more — all experiencing The Infinite One's fantasy as seemingly separate portions of Oneness.

Scooter squints, turns and squeezes his face as he tries to follow what Aum is describing.

222

EARL: You gonna get a stroke.

SCOOTER: I kind of ... understand.

VINCENT: No, you don't.

SCOOTER: I think I do.

VINCENT: You don't. 'Cause I don't.

AUM: Many of the higher dimensions can be accessed by human beings who are living in this level, which is the third level ... the third dimension. Higher dimensions can be accessed by increasing one's awareness. There are many reasons one would desire to access higher dimensions. The primary reasons, from what I see are: To seek and know One Self within the self of the individual. To seek further knowledge of the nature of the universe, and of the universe within the Self. To seek to know oneself in body, mind and spirit. To heal oneself. To heal others. To balance oneself. To access useful information which will progress oneself on one's individual path of seeking. To access information which will progress oneself in their service of others. For exciting experiences, for joy, bliss, mysterious and mystical experiences. For contact with the expanded portions of ones Self — the soul, the Higher Self in order to receive information related to conscious evolution and healing. Some may access higher dimensions in order to communicate with their angelic guides, inter-dimensional, interplanetary and interstellar beings who are on the path of service to others. Generally, using expanded consciousness to communicate with higher-dimensional beings is far, far less important than using it for a clearer view and understanding of your current situation in this world, your life, relationships, and choices. And for sincere revelations of useful, practical information that may help an individual to further know the Self, to heal, or to provide *service to others which is **sincerely** motivated by love of service itself.* It is suggested that sufficient grounding and sufficient healing ... of mind and body, and balance of mind and body is attained before attempting to consciously access higher dimensions. All is available within your self. Within is domain of The One Self.

Nadia whispers.

NADIA: The kingdom of God is within.

SCOOTER: Dimensions. I have no idea what you're talking about.

Aum begins to think about this information. There are so many opposites and paradoxes which can't be accurately described with words or understood by his current limited perceptions. He doesn't know if what he's saying makes sense. He doesn't even know if this information is relevant to their goal. Auh transfers a feeling to him from her heart to his. She lets him know that this feels right to her, and that he should keep going. With some skepticism and doubt of himself, he tries his best to trust and continue. He treads slowly through the metaphysical world within himself. He gathers information quickly, but speaks slowly.

AUM: At this level, the major goal of The One spirit and of all spirits of the universe ... seems to be ... to descend from pure light into the physical material ... to experience all which can be experienced in the physical material ... to learn many lessons in the physical matter ... and to raise the physical matter back up into the purer Light and Sound of Oneness.

SCOOTER: That sounds crazy.

AUM: As physical beings, we evolve by slowly bringing the light of the higher worlds into our bodies and minds ... so that ... we may ... see and know more. We evolve by seeking in many ways, inside and outside, many positive, some negative. As positive beings in the physical world, we evolve ... through compassion, universal love —by feeling and expressing genuine love and compassion for others. We also evolve through wisdom, discernment, responsibility, knowledge, doing things the right way, and making sure that we are moving along our path. Through genuine love and wisdom, we bring more and more light into our bodies and minds. We bring the Higher Light of the higher dimensions into ourselves. As we bring the energy of the higher dimensions into ourselves, we bring more light into the physical planet. This allows us to slowly raise ourselves and the physical planet up into the higher dimensions, while grounding the higher-dimensional light into ourselves and into the physical planet.

NADIA: (Whispering) To bring heaven to Earth.

SCOOTER: Like a merger of the higher and lower.

AUM: Through love, movement, compassion, connection, wisdom and service to all, we seek to unify what you call heaven and Earth in our individual lives. We teach and learn, learn and teach, teach and learn, learn and teach, giving light to others and receiving light from others with patience, allowing, acceptance, tolerance, humility, and compassion. Eventually, we realize oneness of humanity and the Earth.

SCOOTER: This is ... Wait, where are the different layers?

AUM: We are inside of them now. We exist in all of them now. They are also inside of us.

Vincent rolls his eyes.

SCOOTER: Literally? Like ... How ...

EARL: How come we can't see them?

AUM: I ... You can see them. You can become more aware of them ... if you ... *change your perspective of what reality is, and what you are.* Our physical brains, our physical bodies lock us into a particular filter for viewing and experiencing reality. Most humans on this planet remain locked into the same channel for an entire lifetime. Many experience moments of expanded awareness at different times in their lives, but never learn how to consciously tune themselves in order to continuously expand in balance. Many never learn the purpose — what is so important about expanding our awareness? If an individual sincerely seeks inner knowledge of the Self and their reality, they may learn to tune their minds and bodies to expanded states of awareness. Many in this world who you call Scientists have worked hard and discovered extraordinary amounts of information about your reality. This is extremely impressive. However, the more these beings discover, the more they continue to miss and ignore. This is because their beliefs about themselves and the natural world lock them into an extremely limiting point of awareness. Auh and I are beings of the fourth-density level of awareness, yet we are limited in our access to many fourth-density attributes. However, our perceptions are much broader than yours.

SCOOTER: I'm not following.

AUM: I shall attempt to teach what I am learning. I see. Among other things, it is our knowledge, experience, intentions and attention which allows us to consciously become aware of the higher dimensions in a clear and balanced way. And in a way that teaches, and is positive, practical, and useful for conscious evolution, Self knowledge, and service to others. An expansion to a wider amount of awareness changes the way we perceive our world. Expanding our awareness lifts our minds up into the higher worlds while we are still grounded to the physical Earth in our physical bodies.

SCOOTER: I'm kind of lost.

EARL: I'm all the way lost.

BINDIA: Me, too.

SCOOTER: What is consciousness?

Aum closes his eyes. He feels that there is a much better way to get answers from a deeper part of himself, but his mind wanders. He remains doubtful and nervous.

AUM: Consciousness can be defined as ... self-awareness ... ...

VINCENT: This guy sucks.

AUM: It is ... an individualized ... perception ... of experience ...

VINCENT: This isn't going too well, is it?

AUM: I apologize. From what I see, there are many different layers, different expressions of One Pure Awareness. This is like exploring a large, dark mansion with only a candle light.

SCOOTER: Oh.

NADIA: Wow.

AUM: You are self-aware. Aware of your Self as Scooter, as a male human being, as an American. You are all conscious of these things. As your awareness expands, you experience your identity, your world, other beings, and your life in very different ways.

SCOOTER: Okay. Can you explain that?

VINCENT: Why?! What does this have to do with Earth 5.0?!

Vincent gets frustrated and lies on his back.

NADIA: Vincent, get up.

VINCENT: This is taking too long.

He sits up in the circle with the others. Aum tries to regain his concentration.

AUM: I do not know if I am able to explain it.

Auh squeezes Aum's hand. She feels his frustration, as well as his sense of incompetence. This feeling creates blockages in his indigo center, decreasing his self-esteem and his awareness.

AUH: You know it. I trust you.

Aum closes his eyes and breathes. He asks The Creator within for information.

AUM: It is my hope that this helps to clarify. Please forgive me if this is not a good example.

AUH: You know it.

SCOOTER: Like, when we expand our awareness, things change? Like ... when I was a baby, I had some awareness, then I got more when I got older? And now I have more now?

Aum tries to understand more about consciousness and awareness. He searches for the best way to explain it to the children. At this time, Hathora and a few other angels observe what is happening. Each of these angels is being taught specific skills on the nature and use of light energy. They observe the chakras — colorful spinning vortexes of energy in the bodies of Aum and the others. They see that Aum's blue energy center at his throat and his indigo energy center between his eyebrows are dimmer than the other centers. The bodies of Aum and Auh are vibrating at the fourth density level. They have access to much more light and understanding than they are aware of. What limits their ability to see more is the effects of their initial confusion as they materialized in the classroom, as well as the sudden shrinking of their bodies. It is their continued fear, doubt and concerns about remaining on Earth for a very long time.

Hathora observes as Aum closes his eyes and seeks information. Hathora is able to see all of the specific streams of light flowing in and out of Aum's body, mind and spirit. Auh is able to feel the inflowing streams, but not as well as she would feel them if she was better tuned. The children have no idea of the complex streams of light which are flowing in and out of their beings. Nadia is extra sensitive to these subtle energies, but wouldn't know what they mean or how to use them unless she was taught. As Aum asks for help, Hathora sends him a thought that could be used to clear things up. Aum becomes aware of the information sent, but is unable to understand it and even more unable to communicate it to the children. He is unable to make use of the thought. In his doubt, he still tries to move forward.

AUM: I shall provide an example of how consciousness expands.
He breathes slowly.

AUM: In your recent history, many humans were only aware of their own cultures on their individual sections of land. The creation of the vehicle known as the boat allowed them to connect to other lands, and other cultures. This allowed their awareness of the world and of humanity to expand in certain ways. Their view of what the world was … changed. Their consciousness of the world and humanity expanded as they learned more. Eventually, human consciousness went from a … tribal consciousness to a more national consciousness, then to a more global consciousness. With the invention of ships, trains, cars, planes, rocket ships and the internet, human consciousness has expanded to know itself more and more.

SCOOTER: This I understand! Yes!

AUM: At some point, you learned of the atoms and cells in your bodies. You learned much of the physical internal workings of your bodies. That expanded your awareness inwardly … on a physical level at least. You knew more of *what* you were ... on a physical level.

With the invention of planes, you were able to look down upon the Earth. With the invention of the rocket ship, you were able to look back at the Earth in order to see the whole planet from outside. That greatly changed the way you saw yourselves, each other, and your world. This was only experienced directly by very few human beings, but it greatly affected many across the planet. This experience helped to create a large burst of expansion in human consciousness. At one point, you became aware that your galaxy was not the only one in existence. That it was one of billions in the visible universe. From the tribal people living in caves to where you are now, it is your consciousness which continues to expand and change the way you view and experience reality. Many in your world have no appreciation of what this means for you all as a planet.

KAREEM: I understand it.

Scooter shakes himself in excitement!

SCOOTER: I ... understood that ... completely!

EARL: I got it.

NADIA: Me, too.

Aum nods his head and clenches Auh's hand tighter. He takes a deep breath. He feels more confident. This allows his indigo single eye chakra to receive more light. The blue throat center harmonizes better with the indigo center and the lower centers. Aum feels more love and begins to understand more. The green energy center at his heart glows brighter and harmonizes better with the others. Hathora and the other angels see that Aum still has many major blind spots, but is in much better shape than he was just a few moments ago.

SCOOTER: What are you seeing? Can you see how awareness started in the first place?

VINCENT: Scooter, come on, man! Too much!

AUM: Vincent is correct. We do not have the time to seek answers to such a question.

Hathora speaks to them all. They hear her voice coming out of the darkness in the Sudanese sky.

HATHORA: This question would be of great aid to many on this planetary sphere who are seeking metaphysical information at this time, including the ones we have called The Children of Light. It will aid in their inner seeking of The Creator. Your attempt to answer this particular question can also tune and sharpen your use of the indigo and blue energy centers of your being. This would increase your ability to see answers and clearly communicate them to others, thus quickening your movement toward your goal of opening the portal.

Aum thanks Hathora, then asks The Creator within for an answer. Rājā Mārśala comes to Aum's aid. They project a ray of light containing the

228

information Aum is seeking. Aum receives the information and constructs it in his own way, with his own filters. It is normal for some or much of the information to become lost or changed as the receiving being tries to understand it and then communicate it. Although information is lost, Aum takes in more than enough of what is needed to answer Scooter's question. This is because of his asking of The Creator within, his compassion for the children, his better mood and attitude, his confidence, the cleanliness of his body organs, his strong will to learn and get it right, and his desire to serve others. Hathora and the others are delighted. They see all of the complex and intertwining movement of light, sound, thoughts, feelings, openings and closings around and within Aum.

AUM: How did awareness start? This would be as far as I can currently go into the nature of The Infinite One which you call God. It is as much as I shall understand at this point. First, there was ... a ... what I can only think of as ... nothing...ness. The only way I can explain it is that it is ... no thing as we know a thing to be.

SCOOTER: How is that possible? How could something be nothing?

EARL: I think he means that it isn't something in the first place.

SCOOTER: So, how could we be even talking about something that isn't something?

KAREEM: It isn't.

SCOOTER: Isn't what? Oh, it isn't nothing. I mean, it *is* nothing. But if it is, then it *is* there. I mean is *is* something. Is isn't nothing.

VINCENT: I wanna punch somebody hard right now.

AUM: The nothingness is, in fact, everythingness. It is infinite. It is unity. Infinity is ... I cannot describe infinity in a satisfying way for you. Or for myself.

VINCENT: I thought it was nothing.

NADIA: Shhh!

AUM: Alright. Allow me to begin again. I apologize.

NADIA: It's okay. Take your time.

VINCENT: What kind of incompetent aliens are these?

Nadia gives Vincent a piercing side eye. He leans back, not knowing how to handle Nadia's gaze. Auh centers herself. She feels compassion for Aum as he struggles to put the thoughts, feelings, and images into words. She sends him the energy of encouragement.

AUM: Infinity becomes aware of itself. That is where awareness starts. From infinity, there comes a ... point ... of awareness. The infinity becomes aware of ... itself ... in a specific focused point of awareness. It goes from being everything which is not expressed in any specific way ... to being a point where things can be expressed in a specific way. So, infinity becomes aware. It is with this focused point of awareness that infinity created and became everything we know. At this point of focus, there is movement. This movement can be called "Vibration." It can also be called "Love." Everything we know is made of Love. All is Love.

NADIA: God is Love.

AUM: So, then, infinity becomes aware and focuses at a point. At this focused point, there is motion. A spinning motion. As I said, this point of focus in motion is Love. This love is not yet emotional love which we feel between each other. At this point, there is no emotion as yet. It is universal magnetism. It is Vibration. It is a ... vibrating magnetic movement. Vibration expresses itself by moving at different speeds or different frequencies. These different frequencies of vibration create light.

SCOOTER: I'm sorry. You lost me.

NADIA: Me, too.

BINDIA: Yeah.

Vincent shakes his head.

KAREEM: Vibrating frequencies of light?

Aum thinks. Auh breathes deeply, allowing the air to pass through her body in a smooth rhythm. She feels the air in her stomach and her heart. She feels around with her awareness and finds the spot in her chest and her back that *just feels right*. Without knowing exactly how, she opens the sacred space within her heart. She radiates her Powerful Heart-Based Feminine Energy. Aum is In-Spirited and Inspired. He uses the rhythm of deep breathing to center his mind as best as he can. The energies around them become more harmonized.

AUH: Begin again.

AUM: The infinite becomes aware of itself, then focuses itself. This focus creates the movement. It is an intense and constant movement. It is a chaotic movement. This movement can be called vibration. Vibration spirals intensely with intelligence ... in many complex ways. The vibration spins in a certain way to create particles called photons.

SCOOTER: Light.

AUM: Yes, photons are the basic particles of light. The Love creates and becomes light.

SCOOTER: So, God creates *and* becomes everything. I never knew that.

NADIA: Wow! Me neither.
SCOOTER: Okay, so the vibration creates the light. Then what?
AUM: The light spins intensely with intelligence. The intelligent spiraling light creates intelligent geometric patterns. These geometric patterns vibrate continuously, changing more and more, becoming more and more complex. The intense spiraling light spins slower and condenses into thicker, heavier particles of light. I do not know if "thicker" is the proper word. These … denser and slower spinning particles of light create the core of what you call the atom. The slower frequency of vibrating light creates the core of all atomic particles … which create different major layers or levels of existence within the pure awareness. The heaviest and most dense expression of the original light is the red vibration which creates the most solid, "slow-moving" state of matter. One popular name for these levels is "Density." Or you may simply say "level." A density level is … formed by the light vibrating at a certain frequency which creates a certain amount of condensation. The condensed light is the substance or material of all densities. As spirits, we are also vibrating light. As a spirit descends down through the levels of densities, we also change our frequency of vibration as we move from one level to another. The density levels create a certain … kind … a specific filter of awareness for all of the spirits that vibrate at that specific level. In our galaxy, there are seven main large density levels. This design of seven density levels can be called a "density structure," "density frame," or an "octave." Within each one level of density, there are seven sub-levels. You children are focused in what you call the third density level of awareness. You are focused in this third density level because of the particular kind of physical bodies and brains you are using.

Scooter is speechless, sitting with his mouth open, shaking his head slowly. Earl isn't trying too hard to understand it all, but he has the best intuitive visualization of Aum's descriptions, Nadia and Din currently have the best intuitive ability to consciously surf these higher realities directly. Where Earl sees more, Nadia feels more. Din has practiced meditation with his grandfather as a younger child, so he would be able to enter the states needed to surf the higher layers. Vincent is trying hard to wrap his mind around the information, although he wants to dismiss it as nonsense. Kareem is silently trying to understand it while thinking about Allah's Greatness as He has constructed the higher dimensional layers. Din sits with his eyes closed, taking it all in. Scooter connects this information to what he's learned so far about quantum physics and parallel realities. He would be best able to translate Aum's information scientifically.

NADIA: So, God's love creates light and light creates everything.

AUM: Yes. As the light slows down its vibration, it gets denser and denser, and creates the lower density levels. "Lower" is not a perfectly accurate word, but … it will have to work for now. In each density level, the light transforms into a new color. The order of the different colors can be seen in the colors of your rainbow.

KAREEM: And the colors in the ship.

EARL: Ohhhh, yeah!

AUM: Each color is the result of the light vibrating at a certain speed with a certain amount of thickness or density. The violet light is the least dense expression of the light. This density frame is made of seven major levels. From the top down, the violet level would be seen as the first level of the frame. But we will observe the frame from the bottom up. So, the violet level will be seen as the seventh density level. The seventh density level is the least dense of all the density levels. You may say the light is "thinnest" in that level. The speed of light in that density is vibrating the fastest. The violet light spirals with love and intelligence, becoming slower, thicker, denser, creating lower and lower layers of vibrating light. The violet light becomes indigo, then blue, then green, then yellow or gold, then orange, and then red. The red light is the most condensed layer of vibrating light. It creates the atoms, molecules, elements, chemicals and minerals which create the seemingly solid material universe which we physically see, touch, taste, smell and hear.

SCOOTER: Dude! We just traveled down, like, the body of God!

AUM: Although the colors, vibrations, substances and other components change as we descend the levels, the essence always remains the exact same. The essence of all the colors and levels is always the same Original Essence of The Infinite One — Love and Light. The experience and expression of the original essence changes as it vibrates at different speeds and resounds at different tones. But the original essence never actually changes. As we stand here, sit here, speaking, looking, hearing, thinking, feeling and interacting now, all of these seemingly different parts of our experience, including our own souls, are the one original essence of The Infinite One being expressed and experienced in different ways on the surface of one planet in one solar system in one galaxy.

NADIA: So, no matter what, it is all light. And that's God's … consciousness. So, God is every …

She shivers.
NADIA: God really *is* everywhere.
TEARS POUR through her eyes and she feels a chill run through her body.
NADIA: Jehovah! Oooh!
She fans her eyes and wipes the tears away. She chuckles.
NADIA: Jeh - Ho -Vah!
She bursts into tears again.
Earl observes his sister carefully and stays quiet. He knows just how pure
and genuine her love for Jehovah is. Aum and Auh observe Nadia's feeling
of closeness and genuine appreciation for The Creator. They see that this
love is perfectly pure. They see that her conscious framing of The Creator
is filtered through her particular system of religious beliefs. They see that
Kareem's love and devotion to The Creator is just as strong and pure.
Nadia's heart chakra receives a tremendous amount of intelligent energy
through those feelings. She shivers.
SCOOTER: This is the epicest of all epicness I've ever seen. Like, is that
exactly how the universe is made?
AUM: To say it is exact or even very accurate would be deceptive on my
part. These are my opinions and my interpretations. There are an
innumerable number of components which I am not seeing or describing.
There is time, geometry, mathematics, fractals, and also all of the dynamics
of sentient observation by mind, spirit and soul.
Scooter rubs his eyes in confusion.
AUM: It would take a great deal of time and contribution from you all for us
to know more of these components. I would say that what I am learning and
teaching you now is what we need to know at this time. At least I hope so.
It takes a great deal of vital energy and mental focus to bring forth this
information in this way.
   Aum takes some time to sit and rest. The children discuss what was just
learned. After a few minutes, Aum stands up and tunes his awareness
inwards again. Scooter then asks a question about oneness.
AUM: The One is All and All is The One. The Prime Creator, which you
call God, creates co-creators by creating an illusion of "an other" within
The One Self. The other co-creator is able to experience existence as its
own point of awareness, love and light. So The Infinite One creates the
illusion of separation, and the illusion of being more than one being. The
co-creators, including all of us, are smaller versions of The Prime Creator,
each containing the whole perfect blueprint of The One and, will eventually

know itself as an entire universe. Through their own free will and their own point of views, the co-creators create new and unique experiences using the illusion of separation. They create co-creators within themselves. Each new co-creator is able to have unique experiences which The Prime Creator, in its Allness, always contained … but did not experience and express in any specific way without the illusion of "others." The Infinite One does this because it is the All Which Exists. It is All. It is One. It is infinite. The creation of co-creators and co-creators within co-creators allows The Prime Creator to act as if it is many, many, many beings — each with its own specific point of attention, its own free will, with its own unique attributes, roles, designs, substances, goals and lessons to learn. The Infinite One also uses what you call "time." The energy of time is directly related to the level of density of the vibrating light. Time allows The Prime Creator, through co-creators, to experience an infinite amount of unique and specific experiences in different spaces or locations within the denser and denser levels of light material.

SCOOTER: Lost me.

AUM: You may say that I also lost my step in the last two sentences.

AUH: Remember, Scooter, that this is all being recorded. You'll be able to study everything you're learning now over and over again.

SCOOTER: Oh, yeah. Yeah!

NADIA: I understood a lot of it, though. I can't believe I do.

KAREEM: Me, too.

SCOOTER: Okay. Continue.

AUM: So, then ... the awareness of The One descends through dimensions as seemingly separate spirits who are co-creators. This is done so that All That Is can go from infinity, which has been called no thing … to finity, some thing, many things. Looking at the big picture and the fullest attainable truth, it is my understanding that The One is All That Exists. It *Is* What *Is*. The Infinite One has split The One Self into many selves and many parts to vibrate at all of the density levels, to exist as all of the dimensions, to live in all of the dimensions, as all things, and as all of us. The One Creator experiences existence as atoms, molecules, elements, rocks, plants, animals, humans, extraterrestrial beings, angels, vast and powerful light beings, planets, stars, galaxies and universes. There is only One of us actually here right now. Within the center of every atom and the heart of every conscious being is the seed and spark of The Infinite One. When we are able to expand our awareness and raise our personal frequency of vibration, with sufficient balance and self-knowledge, we are able to see through more of the illusion and experience the world with a more and more pure awareness of Oneness. The Infinite One is already all of us. It is our perception of limitations, our lack of Compassion and Understanding, and our innocent or willful ignorance of genuine oneness that prevents us from realizing that.

EARL: So, God is the main player playing all of us like *The Sims*.

AUM: Yes, I see. It is so.

SCOOTER: Did you just, like, see *The Sims*? Like scanned over it?

AUM: I did.

SCOOTER: (Goofy smile) Ah, That's epic!

AUM: The Prime Creator seemingly divides The One Self into many co-creators, and gives them free will to create from their point of view. The co-creators create co-creators within themselves, and give them the attributes to create from their point of view. And it goes on. You are microscopic co-creators.

Vincent rubs his temples.

VINCENT: I'm burning out. Is my nose bleeding? I feel like I ruptured a part of my brain or something.

EARL: Ruptured. Ruptured. That's a weird word. Ruptured.

Nadia rings Earl's ears.

NADIA: Shdp! Stop encouraging Vincent.

EARL: How am I responsible for him?

NADIA: Shut up and let them teach us! Please!

SCOOTER: How can you not find this interesting, Vincent?

NADIA: Something's wrong with him.

VINCENT: I'm just going along with it. I wanna see Earth 5.0.

AUM: There are forms of life which exist in ways that you cannot imagine. There are levels, dimensions and portions of this reality that are impossible to describe with your words. But the point must be stressed that no matter how far out or how deep within it all goes, All That Is *Is* The One Infinite Creator. All co-creators have the spark of The One within them, and are able to fully awaken and realize themselves and all others as The One. Eventually, all spirits, souls, minerals, liquids, gasses, organisms, humans, extraterrestrials, angels, light beings, stars, galaxies, universes, and all of their individual experiences return to the infinite and absolute allness of The Infinite One.

SCOOTER: Allness.

AUM: And so, through all of us, and our individual and collective experiences here and now, The Prime Creator gains a more expanded understanding of The One Self. That is why we are all here. To go through our unique experiences and points of views so that The One may enjoy the creation, and learn more of The One Self through our experiences and reactions to challenges, and our learning of lessons.

NADIA: We help God? Hmm.

AUM: I must clarify that that is a humble opinion from my current point of view.

NADIA: Okay.

AUM: The One uses the parts of The One Self to learn about The One Self. The One teaches All and All teach The One. In other words, The Self teaches The Self. The Infinite Creator uses intelligent energy to create finiteness and limitations. Sound, Love, Light, the densities, the dimensions, time and space are all used to create specific arrangements of the one original essence. These arrangements of energies create specific kinds of limiting conditions in order to experience existence from many single points of attention within The One Creator's essence. For example, The Infinite One has never experienced the unique songs played on planet Earth with these exact instruments, voices, personalities, lyrics, styles, venues, and reactions. Yet, the potential for all of those things have always existed within the Infinity of The One

SCOOTER: Ohhh! I get it!

NADIA: Me, too!

AUM: We are microscopic co-creators with the perfect spark of the macrocosmic co-creator and The One Infinite Creator as our Core Self. It is impossible to not be The Infinite One Every thing is. We may forget it, ignore it, and treat others as if they were not It. But you cannot not be It. You may experience painful separation from Oneness in your individual conscious filter through innocent ignorance, willful ignorance, negative judgment of others, fear, or negative beliefs and actions. But you can never actually *be* separate from Infinite Oneness. *Separation is always an illusion*. It can never be. This is a central point of all we shall teach you.

SCOOTER: Central point.

AUM: The One creates an illusion in order to divide One Self and express One Self as All That Is. Deep within our center, we all know the whole story. Eventually, after all the dramas, pains, and challenges, we all make our way back to fully knowing that we are one with each other, one with all, and that, together, we all are The Infinite One.

NADIA: But this isn't what they teach us at church. I can't believe that.

AUM: Then you may simply choose not to believe that. The gift of free will makes it so that all are allowed to seek in their own way. Therefore, you should not believe anything because I say so, or because any one says so. There are many questions that must be asked by you and confirmed only by you.

NADIA: So, what about the true God and all the false Gods?

AUM: That is a question which I choose not to answer for you for fear that I may infringe upon your free will. For you are young, and have a filtered point of view which contains extremely particularized beliefs about The Creator. These beliefs were given to you by those loved ones and those teachers who teach a very specific system of information which calls for strict behaviors, absolute and unchangeable points of views, and devotion to one extremely particularized characterization and interpretation of The Creator. I shall not answer this question for you. You must seek The Creator within your heart in order to receive that answer.

NADIA: You *cannot* or *will* not answer it?

AUM: I *will* not. I can say that the answer is already within your heart. As you say, *God is Love.*

NADIA: Hmm.

AUH: You guys can ask anything you want, but there are certain questions that we will choose not to answer due to your young age, and due to your religious beliefs. And with Vincent, your atheistic beliefs.

VINCENT: What? Atheistic?

SCOOTER: You're an atheist?

Vincent looks confused. He raises his index finger and speaks sternly.

VINCENT: I — Holy crap. I'm an atheist. Holy … Holy?

AUH: Your beliefs create a very specific filter of reality which allows you to live, as long as you choose to, in a very focused way where certain possibilities of experience are locked out and seem impossible while other possibilities are seen as the only absolute and unchangeable truth. This is not only true of religious and atheistic points of views. It applies to all beliefs about all things, including yourself, others and the world around you. The information that brings these teachings to you now is not only coming directly from Aum and me as individuals. You can say that this information is coming *through* us from many points within and outside of the planet. It comes *through* us from our core.

Auh smiles and enjoys using the slang of The Young Ones.

AUH: Of course, when you ... "break it down" ... "at the ... end of the day ... this information comes *through* us from ...

All seven students Speak At Once.

STUDENTS: The Creator! NADIA: God! KAREEM: From God!

AUH: Exactly!

They laugh!

SCOOTER: If the information is already here, why don't our parents and teachers know this?

As Aum speaks, this portion of the Sudanese desert increases in vibration. Everyone in this space receives a greater opportunity to consciously sync their bodies and minds deeper into the purer love, light and unity of The One Original essence.

AUM: The information is ancient and has not been placed into mainstream consciousness in your recent history for many reasons. This information is, above all things, intended to be used for conscious evolution.

AUH: Right. We seek within in order to increase awareness of the ... literal, right-here-right now, direct presence of the One Creator. The presence of the Source of existence. The Original Essence. This Source/Essence is *what you are. Full awareness of it lies deep within* the mind, and then beyond the conscious mind of all self-aware beings.

AUM: Correct. Accessing this state of awareness often results in your personal radiation of The Essence through your personality, actions, talents, and skills. As you progress, you face your challenges, learn your major life lessons, and radiate the Joy and Bliss of consciously experiencing the presence of The Creator out to others and the planet. This teaching is very different from what you have learned before. Many of these teachings do not align with what you currently perceive, or what you have been taught. It can be a painful emotional experience to have the mental perception of all you have known before change so quickly. So, we ask you again, to just listen. You do not have to make any permanent changes in the way you see things. Take it in. All is being recorded for you to use later. It will be used for study and practice.

NADIA: Okay.

AUM: We have to respect your free will. It is a challenge for us to determine what we will teach you at this time and what should be left for you to confirm on your own. This does give us the chance to remind you all of a central point of all of these teachings: That you are able to receive answers from The Creator directly through asking, through your intuition, through silence, through eating the purer foods, through joy and bliss, through discipline, and through seeking with a free mind and a truly-opened heart. The answers to many questions are very clear and obvious once you are able to let go and allow the essence of The One Self, your Source, to flow through you.

VINCENT: No. I'm definitely not an atheist.

AUM: For answers to the questions which we shall not answer, we recommend that you ask The Creator. If the term "Creator" or "God" brings too much of a religious feeling to your mind, you may say "Source," or Universe, or Essence. You exist and therefore you came from a Source, and since there is no separation, you are that Source. If you can accept that this Source is intelligent and has designed reality to assist you in your evolution, then you may call upon your Source Self for answers and guidance. We choose to speak of The Source as Creator. The Creator we speak of is infinity and Unity of all. This is tricky to get your mind around. We've used the term, "All That Is." This is speaking from a point of view of one individual. The term, "All That Is", like all terms, is an attempt to point towards something ... in an attempt for us as spirits to become more aware.

Aum stops and thinks.

Aum: Infinity is not many things. Infinity is not even the idea of One Thing. Infinity is Unity of existence. From the third dimension, Compassion and Understanding are the primary tools which are required to truly know Unity. Therefore, what we mean when we say "The Creator" is That Which Is the ultimate Unity of existence itself. Within Unity are the answers to all questions presented by all souls within existence. Each soul has their individual transmitter and receiver to ask and receive any answer they seek. So, we say, ask The

Creator. After asking, open your minds and hearts. Then, you may either actively seek the answer by doing research, or by asking a trusted teacher. Or you may temporarily let go of seeking the answer, then do something which gives you love and joy. Or you may spend some time in peaceful silence, in either a kind of passive, letting-go-and-flowing-with-all meditation. Or/And a more contemplative, thinking, analyzing meditation. If the question is asked sincerely, and you are open to the answer, you will receive the answer in some way after it is asked. It will always be up to you to decide whether the answer is correct or incorrect, useful or not useful for you. What we teach you now should absolutely not automatically be taken as absolute truth. For our filter at this time is very much cleaner than your own, but far, far from perfect.

For the first time in their lives, all of the children experience a *United Body/Mind/Spirit Focus and Flow in the Unity of The Present Moment. For a few moments within the third dimensional world,* they consciously experience The Eternal Now. The energy radiates from Africa and is shared with the entire planet. The moment flows and the energy is integrated.

AUH: Nadia, it is helpful to have a healthy amount of skepticism at this point. All of you. Time in silence and stillness, and an opening of the heart and mind will be needed in order to make things more clear. Try to not completely make up your mind right now on anything new. As long as you choose to remain with us on this adventure, we ask you to listen. And I'd like to repeat that you should only accept the ideas that feel right to you at this time. And ask questions or reject what does not feel right. Let love and goodness be your guide to determining what is right for you at this time.

NADIA: It's not a lot that don't feel right. I just don't want to anger God by believing in other gods or anything.

AUH: I understand. In your confusion, know that The Creator understands what you are feeling and experiencing *completely.* The Creator is not …

Auh wants Nadia to know that The Creator is not angry at her. She observes the fear Nadia holds for God if she doesn't do the right thing. She observes Nadia's thoughts and memories of biblical verses where it is written that god becomes enflamed with fiery jealousy and

murderous anger! She observes the effect of this
fear on nadia's emotions, brain patterns, self-worth,
nerves and body functions. She then observes Nadia's desire to
avoid punishment and just do the right thing; to be a good human being
who obeys God and does what she is told in an innocent attempt to be close
to God. Auh thinks about Nadia's free will. She realizes that it would be
inappropriate to tell Nadia that The Creator does not become angry at her.
AUH: The Creator … understands you in every way.
NADIA: Okay …
AUM: I would like to repeat that, as this information comes through us, it
comes with our personal filters, by our brains, our experiences, and our
current state of mind. We connect to this intelligence and we communicate
to you our filtered interpretation of what we are feeling and seeing. Also
remember that each one of you also have a direct connection to this
information. If any of you feel too overwhelmed by this experience and this
information, we can return you to your life on this Earth with no memory of
this experience.
NADIA: Oh, no, I'm staying!
She laughs, then sighs.
NADIA: It's just so different … than what we know.
VINCENT: That's what I'm saying! By the way, it's different "from" what
we know, not "than" what we know.
NADIA: Shut up.
VINCENT: No, no, I'm not saying you're stupid 'cause I think the same
thing. All of this *is* different *from* … what we know. "From."
Nadia gives Vincent the side-eye.
Auh walks over to Nadia and gives her a hug. She feels a tremendous
amount of empathy for Nadia's difficulty with this.
AUH: The answers will come.
NADIA: I have faith.
AUH: More than most, darling.
 Auh returns to the center of the circle. They're all silent for a while.
SCOOTER: Welp! That's a butt load of new stuff we learned in just a couple
minutes. Stuff that, I dunno, maybe they should teach us in church, or in
school?
VINCENT: This is definitely a really, really well-done prank. They went all
out for this one!
EARL: Get off that prank stuff, dawg.

241

VINCENT: I'm only half-joking now.

DIN: We're on a real spaceship with real aliens.

SCOOTER: Yeah, they *are* real aliens. I mean extraterrestrial human beings.

DIN: What's not to believe? We *are* really here in Africa now.

SCOOTER: Let's get back to the ... consciousness thing. We have to ... um ... expand our consciousness. How do we do that? How does it even expand? Like, what does that mean, really?

AUM: Allow me to attempt to simplify this.

VINCENT: Please, God.

NADIA: Stop saying God's name in vain.

AUM: As consciousness vibrates and descends through the layers, it may be called Involution — The Involution of Consciousness. As consciousness expands from the lowest layers up, it may be called Evolution.

SCOOTER: Involution. Evolution.

AUM: Let us look at consciousness as it expands from the lower to the higher. Look at the rocks on the Earth. Look at the dust, the water, the gasses, feel the wind. All of these portions of the creation vibrate at the first level of density, the mineral level. This is the red light. Compared to the other levels, the minerals exist at a very low frequency of vibration within The awareness of The Infinite One. From your perspective, they seem to have no awareness at all, but they are made of atoms. These atoms are made of light vibrating at a certain frequency. The atoms which make up the rocks create the illusion of solidity which allows us to experience the most solid level of density. Every atom which makes up the rocks and the ground ... is ... the intelligent awareness of The One experiencing The Self at one major level of existence. Awareness on this level also includes the molecules, elements, chemicals, gasses, liquids, and fire. The difference between your human awareness and the awareness of those of the mineral kingdom is that they are not aware of themselves. From the lower layers moving upward, the mineral kingdom can be seen as first-density awareness. Do not think of the first density awareness as being inferior or less important than the awareness of higher densities. First-density provides a function which sets the foundation for second and third density beings to live in the physical world. So ... first-density awareness is the mineral kingdom. Second-density awareness is the plant and animal kingdom. The microscopic beings, plants, and the majority of animals vibrate at the second density level of awareness. They have more of a group awareness. Your genetic coding, DNA molecules, cells, bones, skin, brain, and other organs vibrate at the first and second-density levels of awareness. Plants and animals are more aware than the minerals in the rocks, but less aware than the conscious mind of the human being. The plants and animals are vibrating at a faster speed of light than the minerals, but at a slower speed of light than humans.

KAREEM: Okay. That is the first and the second.

AUM: Correct. Your human awareness vibrates at the level of third-density awareness. The third density level is the level of Self-Awareness. A few members of the animal kingdom also vibrate at, or close to, the level of self-awareness. You are aware of your self as a separate individual being, and as a being who is part of a social community with other individual self-aware beings. You are able to acknowledge and say, "I am." The beings of the lower levels do not know themselves in this way. They are aware, but do not have such a sense of selfhood. Do you understand?

KAREEM: Yes!

NADIA: Yeah. I got it.

SCOOTER: I think we're getting it.

EARL: Definitely.

DIN: Me, too.

AUM: The third density awareness is able to become aware of the spirit. The first and second-density beings are necessary for third-density beings to exist on a planet such as Earth. The lower density beings exist and create with intelligent awareness that is not less important, only different than yours. At the third density level, knowing yourself as a human being, you are able to live and create with self-aware intelligence. In the same way, there are beings who vibrate at much higher levels of awareness than you are. Auh and I vibrate at, from my understanding, the lower-fourth-density level of consciousness. You all have access to the fourth-density level because the Earth is currently vibrating at the fourth-density level. You all are vibrating, shall I say, in between the third and fourth-dimensional levels. Being fourth-density beings, Auh and I can use our higher psychic and truly magical abilities with better clarity and accuracy. You also have these abilities to speak telepathically, to heal yourself and each other, and to receive clear light information from intelligent infinity. You have just never tuned in and used these abilities. You refer to us as aliens, or extraterrestrials. There are beings at even higher levels of awareness. You call these beings Angels, Lords, Gods, Devas, Light Beings, Ascended Masters, Christic beings, Oversouls, Archangels, Angelic Creator Gods ...

just to name a few. The same way you experience time, space and events very differently from the minerals, plants and animals, these beings of higher awareness experience time, space and events very differently than you do. What you do not know is that you can widen, or expand your awareness past the "average" day-to-day level of awareness. When you do, you can become wiser, more loving, or much more skillful at an activity. Your brain works much more efficiently. Mental efficiency is something cherished by many self-aware beings. Expansion of awareness, with sufficient balance, helps the mind to operate with much greater efficiency. Also, with expansion of awareness, many will become aware of the angelic and God-like aspects of themselves. That is what is revealed more and more as you expand your awareness. For now, we will focus on raising our awareness up enough to accomplish our goal of opening a portal. When awareness is expanded, you will usually receive challenges in order to make you stronger, to help you make new choices, make changes, seek what is needed, and let go of what is no longer needed. Challenges help you to seek and learn your lessons in an honest way. As awareness expands, you are granted more and more personal access to what you call "heaven." While you still exist within a third-dimensional body, it is within your awareness that this state of heaven is accessible for you in this lifetime.

NADIA: Luke 17:21. The kingdom of God is in your midst.

SCOOTER: Jesus said that, right? He meant that literally?

EARL: Wait. If he meant it the way you sayin' it, then that's … important, right? Like, very important?

SCOOTER: The most important thing ever!

AUM: Do you believe it to be the most important information to know?

SCOOTER: It's very important.

AUM: If you feel it is so, then let it be so for you. I would agree that it is very vital information.

AUM: Through sufficient compassion, forgiveness, service, and freely-given love, you build up the energetic current of your mind, body and soul so that it matches the energetic current of the fourth-density vibration. This is how you attain what you call Salvation after the physical death, and be born upon the new Earth.

NADIA: New Earth?

SCOOTER: Mr. Lightman taught us the same stuff yesterday. I mean earlier. Holy crap, I didn't realize it's night time in Africa. It was just daytime.

DIN: Duh.

VINCENT: Wait, what?!

EARL: Ohhhh!

Only Din immediately realized the change in time zones. The others are surprised that they didn't realize this earlier.

SCOOTER: So, heaven is in our midst. Jesus was right. Jesus was third-density right?

Scooter does his goofy smile.

SCOOTER: I said "density."

AUM: He incarnated here as a third-density being, but came from the fourth — the density of Love and Understanding. He was born into a third-density body and faced the same challenges faced by other third-dimensional humans. He had to work through many difficulties and challenges. Working with the energy of love, he greatly expanded his awareness and worked to align his human self with his Source Self. He fine-tuned his ability to work with intelligent energy. When a human being does this, he or she has better access to useful information and knowledge from the higher and lower density levels. Being aware of himself and all else as Love, he was able to shift, change and work together with the intelligent atoms, minerals, cells and microscopic second-density beings.

NADIA: So, that's how he healed people!

SCOOTER: Ohhh.

AUM: He was able to see that compassion, love and unity are the way to expand and evolve. He was able to use his mind to work with the conscious elementals of water, earth, air, fire, and spirit. Expanding his consciousness allowed him to consciously communicate with the atoms and molecules within the water. Through intention, focused thought, and strong feeling, he transformed the water in what you call wine. Expanding his awareness allowed him to use his mind to lovingly cooperate with the original essence in order to heal a dis-eased body.

EARL: Nadia just said that.

AUM: Yehoshua expanded his view of himself and the world.

SCOOTER: Who?

AUM: Yehoshua —

VINCENT: Bless you.

NADIA: Yeshua is Jesus.

AUM: Correct, Nadia. Yehoshua or Yeshua is what this being was called at the time he physically walked upon this planet. All of the things he was able to do, you all hold within yourselves. One major difference between you and him is that he chose to seek and become fully aware of himself as a third-dimensional human, as a spirit, as Love, and as Unity with all of creation. You all are not aware that you are spirits. You are aware of yourselves as physical bodies and imperfect human personalities.

SCOOTER: Mr. Lightman told us that we are spirits.

SCOOTER: So, wait. Whoa. The rocks and bacteria are lower. We're higher. Angels are higher than us? It's like we're all one big family.

VINCENT: That's crazy!

EARL: So, you believin' it now?

VINCENT: I mean, it sounds like they're putting parts together that make sense. But I'm just listening.

AUH: That is a good attitude to have, Vincent. Be skeptical enough, but remain open. Trust yourself. Take in what makes sense, ask questions, and reject what doesn't work for you.

VINCENT: If you say so.

EARL: It sounds right to me.

AUM: Expanding your awareness can give you plenty of useful knowledge. If you learn to focus and use the energy with love, humility and wisdom, you will become much more powerful beings. This would allow you to serve and play your part in making the world a better place, and eventually, bringing forth what you call heaven on Earth. An expanded awareness makes it much easier for you to see that you and all others are a part of the same One. This has been called Unity-consciousness. Unity allows us to know that the spirit and the matter are different vibrating speeds of consciousness within the original essence of The Infinite.

SCOOTER: So, the spirit turns into the matter.

AUM: Yes, but the spirit never disappears. It is simply condensed into a denser essence until it is experienced as solid. What appears to be solid is only a holographic projection produced by the electric signals within your brain. The solidity is an illusion within your minds.

Vincent shakes his head.

VINCENT: We live in a hologram now?

AUM: It is yourself who exists as awareness, as spirit, and as a mind living within the holographic illusion of a physical body.

Vincent thinks about that.

AUM: Atoms are able to exist as ghost-like waves and as solid particles. Your complex brains allow your minds to perceive the atoms in certain ways so that you may experience the seemingly solid holographic reality through your five senses.

Vincent shakes his head and speaks sarcastically.

VINCENT: Aren't we supposed to be going to another planet? Why do I have the suspicion that we're gonna go through a whole lotta stuff, then somehow, something is gonna happen that mysteriously stops us from going to the so-called new planet?

He shakes his head.

VINCENT: As the only logical person here, I have to say something. I've held my tongue long enough.

EARL: About what?

VINCENT: I see this for what it is. It's obvious. This *is* a hologram. We're hooked up to some new technology. If you see all the devices and the stuff they have planned for the future, slipping us into a hologram is definitely realistic and doable. My theory is that we're in a hologram and being filmed as a big prank, or more likely, a serious experiment. Mr. Lightman was a part of it. That's why he told us all that stuff. The exact same stuff they're saying now.

NADIA: Are you being serious right now?

DIN: Why would they do this?

VINCENT: A social experiment. To see if we'll ... believe it. Or to ... learn a lesson or something.

SCOOTER: Why is this so hard to believe? You're actually in Africa right now.

VINCENT: I'm separating the truth from fantasy. They messed up when they said "hologram." They sound smart because some really good writers wrote this stuff. I feel so good about myself right now because that is definitely what's going on here. I dare any of you to tell me I'm wrong. Raise you hand if you think I'm wrong.

They all hesitate, then Earl, Scooter, Kareem, and Din raise their hands. Bindia then raises her hands also. Nadia keeps her hands down.

EARL: You believe this is a hologram too?

NADIA: It has to be. A lot of the stuff they're saying goes against the bible. If it's real, then the bible has to be wrong. And that can never be true.

VINCENT: Thank you! Even though you believe the dumb Bible crap, you're making more sense than all of them right now.

The others look at him.

VINCENT: What? It's not real. Aliens on a ship?! God becoming rocks? What?! They're just saying stuff that seems to make random things make sense. It's psychological tricks. There are no aliens or angels or gods. There is a perfectly logical explanation for everything. I guarantee one-hundred percent that when this is over, we'll get the explanation. Every time people think something paranormal is happening, there always ends up being a reasonable answer. And people who want there to be magical stuff are never convinced. Our parents are behind this. We all know they have the technology, and the dead giveaway is Mr. Lightman telling us all that stuff this morning. And the hologram they just said we're in. They knew you guys would be that gullible. I'll go with the alien storyline, and the higher dimensions, and living Earth thing. I'll stay for the lessons and the cool special effects. I see the value in the lessons they're trying to teach us, but I don't buy the annoying New-Age religious pseudoscience. That's the worse. God, heaven, all that crap. Come on, man. I'm just sayin'.

EARL: I'm done with you, homey. You messin' this up for us right now.

SCOOTER: Yeah, it's real to us. This is reality. And we're learning the truth about said reality. So, if you —

VINCENT: About what reality? Did you say, "Said reality."

SCOOTER: Yeah, we're learn —

VINCENT: You said, "We're learning the truth about said reality." "Said?" I hhhate people who try to talk like that.

SCOOTER: You hate everybody.

VINCENT: "Said" reality? That's like people who say "thus", or "hence."

EARL: You done?

VINCENT: You're the type to say, "If I may say so myself." That whole phrase is a … powerful … gathering of nonsense. "If I may say so myself." You said it yourself! Who else may say it for you? How can … (Scoffs) "Said reality."

AUM: Vincent, Nadia, we offer to immediately release you from this adventure, and allow you to continue your third-dimensional lives uninterrupted.

VINCENT: Oh, you gonna use the M.I.B memory forgetter thing?

Aum scans Vincent's brain to get an understanding of the device.

AUM: The result will be a loss of the memory of this experience and the knowledge given, but the method is very different. Do you Nadia, or you Vincent, wish to discontinue this experience at this time?

EARL: Go. Man up! If it's fake, you'll be done with it, and you gonna see the truth.

The others look at Vincent and Nadia. They look at each other.

SCOOTER: If it's fake, then you get to find out now. Obviously there isn't any real memory eraser, right? It's an experiment. So, if you really know it's fake, just end it.

VINCENT: No, I'll stay.

EARL: That's what I thought. You know it's real.

VINCENT: I know it's fake. But I know it's fun.

SCOOTER: You know it's real.

AUM: And you, Nadia?

NADIA: I don't feel right listening to stuff that teaches these different stories about God in the Bible. But I'll stay, too. I'll do what you said before.

AUH: I recommend that you hold onto the beliefs that you've been given. And you, Vincent, hold onto your beliefs about reality.

Auh scans the information in a few versions of the holy Bible. Within the Akashic records, she scans many of the different interpretations of biblical texts made by human beings. She observes the great confusions within the book and the confusion that surrounds the book. She observes the information that was lost in translation. She sees the misunderstood texts, the lies, and the half-truths. She sees the symbolism that is often interpreted as literal. She sees the mixture of history and mythology. She sees the location and the events described in the Bible which took place on higher planes of Earth. She sees the many books which were rejected by the church and the heavy edits done under the authority of councils, kings and other individuals in positions of authority — each with their own self-serving agenda.

AUH: You'll need more time to learn what you need to learn. Remember that you'll have all of this information for study. I will say what we've been saying. If you are going to stay, accept what feels right to you and reject what does not. The confusion is a major part of the process of coming to know The Creator. Open your heart to The Creator.

NADIA: Okay.

Vincent sits back in his chair and stretches.

VINCENT: The sweet smell of logical victory.

SCOOTER: You didn't win.

DIN: Yeah, you lost! You would've won by leaving.

VINCENT: Okay, then, let's go to Earth 5.0. What were we talking about? Nothing is everything, but everything isn't is is not nothing though as long as that thing over there —

NADIA: Shut up! What was he talking about again?

KAREEM: You talked about Jesus.

NADIA: Oh, yeah. That was the best stuff.

AUM: We were discussing Yeshua and the presence of The Creator within.

The kids return to sitting neatly in the circle. Aum gives them a few moments to adjust themselves and focus.

AUM: I used the one you call Jesus as an example of how expanding your awareness can be mastered and used with love. The consciousness of The Infinite One is every where. It is every thing. It is every grain of sand in this desert, every moment in time, and all movement through space. It is even the so-called empty space right in front of your eyes.

VINCENT: Din, why are you all quiet? You're not asking any questions at all.

DIN: I'm listening. My grandfather talks like this all the time. I never heard it like this, though. But I know that they are telling the truth.

Vincent exhales, frustrated.

VINCENT: Can you do some mind trick and make me understand this crap?

AUH: We can't take away your free will, honey. If you see this as crap, then it's crap. Seeing this as crap is just another point of view of The Creator expressing The One Self as Vincent.

Vincent closes his eyes and inhales. He shakes his head.

EARL: Man, you said you gonna flow with it, so flow with it. We don't need to hear how fake it is every two seconds. Chill.

VINCENT: Okay. I'll shut up.

Bindia, Nadia, Scooter and Earl all breathe an exaggerated sigh of relief at him shutting up.

VINCENT: Funny. Funnaaaaayyyyy!

SCOOTER: Oh, wait! Dude, so God's consciousness is The Force! Mr. Lightman said it earlier!

Scooter stands up and takes the stance of a warrior.

SCOOTER: Consciousness creates everything. It is The Force. It … surrounds us …

Earl stands up and waves his arms like a warrior.

EARL: Penetrates us …

SCOOTER: It binds the galaxies together.

AUM: This is a poetic description of the nature of consciousness.

The guys laugh.

EARL: That's from Obi-Wan Kenobi. *Star Wars*.

Aum downloads *Star Wars* into his mind. He receives a few other fictional

stories that contain information about consciousness and intelligent energy.
AUM: I see. Consciousness *is* The Force. Consciousness is the matrix of all
matter. It is everything that you see, hear, touch, smell, taste, think, feel,
speak and do. If you begin to understand this energy, you can then learn to
use, live and create your daily lives with it. You'll learn that *you are* this
powerful and intelligent energy. If you can come to know this personally,
you will know your intelligence and know your power.
AUH: You guys have the chance to know it so well. You'll be a powerful
generation. You'll be able to help your planet through this transition.
BINDIA: O...kay. You lost me at "powerful generation." Powerful
generation? Intelligent? Us? Have you seen YouTube? You ever seen
somebody in this powerful generation light themself on fire, or swell their
lips up for likes? Or do a back flip off the top of a garage on a table?
AUM: You are powerful co-creators of reality. You have the power of The
Creator within you. You may use that knowledge to jump off of a garage if
you so desire. Or you may use it to create a beautiful piece of music or art.
Or you may use it to give love freely, or to help a fellow human being in
need. At this point, we need to use it to open the portal.
DIN: Aren't there different levels of consciousness? Like cosmic
consciousness and soul consciousness.
VINCENT: Come on! Can we open the portal?!
DIN: We're learning.
VINCENT: It's too much crap to learn!
NADIA: Stop yelling!
VINCENT: Can we fast forward the storyline? Let's get off this nasty planet
with these stupid people, and get to Earth 5.0!
Aum begins to feel tired.
AUH: Aum, your vital energy levels are falling. Let me see.
Auh closes her eyes. When she does, she gets a strong feeling. She sees
much more than she expected.
NADIA: Shh.
AUH: I can see what Father wants us to do. We need to learn a little bit
about how creation works.
VINCENT: Why?
AUH: Silence, please.
Auh tries to remain as focused as possible while the information comes in.
AUH: You guys need to pass a test. The test ... is going to be in the
missions. To complete the missions, you have to know some of the basics

of how creation works. To learn the basics of creation, you have to play ...
a game.

DIN: So, let's go, then.

AUM: A test? A mission? What is this game? What are you saying?

VINCENT: Let's go, then!

AUH: I can't see.

NADIA: Shhhh.

VINCENT: Yeah, Din, shut up!

DIN: You shut up! Who the hell wants to hear you talk?!

AUH: You'll have to get seven ... crystals. Each of you is going to collect
one crystal. When we collect all seven, we'll be able to use the energy in
them to open the portal.

VINCENT: You know I'm not scared of you!

DIN: Oh, and I'm supposed to be scared of you?!

AUM: Where are the crystals?

   Things get more unclear for Auh.

AUH: I can't see.

She tries to focus, but the messages come in with a lot of static.

AUH: Let's just go on. We will be guided.

AUM: Very well, then. Let us go on to the tests.

AUH: No, wait. First, they need to play the game, then the missions.

Din reaches over and tries to hit Vincent, but Earl and Scooter keep them
apart. Aum tries to think but gets frustrated.

AUM: We do not have time for a game. I do not want to be here much
longer. Can we go on without the game?

AUH: I don't know. I think they need to learn something before they gather
the crystals.

Din spits at Vincent and misses.

AUM: Cease! How can you ... creatures live like this? This is why you are
stuck where you are! Such low, dark, petty entities!

AUH: Aum!

AUM: Anger.

Aum begins to scratch his skin furiously.

AUM: I cannot adjust to this ... world. Let them go through the missions, get
the crystals, and open the portal now!

AUH: I feel that the game is needed.

AUM: Why?

AUH: I don't know why. I can't see anymore.

EARL: Because Vincent messed up the vibe.
AUM: Let us take them to the tests.
AUH: If you say so.
EARL: I wanna play the game.
DIN: I just wanna get to Earth 5.0. Let's do the missions.
AUM: So, then, let the missions begin.
VINCENT: What the hell are the missions?
The children gather around Auh. She closes her eyes and seeks knowledge about the missions.
AUH: You're all going to have to complete an individual mission. On the mission, you'll have to go into a town and meet the people who live there.
   She moves her head around in circles as she tries to maintain a balance of the incoming signals from above.
AUH: There will be someone who needs your help. A situation that has to be fixed.
A clear glass box appears on the ground nearby. Inside the box is a glowing red spinning crystal that is in the shape of a Merkaba.
KAREEM: What is that?
NADIA: Look at the glow! It's beautiful!
AUH: That's your key to Earth 5.0. On the mission, you'll have two challenges. When you pass the first one, the box will open, and you'll receive that crystal in your hand. But the crystal won't be able to open the portal, because it won't be activated. You'll have to pass the second challenge in order to activate the crystal and receive the energy that'll open the portal. The portal can only open when the energies of all seven crystals are combined.
BINDIA: I knew it was gonna be long. I knew it!
EARL: You wanna go back home?
Bindia shakes her head, frustrated.
AUH: If, for some reason, any of you decide that you don't want to go to Earth 5.0 anymore, your crystal will be activated by those who watch over us. If any of you fail to activate your crystal, we'll have to live an entire lifetime on this planet in this dimension.
VINCENT: Awww, man. Something tells me *that's* what's gonna happen. They set this whole thing up so neatly.
AUH: There is one more thing. Even after you receive all seven crystals and enter the portal to Earth 5.0, you will have to spend time on a "transitional" Earth in order to learn the ways of Earth 5.0.

253

EARL: See, that's messed up. Why it always gotta be something?

VINCENT: I knew it.

BINDIA: Me, too.

KAREEM: That's okay with me.

NADIA: Me, too. Can't get everything for free.

AUH: You will have to continuously live in the ways of compassion and unconditional love in order to permanently match your vibration to Earth 5.0. Without proper tuning and balancing, the intensity of the purer vibration of love will be too much for your lower-vibrating body/mind/spirit being to live in comfortably. And so, this transitional Earth will be the place where you can practice the ways of universal love and service to others by repeatedly facing challenges and honestly making the choice of love.

DIN: So, what's that? Earth 4.5?

AUH: Okay. Call it whatever you want. Your family and friends will be there. Life will be better. You'll know more and see more. But you will be challenged with the same challenges that you're facing on this Earth. The lessons you learn on this adventure will be used to work through those challenges and evolve consciously. By the end of this adventure, you will be more-than-ready for those challenges. Life will be much easier on the transitional Earth. I promise you that. As you learn, your awareness will expand very rapidly. You will know that you are no longer on this Earth. You will be mentored by patient, loving beings whose only duty is to see you move on to Earth 5.0.

VINCENT: How long are we gonna be on this other Earth?

AUH: You have up to six months to put everything you know into practice. If you have not sufficiently learned the ways of universal love in six months, I believe you will return to this version of Earth.

Remember, there will still be a lot of duality and many challenges on the transitional Earth. If you learn your lessons quickly, you'll move on to Earth 5.0 quickly. You may be on the transitional Earth for a few weeks, or for the whole six months.

NADIA: That's fair.

EARL: You would say that.

KAREEM: You will keep teaching us more lessons, right?

AUH: That's what we're here to do — teach you and learn from you.

NADIA: Okay, so we're gonna get the crystals, then open the portal, and go to Earth 4.5 or whatever.

AUH: Exactly. The first mission is here in Sudan.

DIN: So, who's gonna go first?

AUH: You, Din.

DIN: Yeah, let's get this over with.

KAREEM: How can you be so brave?

DIN: I just wanna get outta here right away. Where do I go?

AUH: (Pointing) That way. You'll find out what your mission is when you get there.

DIN: Me alone? In the dark?

AUM: You can be assured that you are safe. We are being protected and observed by beings of light. No harm will come to you at all.

DIN: Okay.

KAREEM: You say "okay" so easily?

Din looks at Aum and Auh. He pauses for a moment. Earl and Scooter rustle Din's hair and give him good luck slaps all over.

EARL: Go get 'em, boy.

SCOOTER: We're counting on you.

Auh takes out a small earpiece and places it over Din's ear.

AUH: This will allow you to speak to us when you need help.

SCOOTER: Aren't you already speaking to us through your mind?

AUM: Are you ready?

Din nods and walks away from the desert area, through some bushes, and into a very poor Sudanese village. This village is much poorer than most in the country. Din feels very different, as if something in the environment has changed. There are some adults and children having a small celebration. A fire is lit. The celebration is winding down. They've run out of food. Some of the people are skinny and malnourished. They live in small huts and walk on dirt roads. They mostly wear dirty, tattered clothes. As Din walks along, a group of younger children swarm around him. Most of them speak Sudanese Arabic, but two speak English. One is a boy named Atif.

ATIF: Hi!

DIN: What do you want? Wait, is this my mission?

ATIF: Food!

DIN: I don't have any money.

He goes through his pockets and pulls out five American dollars.

DIN: Whoa! Wait. Um. Do I have to buy food? Is that the mission?

Back in the desert area, the others are standing outside of the ship. They hear Din's voice on the loud speakers inside the ship.

ATIF: Buy food from the lady!

DIN: What lady? It's night time.

ATIF: The lady sell food at night time.

DIN: Okay. I'll get the food. Where's the lady?

They point in the direction.

DIN: What kind of food?

Din speaks to one of the adults. He learns what kinds of food the children need. The children go with him and he buys bananas, bread and a few other things. He then heads back to the village and gives them five bags full of food. They all hug him. They scream thanks and praises for him as they dig into the bags and share with each other.

Din speaks into his earpiece.

DIN: Did anything happen?

AUM: Not as yet.

DIN: Why isn't it working? I did all that for nothing?

AUH: Look around. There must be something else left to do.

Din gets frustrated. He looks around and sees the children playing, laughing and eating the food. He looks for clues to accomplishing the mission. He removes the bread from one of the bags and searches inside. He then searches the bag of fruits. He looks all around and sees nothing that he thinks would get the box to open. Then, a bald-headed girl named Akeyo comes up to him with a big smile and offers him an apple. Din doesn't look her in the eyes. He just shakes his head.

Akeyo frowns and runs back with her brothers and friends.

DIN: Is it open yet?

AUM: No. I am looking at the energy field around the box. It is vibrating at a very high rate of frequency.

AUH: You have to match the speed of light vibrations in your body with the speed of light vibrations in the box.

DIN: I really don't know what that means.

VINCENT: See? All of y'all are just pretending to understand.

AUH: Hold on.

DIN: Great.

Din sits against a hut that's built with wooden sticks, straw, mud, and grass. Some mud on the side of the hut gets onto his shirt.

DIN: Uh! This is disgusting.

He closes his eyes and leans against the hut. He opens his eyes a few minutes later and sees the children dancing, singing and celebrating as they eat the food. He looks at them as they perform an African dance that looks goofy to him. He looks at the way Akeyo stuffs the bread into her mouth and chews it while dancing. He listens to the children singing a catchy Sudanese song. He sees them enjoying themselves and it makes him smile. He begins to feel good just knowing that it was his help that caused them to feel this joy. Akeyo comes over to him again and offers an apple. He takes it.

DIN: Thank you.

They both smile. Din gives Akeyo a hug.

Akeyo: Dance. Come! Dance!

DIN: Oh, no. I don't dance.

Over the earpiece, he hears the voice of Aum.

AUM: The box has opened.

DIN: Yes!

AUM: What did you do?

DIN: Nothing. I'm coming!

AUM: Wait! You must still activate the crystal.

DIN: Oh, man! How do I do that now?

The crystal materializes in Din's hand as he stands in the village.

AUM: The crystal has vanished.

DIN: I have it! It just appeared out of nowhere! That was cool!

AUM: You must activate it by matching the frequency of your mind, heart and body to the frequency of the energy within the crystal.

DIN: What energy?

AUM: The energy within your being must match the energy inside of the crystal. What did you do in order to open the box?

DIN: I don't know. I just took the apple the little girl gave me. And we smiled. Was it because I was nice?

AUM: Be nice to all of them.

AUH: Don't just be nice. Give love honestly, freely. From your heart.

　Aum speaks to the other children.

AUM: He opened the box by matching the frequency of vibrating light in his heart to the frequency of vibrating light in the box.

SCOOTER: One more time, what's vibration again?

AUM: Remember that everything in our reality is vibrating conscious energy. Things, objects, people, thoughts, your mind, heart, all vibrate. Some things vibrate at very high frequencies. Others vibrate at lower frequencies. Remember that solid material objects vibrate slowly. It is, in actuality, vibrating very quickly. But solid matter vibrates slowly when compared to other sates of energy such as thought. Thoughts and emotions vibrate at much, much higher speeds. Emotional love, compassion, and joy vibrate at very, very high speeds. Thoughts and feelings of fun, excitement, peace and love vibrate at extremely high frequencies of energy also. In this context, when we say, "high vibration," we are speaking of a frequency that is purer or closer to the state of Oneness. The closer an individual or a thing is to unity, the higher the vibration will be.

AUH: Basically, feel good to vibrate faster and more in alignment with Source.

KAREEM: You feel good and feel God.

AUH: Exactly.

EARL: I like that!

Earl gives Kareem a fist bump.

AUM: Thoughts of fear, anger, hatred, and sadness vibrate at much slower frequencies. You may say, "These are lower vibrations."

AUH: Basically, you want to vibrate at a higher rate in order to expand your awareness.

AUM: But, when vibrating at very high rates, especially during spiritual work, it is important to remain grounded, balanced, and to have a sufficient level of understanding and discipline. Without grounding and discipline, a high-vibrating individual can become lost, confused, and possibly become a danger to themselves and others. You must find that balance.

AUH: Right. There are lots of ways to raise your frequency of mental vibration. Things like sitting or laying in silence, stilling your mind. Meditating helps to expand and balance your awareness. Heartfelt prayer, worship, devotional practices to The Creator can also help to expand your awareness. Laughing, dancing, enjoying music, and playing games can speed up the vibration of your mind, body, and soul. Experiencing high excitement, desire, following your passion, and living your passion can raise your vibes. Being around the ones you love and doing good things for other people are some of the primary ways of raising your vibes. Resolving an argument through genuine forgiveness also raises your vibrations.

EARL: So, we raise up our vibration? You mean speed it up.

AUH: When we say terms such as "vibrational frequency," "vibrational strength," "vibrational rate," "vibratory frequency," or "raising vibrations," — those terms, in general, are usually referring to the frequency/speed of vibrating energy. Or the purity, or the strength of energy. Or the closeness

258

to the purer energies of Source. This can be in relation to a material object, a situation, or a thought, a feeling, an individual, an experience, or a place. Some examples are: "I feel really guilty and ashamed. My vibratory frequency is very low." "I feel excited. My vibratory rate is higher." "I feel the presence of The Creator with me now. I am Source. My vibrations have been raised to a very high rate of frequency." "I am inspired and motivated to do something amazing. My mind is vibrating at a very high rate." Or as you guys would say, "I have good vibes."

SCOOTER: I get it.

AUH: Again this is within the context which we are teaching you now. These terms and definitions we give you now can sometimes have slightly different meanings as you explore other aspects of reality and our consciousness. Mentally, the speed of vibration can affect how clear your thoughts are, your memory, your focus and concentration, and your level of creativity. Vibratory frequency can also affect how much information you can receive at any given moment, and the quality of that information. It can also help with generating great ideas, genius-like ideas, business ideas, creative ideas. Your vibes affect your overall mental function. Emotionally, your speed of vibration deals with your level of love or fear. These include feelings of excitement, appreciation, gratitude, satisfaction, happiness, joy, bliss, as well as fear, elitism, arrogance, pride, greed, shame, guilt, sadness, anxiety, and depression. Physically, speed of vibration can affect atoms, molecules, matter, and your environment. More importantly, it can affect your physical health. Your vibes affect your cells and organs. Overall, within an individual, changing your rate of vibration can change your experience of reality a little, a lot, or a whole lot. You can go into a slight shift in awareness, a slight daydream, a deep trance, or shift into a completely different or parallel reality. Does everyone have a better understanding of what we generally mean when we say "vibration" and "frequency?"

EARL: I got it now.

KAREEM: Me, too.

Earl raps the lyrics to the song, "By Design" by Kid Cudi.

EARL: "Oooooooh, tap into the frequency, love. Oooooooh, tap into the frequency, love... And the choices you make ... are all by design ... Come on, don't mess up the Fung Shui."

EARL: Helpin' people really do feel good. That turns up my vibrations a lot. Can we say, "Turn up my vibrations?"

AUH: As long as you understand what it means, you can describe it in that way, of course.

EARL: When I help people, my vibes get turned up!

SCOOTER: Not if they don't work for it.

VINCENT: No, helping does feel good.

NADIA: Shame on you, Scooter. *Even Vincent* knows it's good to help others.

SCOOTER: I don't care. I help. Just not lazy people.

KAREEM: So, that is what I was feeling when I serve the homeless people food at the shelter. I felt so good.

AUM: Yes, exactly. That *good feeling* is how the higher energies of Oneness affect your body, through the faster vibrations of the energy of your mind. It gives your body more vital energy. It seems as though doing good for another being is one of the greatest ways of raising the rate of your vibrations. On a spiritual level, giving love *freely, with no ulterior motive,* is the greatest gift of all to others and yourself.

SCOOTER: You believe that?

AUM: I do not base this on a personal belief. I see this as a function of the metaphysical laws of our reality.

KAREEM: Just as Mr. Lightman said.

SCOOTER: What's metaphysics again?

AUM: The short answer — the metaphysical world is the world ... beyond the physical. It consists of those things in the world of the invisible. The vibrating, the sound, the spiraling, the light, the thoughts, emotions, the karmic energies, the ideas, the philosophies, all exist in the metaphysical world. Obviously, they greatly affect your experience in the physical world. The traveling of various subtle energies between space-time reality and time-space reality is metaphysical. The activities of various subtle energies between spirit, mind, body, people, events, situations, animals, objects and so forth are all metaphysical. Meta, in this case, means "beyond."

SCOOTER: Beyond physical.

AUM: Therefore, when you give love freely, you receive energy on a metaphysical level. This is one of the many, many components which affect the state of your body, your brain, and the way you feel. Along with the many other ways mentioned, you can raise your vibrational rate in order to expand your awareness or to
better align to the Original Essence.

AUH: So, feeling good and making others feel good is a very important part of —

KAREEM AND NADIA: Feeling God.

They hear Din on the ship's speakers.

DIN: I don't know how to activate the crystal! I'm getting pissed.

AUM: You must change your attitude. The energy that was needed to open the box had a certain frequency of vibration. Your heart and brain activity matched that frequency of the crystal when you were nice to the children. The mental thought, emotional feeling, spoken words, and physical actions which you chose to experience at that moment is what caused the box to open and granted you the crystal. This time, you must choose the experience which will activate the crystal. This means that you must change your attitude.

In the village, Din lays the crystal down on a bench and joins the children in their dance. As awkward as it feels, he tries to sing and dance along. After five minutes, he gets tired and stops dancing.

DIN: How will I know when the crystal is activated?

AUH: It should light up.

DIN: So, it's not activated. I've been dancing for a long time. I'm being nice. I don't know what else to do. I'm done.

Din walks out of the village and back to the desert with the others.

DIN: Figure it out before I go back. I don't wanna dance anymore.

VINCENT: You were dancing?

AUM: Auh, what do you feel? Did we do something wrong?

VINCENT: I would've loved to see you dance.

AUH: I'm not sure.

EARL: So, what now?

AUM: I think we're missing something vital. We need to meditate.

KAREEM: What does meditation do?

Aum and Auh sit on the ground and prepare to meditate.

AUH: It quiets our minds and allows us to get in better tune with the higher vibrations of Source. It helps with intuition and direct knowing. To find answers. It kind of gets us out of our minds.

VINCENT: And why would I wanna be outta my mind?

AUH: It slows down, or kind of ... organizes our experience of incoming thoughts, making it easier to see and receive the information we need. It also makes it easier to select the thoughts which you prefer. This kind of meditation also helps me to search my feelings better. There's stillness, and then there's flowing. When I sit in silence, things become clearer. I feel more and know more.

NADIA: Psalm 46:10. "Be still, and know that I am God."

KAREEM: And you get all the answers?

AUH: The ones I need. It kind of puts me in the zone. Then, after I'm finished, I get feelings, random impulses, hunches to just do certain things — things that usually end up being the right thing to do. Even when I'm not sure how or why I did it. Please give us some silence. The children move away and speak quietly, leaving Aum and Auh to meditate on the ground in the dark Sudanese desert. After seven minutes of flowing, Auh opens her eyes.

AUH: The game! They have to play the game.

AUM: You are correct. I was incorrect. My frustration prevented me from seeing. I am sorry.

AUH: It's understandable.

AUM: How do they play the game?

4

FOCUSED MANIFESTATION
LET'S PLAY
THE GREATEST VIDEO GAME
WE ARE CREATORS
BASIC INGREDIENTS OF CREATION
ACTIVATE YOUR SUPER POWERS
WILLPOWER, THOUGHTFORMS, WAVES & PARTICLES
SPIRITUAL-MENTAL-ELECTRO-BIOLOGY
DESIGN A BETTER LIFE AND PROVIDE SERVICE TO OTHERS
THIS IS THE WAY OF THE NEO-CHRIST

Auh stands up. Aum does also. She calls the children over.

AUH: Reach into your pockets.

They all reach into their pockets and pull out their cell phones.

VINCENT: What The hell?!

SCOOTER: This is like a movie! That was magic!

VINCENT: Oh, looks like I *will* be tweeting!

NADIA: They won't let us tweet!

VINCENT: Twitpics from the cockpit!

NADIA: That sounds disgusting!

AUH: Do you really think we're gonna let you do that?

VINCENT: OH, COME OHHHNNN!

NADIA: Told you.

AUH: You have no connection to your internet, and you have no way of contacting anyone you know.

VINCENT: I … I can't do this!

AUH: You now have a *Spyrit App*. This is an application that will allow you to play the game. Sit on the ground in a circle.

They sit in a circle on the desert floor.

AUH: Select the *Spyrit* app and press the number four.

They press the button and a large dose of Higher Light radiation bursts out of the phones and goes into their physical bodies. They see a R   I   P P   L   I   N   G   E   F   F   E   C   T in the area all around them. The waves ripple through the ground and the sky. The radiation exposes an outline of rainbow-colored light around their physical bodies. It also exposes their energy centers/chakras.

SCOOTER: The colors!

NADIA: They're just like the colors in the ship!

KAREEM: What do they mean?

DIN: Our chakras!

BINDIA: And our auras.

AUM: The colors relate to the major portions of the dimensions and densities. They also relate to what you call the rays, the elements, and your energy centers or chakras. They also relate to many other aspects of our reality, and can be found in many systems of teaching and seeking on your planet. I will mainly explain the colors as they relate to the energy centers within your bodies. You now know that we, you, all of us, are nonphysical spirits who are focused into this holographic arena in order to experience an apparently solid, physical world. Remember that our universe is made of pulsations of love, tones of sound, and colors of light. The colors are the result of the different vibrating frequencies of light as The Original essence is separated and expressed through the descending layers of the different densities and dimensions. The Original essence is finally grounded into the deepest vibration, the red vibration, where it becomes the most dense with matter. Within the atomic and mineral kingdom, the essence holds the illusion of being solid, and is experienced as "real" through the electrical signals of your brain and your five senses. Your physical body, your personality, along with your mental, emotional, and social interactions are the end result of seven vibrations and colors of light all grounded into the yellow, orange and red vibrations.

SCOOTER: Huh?

AUM: I will present to you a much more detailed explanation of the energy centers and their functions within the different layers of your being a little later. This includes your glandular system, hormones, sexuality, social life, universal love, communication and so on. At this time, I will explain the basics in a very simplistic way. Your chakras are made of specific energies and information which create your conscious/spirit, etheric, mental, emotional, physical and chemical fields/bodies. They are spinning vortexes of focused light energy which process information and allow us to have a particularized experience within the densities. The energy centers sync neatly with and within the dimensions and densities. For the purpose of our teachings, the lowest center will be viewed as the first. The first energy center is often called the root or base chakra on your planet. It is the red vibration, and its energy creates your chemical body. Its energy is mainly focused at the base of the spine, your genital area, and flows through your hips, legs, knees, ankles, feet and toes. The second center is the sacral or naval center. It is the orange vibration. It creates the biological humanoid body without self-awareness. Its energy is mainly focused under and around the naval area, and the lumbar, mid-to-lower region of your spine. The third center is the solar plexus center. It creates your chemical, biological body with self-awareness. It is the yellow vibration. Its energy is mainly focused at the solar plexus, above the naval, under the chest, and in the middle of your spine behind your solar plexus. The fourth center is the heart center. It is the green vibration. It creates the astral/emotional body. Its energy is focused in the middle of your chest and at area of your spine behind your chest, just between the shoulder blades. Its energy flows through your shoulders, arms, hands and fingertips. The fifth center is the throat chakra. It is the blue vibration. It creates your mental body which is your light body. Its energy spins through the middle and upper portions of the trapezius muscle, your throat, Adam's apple, neck, chin, within and around your mouth, your tongue, lips, nose, ears and cheekbones. The sixth energy center is often called the single eye or third eye center. It is of the indigo vibration. It is your etheric body. You may call this your "spirit body" or even your "light body." It is the very Light itself which forms all of the lower colors, bodies and chakras. Its power is focused within your pineal gland, between your eyebrows, and in your frontal lobe. Its energy flows around your eye sockets, in the forehead area, your nose, nostrils, eyebrows, temples, and many sensitive areas in the back and top of your head. The seventh energy center is called the crown chakra. It is of the violet vibration. It has been called the Buddha body. It is the awareness of the complete and total being. It is the chakra that holds the information for all other chakras. Its energy is focused at the top of your head, your entire brain, all around your head, your nervous system, and flows throughout and around your entire body.

DIN: That's cool!

AUM: It often takes an entire lifetime to personally learn and experience the deepest metaphysical information of these centers with great balance. We will present much deeper information on the chakras a bit later.

BINDIA: Okay.

AUM: There are many smaller points of spinning energy centers whose energy flows through your joints, nerve endings and other sensitive body parts. There is another strong center of energy which is called the spiritual heart. It is located above the heart chakra and relates to the thymus gland. It deals with knowing your core, your center, unconditional love, forgiveness of yourself, others, and of life's drama, acceptance, and also your natural telepathic connection to all of existence.

The children look down and see the light energy coming up from the ground and surrounding their bodies. The radiation from their phones travels through two streams of light that spiral up from the root to the crown of their bodies. As the energy spirals up, the chakras spin faster and get much brighter. The feeling is unlike anything they've ever experience in their lives. Kareem trembles.

KAREEM: How is this ... real?

EARL: Oh, yeah, baby. I'm lovin' this! I! Am! Loving! This!

SCOOTER: Whoa! Whoa! Whoa!

NADIA: It feels ... so good. This girl is on firrrrrrre!

BINDIA: Is this stuff safe?

VINCENT: Iihh ...

A beam of light shoots down from the sky and into their heads.

EARL: Oh! Oh! Oh! TurnUpNTuneIn, Baby! Dat's da Goodness! Look at God! Turn me up! Turn me up! Look! At! God!

Another beam of light shoots up from the core of the Earth. The two light beams flow through the energy centers from both directions and meet in the spiritual heart center. Their feeling of connection to the higher dimensions is greatly enhanced. Their heads tickle as their brains receive a massive amount of light. The pineal gland in the center of their brains begins to vibrate at a much higher rate. The fluids of the brain and the light from above allow their pituitary glands to harmonize with their pineal glands. Both hemispheres of their brains begin to function in near-perfect harmony. Their thalamus, cerebrum, cerebral cortex, and cerebellum also harmonize to tune their minds deeper into the vibration of the fourth dimension.

AUH: This is breathtaking!

AUM: Your bodies are vibrating at a much higher rate of frequency. You are more full of light and life. Your bodies are less dense of matter, but more dense with light. Your consciousness has been expanded.

Aum observes them and thinks for a while.

AUM: This seems to be a simulation. It is a temporary expansion of consciousness. It is specially designed for this game.

SCOOTER: We're not in the third dimension anymore?

AUH: You are still in the first, second, and the third dimensions, but your awareness has been expanded. Your awareness now reaches much higher ... Pardon me ...Wider into the fourth dimension. You are now able to access some of the more evolved parts of your human self and the experiences they bring.

DIN: What does that mean?

AUH: Your thoughts, feelings, beliefs, and expectations manifest into the physical world much faster.

SCOOTER: Manifest. I like that.

AUH: If you believe it, you can create it. Miracles, magic, and superfast manifestation are now possible. Everything seems to be just as it was in the third dimension. The difference is that the third-dimensional constraints of linear space and time are no longer a factor. Whatever you can think of, you can manifest very quickly. Telekinesis, levitation, and all kinds of magical experiences can be enjoyed and played with.

AUH: Now you have to compete against each other.

DIN: We have to fight?

AUH: No. Create a game and play it. The light will guide you and cooperate with whatever you desire. The elements of Ether, Earth, Water, Fire, and Air are ready to work with you.

AUM: We will observe your conscious activity as you play. BINDIA: And what does this have to do with the crystals?

AUH: This should teach us how to activate the crystals.

AUM: By watching your conscious activity, we hope to receive information about how you use consciousness to create ordinary events in your daily lives. This should teach us exactly how to match the frequency of vibration that will activate Din's crystal.

AUH: This is a game and you are the players, and the characters.

VINCENT: Awww, man! This is the ultimate 3D game!

EARL: I been waitin' for this day my whole life! This ... is... dope!

BINDIA: I feel weird. I feel funny. I feel weird. Like, funny like.

AUH: The purer energy of spirit is surging through your body. You'll get used to it. Enjoy it. Play.

DIN: Let's fight. Can we fight?

AUM: Yes. Enjoy yourselves.

SCOOTER: Right here?

AUM: You are powerful warriors with super powers! Use them!

SCOOTER: What can we do?

AUH: Whatever you can imagine. If you believe something is possible, you can create it and experience it right away.

The children stand around awkwardly. Vincent walks up to Earl and SLAPS THE BACK OF HIS NECK!
EARL: Aw, hell no!
Earl shoves Vincent.
AUM: Use your imagination.
VINCENT: Imagination? What is this? Kindergarten?
AUM: Do not think of imagination only as a childish plaything. It is a powerful tool of creation. It is an important link between your human mind and your expanded levels of consciousness. Through imagination, all things are created.
EARL: So, I could do like Ryu from Street Fighter and ...
Aum slows time down and observes closely as a thought is received by Earl's pulsing crown chakra. The thought pulses into the single eye chakra where Earl sees a clear image of himself shooting a ball of fire out of his hands. The sixth-density etheric light organizes the rest of the process. From Aum's point of view, the intelligent energy seems to travel down to Earl's throat center and he vibrates it into his reality.
EARL: ... Shoot a fireball out of my hand?
The intelligent energy travels down to Earl's heart center where it mixes the energies of thought, light and sound with the emotional feeling of excitement for actually shooting a fireball out of his hand. The combined energies shoot down into the solar plexus center as the root and naval centers shoot their energies up into the solar plexus and heart. The intelligent light energy forms the atoms, molecules, minerals and chemicals needed to create fire. This allows Earl to manifest physical fire in his hand. He's freaked out at first, but then gets chill. He shakes his head, laughs and forms the fire into a perfect ball.
EARL: Oh! Oh! Look! THIS IS TIIIGHHHHYYYYYYYT! Look!
SCOOTER: What the hell?!
NADIA: That's gorgeous!
DIN: I can't believe this is happening!
KAREEM: Me, neither. It feels like it's not real!
Earl looks at Vincent. Vincent is literally in denial.

VINCENT: No. What is this? Seriously, y'all got to be jokin.'
EARL: No joke, bruh. HADOUKEN!

Earl throws the fireball at Vincent. It HITS him in the chest and sends him FLYIN BACKWARDS. He CRASHES into a huge ROCK AND BREAKS it up into many pieces.

KAREEM: Whoa!
NADIA: Oh, my Goodness!

Nadia covers her mouth in shock. Scooter shakes with excitement and screams at the top of his lungs.

SCOOTER: This is epic! This is epic! This is epic!
DIN: That was awesome! Can we beat the hell out of each other?
AUH: Just have fun. Play any game you want. Just do it with joy.
EARL: Let's play tag! Light tag!
AUH: That's perfect. Begin.

They all use their imaginations to transform their clothes into cool costumes with different designs and colors.

Vincent gets up and looks at his chest.

KAREEM: How come he is not burning?
AUH: Your bodies are made of light. Everything is designed specifically for this game. Don't worry about the technical stuff. This is time to play and Be *The Children of Light*.
VINCENT: Can we play somewhere else?
BINDIA: Yeah, like back in New York?
AUM: You can play anywhere in the world.
BINDIA: New York.
VINCENT: Why New York? We live there. We can go anywhere.
BINDIA: I'm going to New York.

Bindia's thought of New York causes the others to think of New York also. The d e s e r t a n d t h e s k y a b o v e R I P P L E and t r a n s f o r m i n t o M a n h a t t a n.

Scooter ROARS with uncontrollable excitement!

SCOOTER: AAAAAHHHAAAAAYYYYYYAAAAAAAAHHHHH!!!!!

DIN: Cool! Can we fight instead of playing tag? I want to be able to really hurt you guys without getting in trouble.

VINCENT: You are angry, bro.

DIN: Can we?

AUH: Yes, but have fun. Not in anger.

NADIA: No. I don't wanna fight.

EARL: So, let's play tag! You're it!

Earl taps Bindia on the shoulder then SHOOTS up into the sky, leaving a huge crater in the ground under him. He soars through the clouds. Bindia jumps and tries to fly, but lands on the ground.

AUH: *You'll See It When You Believe It.* Believe it first.

She jumps again, squeezes her eyes and uses her imagination to hold herself afloat above the ground.

AUH: Don't strain. *Let it be obvious that you can do anything.* Know with certainty that being limitless is just the way things are. Your thoughts create your reality.

Bindia relaxes herself and floats, then flies up into the sky and chases after Earl. The rest of them get the feel for flying. They follow Earl and Bindia up into the sky above New York City. Bindia looks around. Earl is nowhere in sight. She sees that Kareem is closest and chases him all the way to the Statue of Liberty. He circles around the crown of the statue and she pursues. He speeds up to the speed of light and then vanishes. Bindia looks around, confused.

As she looks around for the others, she sees the left eye of the statue blink. She goes in for a closer look just as THE GIANT ARM OF THE STATUE SWINGS the torch at her. She realizes that Kareem has become the statue. He swings wildly, trying to hit her, but she dodges with skill.

BINDIA: If you touch me, you're it!

KAREEM: Nohhh! Nohhh! I can hit you without being it!

He swats her down and she PLUNGES into the Hudson River. Kareem laughs, then frowns as a huge great white shark JUMPS out of the water and BITES a chunk of the statue's lower half.

Aum and Auh sit in Central Park with the physical bodies of the children surrounding them. The children don't realize that they're using mental/astral projections of their own minds to play the game.

Aum and Auh sit with their eyes closed, watching the game through their indigo-ray single eye centers.

Over the Hudson River, Kareem's consciousness leaves the Statue of Liberty after the shark has ripped it apart☐ The shark flaps its fins, flies out of the water, and transforms into Bindia, flapping her arms with a big smile on her face.

BINDIA: Kareem is it!

KAREEM: That's not right. There are no sharks in a river!

BINDIA: I thought about it, so I can make it happen!

AUH: There — Thought. Thought is the primary TOOL that is used for focused manifestation.

Earl flies over the Hudson River.

EARL: Wait! Kareem! We can't just mess up the city like that! You better put the statue back!

KAREEM: Okay.

EARL: What's wrong with you?!

KAREEM: Sorry. It is fun! I am finally having fun in America!

EARL: And I'm finally showin' some responsitivity! Fix it.

Earl hovers over the river as Kareem mentally creates a new Statue and places it where it belongs. A HUGE WATER SPOUT RISES out of the river and TWIRLS INTENSELY. It engulfs Earl and pulls him deep down under the water.

KAREEM: I fooled you! Now you are it!

Kareem sees Earl resurfacing. He flies away. Vincent, Scooter, Din and Nadia watch on foot near the river's edge. Earl flies out of the water and goes after them. They fly away. He chases Scooter through the New York skyline. They ZOOM between the buildings. Scooter speeds up and touches down on 42nd street in Times Square. Earl sees that he has landed, but can't find him among the hundreds of people in the area. Earl lands on the ground and tries to spot him.

EARL: Hold up …

He looks carefully at the crowd of people, then walks up to a tall man who's waiting for the traffic light to change. As he's about to cross the street, Earl SLAPS him in the face!

MAN: Excuse me, young man?!

EARL: You're it!

SCOOTER: Oh, come on!

Scooter reveals himself as the tall man and the hundreds of other people nearby. He unites the hundreds of bodies into one.

AUH: He became all of them and then one again. The One is all of us. And, in unity, all of us are The One. Just as we taught them earlier. This is a fundamental LAW of focused manifestation — to know that The Source of creation is every One, every where, and every thing.

AUM: Of course! The One is All, and All are One.

SCOOTER: How did you know it was me?

EARL: Dunno. I just had a feelin'. Can't really explain it.

AUH: Earl used his Intuition. His direct knowing. The ability to use your inner knowing, seeing and feeling is another important tool for focused manifestation.

Scooter runs after Earl, then sees Vincent and Nadia standing on a street corner nearby. He walks towards them.

SCOOTER: Hey guys. What if we ...

He LUNGES at them! They zoom around the corner and hide behind a garbage dumpster. Vincent peeks out to see where Scooter is. He's nowhere in sight. Nadia looks around, then looks up. A pigeon perched on a ledge above drops a chunk of bird droppings on her forehead.

NADIA: EEEEEEEEWWWWWWWWWW! TIME OUUUUT!

She gasps when she sees that the pigeon is Scooter.

SCOOTER: You're it!

Vincent points and laughs hysterically.

VINCENT: I'm dead! On your forehead! He just let it out all over your forehead! I'm sorry, but that's funny!

Nadia turns to Vincent. He runs away and transforms his body into a yellow New York City cab. Nadia creates her own car — an Aston Martin DB9 convertible. She gets into it, drives and chases after the yellow cab that is Vincent. The cab speeds down the road and turns the corner as Nadia follows in the convertible. They zoom, twist, and turn down the streets until Vincent comes to a group of huge garbage trucks blocking his way. He's unable to stop in time. The convertible comes at him full-speed and Nadia ejects herself out of the car and flies up into the sky. She transforms into an eagle. Her car SMASHES into the cab that is Vincent and they both CRASH into the garbage trucks. The GLASS and METAL CRUNCH, BURN and TWIST with a ROAR and they EXPLODE IN A FIERY BLAST!

NADIA: You're it!

VINCENT: I like that! You got some skills. I'll give you that!

Vincent uses thought and light energy to heal his body of light.

AUM: His lightbody was damaged. Hmm ...

Vincent then flies up into the clouds to observe the city. He spots Din first and chases after him. Din uses light speed and ZOOMS to South America. He finds himself in Venezuela, but Vincent isn't far behind.

VINCENT: I see you!

Din lands and runs through a small neighborhood. As he runs through an alley, he causes a few birds to scatter and fly up into the air. He decides to disguise himself by transforming into one of the birds. He flies up and sees a terrifying group of sharp teeth coming towards him. It's a tiger leaping from a rooftop. It bites into the bird that is Din and eats it in mid-air.

VINCENT: You're it! I saw you! I saw you! You think I didn't see you! But I saw you!

The tiger falls towards the ground, then transforms into Vincent. Din exits Vincent's stomach and heals his light body. Vincent flies back to North America. As Din follows, he hears Nadia yelling his name. He sees that the others are in St. Louis, Missouri. He gets there and sees everyone standing on the famous Gateway Arch monument. He rushes towards them but they don't move. He slows down and stops. He's suspicious.

DIN: What are you guys up to?

EARL: Nothin'. (Shrugs) Just chillin'.

KAREEM: Come and get us!

DIN: No! I'm gonna come at you and ... a ... a tornado is gonna eat me up or something.

A tornado FORMS and RIPS APART the Gateway Arch! The tornado throws everyone up into the Earth's atmosphere.

EARL: I'm out!

Earl flies into outer space.

AUM: It is a mirror.

AUH: Where?

AUM: The laws of creation. We create from within, and project our creation into the illusory matter. Whatever we think and feel on the inside is mirrored on the outside. And whatever we project comes right back to us. The energy which is sent out is the exact energy which is received.

AUM: He also spoke the tornado into existence.

AUH: The power of The Word is another fundamental tool for focused manifestation. Thoughts and words are fundamental tools of creation.

AUM: The mirror effect and oneness with all are fundamental laws of creation in this Logos. We should store this information in an orderly way for them to study.

Auh creates a device with a screen and buttons. On one of the buttons, she creates the word "Thought." On another is the word "Word."

Meanwhile, Earl is in outer space.

EARL: Come on!

The others fly outside of the Earth.

DIN: Come on, guys! Let's fight instead of playing tag. Or are you guys scared?

KAREEM: I'm not!

BINDIA: Me, neither!

DIN: Then I'm gonna destroy you first! Ha ha ha haaaaahh! (Clears throat) Um, excuse me, Aum? Can we play fight?

AUM: You may.

Din feels extremely powerful. He continues laughing maniacally as he gathers energy from all around. Bindia and Kareem fly away from the Earth and Din chases them. Bindia holds Kareem's hand and speeds up to reach the speed of light. She goes even faster than that and zooms towards the closest star system to our sun. This star system is a double-star system called Alpha Centauri A and Alpha Centauri B. Bindia and Kareem stop. Kareem is dizzy.

KAREEM: Too ... fast.

Bindia turns around and sees Din coming towards her. As he's about to tackle her, she times his approach just right, grabs his ankle, and uses his momentum to spin him around and around. They both spin as Bindia holds onto his ankle. Din slips out of his boot and leaves Bindia holding it. The momentum sends her tumbling uncontrollably through space towards Alpha Centauri B. She's barely able to stop within a thousand miles of the giant ball of fire. She breathes a sigh of relief, regains control, turn around and sees the terrifying sight of the star Alpha Centauri A coming right at her! It was thrown by Din. The two stars collide and create a COLOSSAL EXPLOSION that is strong enough to disintegrate Bindia's light body! Kareem and Din speed away to avoid getting caught in the MONSTROUS BLAST!

KAREEM: She's gone!

DIN: You're out! Ah! Ha ha ha ha haaaaaahhh!

KAREEM: Is she okay?

In Central Park, Bindia opens the eyes of her physical body, which is lying on the grass near Aum, Auh, and the physical bodies of the others. They're all lying down in a circle — in the same order they sat in on the desert floor.

Aum and Auh explain that what she experienced was a mental projection of her consciousness into a fourth-density simulation.

BINDIA: It seemed so real!

AUM: Did it? Would you believe that the physical body you sit in now is also a mental projection of your soul into the third density simulation? This is the body you've known all your life. It also seems so real, does it not?

BINDIA: Why did I have to be first out? That sucks! I didn't know we could get eliminated.

AUM: Neither did we. It seems beneficial. It creates a path to the ending of the game. I expect that we will have all of the answers needed to activate the seven crystals.

Bindia looks at Auh's device.

BINDIA: What's that?

AUH: It's just a — a gadget that kind of organizes some of the components of manifestation.

AUM: It is very basic, but I am sure that it can help you all to better understand some things about intentional manifestation. This can help us to pinpoint a more exact method for activating Din's crystal.

BINDIA: I ... actually understood that.

AUH: I forgot to add "intuition."

On the screen of the device, Auh creates the symbol of a spiral with the word "Intuition" under it.

AUH: You can use the device to watch them play from different points of attention within the galaxy.

Bindia looks at the screen of the device to see the game continue. Aum and Auh close their eyes and look on.

Out in space, Kareem is still light years away from Earth.

KAREEM: I need to go back.

He creates a vortex which seems to tear the fabric of space-time. He designs a tunnel that he believes will create a shortcut back to Earth. He enters the tunnel and moves through it. He sees what appears to be the exit. He exits the tunnel and is immediately SUCKED INTO A BLACK HOLE where his light body gets completely disintegrated. Earl floats in the distance, laughing hysterically.

EARL: He went right in! He he he heehhh!

Kareem opens his physical eyes in Central Park. After shaking off the excitement and learning about the mental projection, he watches the game on Auh's device.

SCOOTER: Oh, I forgot about black holes!

EARL: I remembered that from science class. I pay attention sometimes. I am wise, y'know?

AUH: Wisdom.

A meter with the word "Wisdom" appears on the screen.

AUM: Of course. Wisdom gives balance, order and guidance to the chaotic energy of love. We move and transform in love while being guided accurately by wisdom.

   In outer space, Nadia takes the form of the beautiful goddess Venus. She strikes a pose of an empowered woman.

SCOOTER: What are you supposed to be?

Nadia laughs. Scooter rushes her with a kick! She sidesteps him and blows a breath of toxic acid that burns his light body and throws him thousands of miles towards the planet Venus. He enters the acidic atmosphere and tries to gain control. When he finally does, he gets Nadia's left fist to his jaw, then a stiff kick to the stomach! She gives him another kick, then another, and another! She comes for another kick and he grabs her feet, spins her around, then hits her with a series of punches! He gets her in a sleeper hold. She flies upwards into the Venusian sky, then slips out of the sleeper hold. She laughs and causes the sulfuric acid in the atmosphere to become thicker. Scooter's light body is affected by this.

SCOOTER: How?! This isn't fair!

The planet begins to rain sulfuric acid all over Scooter. He begins to itch and his skin burns.

SCOOTER: Come on! How could a light body burn? Why isn't it raining on her? Rain on her!

NADIA: Silly boy! I am Venus!

Scooter is weakened. As they float above the planet's surface, he looks down and sees an ocean of liquid sulfuric acid.

SCOOTER: I'm outta here!

Very slowly and weakly, he flies up, up, up.

NADIA: No, wait! Give me a hug first!

A huge wave of liquid acid RISES up from below, ENGULFS HIM, and dissolves his light body.

   Scooter opens his eyes in Central Park. They explain the mental projection, then he watches the game on Auh's device.

Nadia laughs as she flies high above Venus' surface. She hovers. She's able to feel the presence of others nearby.

NADIA: I know y'all are here!

She looks around nervously. Vincent and Earl are watching her from two ends of the planet. Both are charging a large amount of plasma energy in their hands, ready to fire. They speak to each other mind-to-mind.

VINCENT: This is gonna be like the power of the death star.

EARL: Yeah, we might blow up the whole planet.

They both aim their plasma as accurately as they can. Vincent imagines a graph with the exact coordinates of Nadia's location. Nadia calls out for them.

NADIA: Vincent?! Din?! Earl?! Come on! Let's just play!

VINCENT: Aim!

EARL: I am aimed!

VINCENT: Use the graph! You can't miss.

EARL: I don't need it! I know I'm aiming right!

VINCENT: You're gonna miss her. Use the graph!

EARL: I'ma just shoot it and hit her! I feel it! Trust me! Go!

They shoot the plasma at Nadia. Two thin beams of hot concentrated plasma completely destroy Nadia's light body! She opens her physical eyes in Central Park.

NADIA: I knew it! I should've flown away when I had the chance!

 In outer space, Vincent and Earl give each other a fist bump.

EARL: Told you I'd hit it! I don't need no graph.

VINCENT: I did. I would have missed without it!

AUM: Again, intuition was used.

BINDIA: What's intuition?

AUH: He just had a natural feeling that he can hit the target without thinking too hard, or using machines, or having to learn it from anywhere outside of himself. Din will have to use his intuition to activate his crystal. All of you will.

AUM: And look! Logic. Vincent analyzed the location and the distance. He calculated the odds of hitting/missing, and then used the graph to get a precise aim.

The word "Logic" appears on the screen across from the word

"Intuition." A symbol of the gammadion cross appears under the word "Logic" across from the spiral symbol which is over the word "Intuition."

In outer space, Earl and Vincent celebrate their elimination of Nadia. They fly away from Venus and catch their breaths.

VINCENT: Let's get rid of Din, and then face each other.

EARL: A'ight.

They both suddenly feel an intense physical vibration nearby. When they look up, they see that Din has thrown the entire planet of Jupiter at them! Just as Jupiter is about to collide, Earl and Vincent use their minds to RIP THE PLANET INTO TWO PIECES! The THUNDEROUS ROAR is EAR-SPLITTING and COMES WITH A MASSIVE AMOUNT OF ENERGY! The halves of Jupiter zoom by on the left and right of Earl and Vincent. Earl struggles to fly away, and does. As Vincent tries to follow, he gets caught in the gravitational pull of the passing halves of the planet. The BARRAGE of gasses, dust, and other substances MERCILESSLY PUMMELS, POUNDS, BURNS AND DISINTEGRATES his lightbody. His awareness returns to his physical body in Central Park. He feels cheated. He complains for a while. When they explain the holographic projection to him, he goes off about being right about the prank. He then watches Earl and Din on Auh's device.

EARL: Okay, Din! You caught Vincent lackin', but Earl don't lose!

DIN: I took your best friend out! And just knowing you're next makes me feel so good.

AUH: Feeling. He feels happy and sure that he'll win. Feelings and emotions are fundamental tools for focused manifestation.

The word "Emotion" appears as a button on the device. A meter with the word "Feeling" then appears on the screen.

AUH: And look! The emotions mix with thoughts. We mix thoughts and emotions — emotions of either love and satisfaction or fear and dissatisfaction. We mix the thought and the emotion to create the feeling!

AUM: It is an ingenious mixture of creative ingredients — Cosmic alchemy. But look. Feelings and desires also work closely. We must

desire something before creating it. Desire is fundamental for
focused manifestation.

The word "Desire" appears as a button on the device.

In outer space, Earl and Din exchange blows. Stiff kicks and
punches to the body and head send them all over the solar system. Din
hits Earl with a SKULL-CRACKING HEAD BUTT that HURLS HIM
towards the Earth.

NADIA: Earl!

SCOOTER: That was hard! Really hard! Din has always been —

VINCENT: Hard-headed?! Haahhh!!!!! No! Not ... funny!

NADIA: What is wrong with you?!

VINCENT: I haven't found anything yet. Why?

Nadia shakes her head. They all look at the device to see Earl falling
down to North America.

AUH: Actions, of course. Physical action is a primary tool for focused
manifestation in the physical world.

AUM: We think, feel, speak and act as we experience physical reality.

The word "Actions" appears as a button on the device.

Earl is back on Earth. He's weak and dizzy. He flies to Canada while
trying to restore his physical and vital energies. He mentally connects
to the water, air, snow and ice around him in order to create a storm.
He loses focus of thought as he continues to feel the effects of Din's
head butt. As Din comes down to the Canadian/American border, Earl
tries to intensify the storm in order to freeze Din. He spins all of the
elements of the storm into a vortex. The storm is weak and the vortex
is uneven. Earl's thoughts aren't focused enough and he doesn't feel
the high excitement and enthusiasm needed to direct the energy. Din
easily pushes through the weak storm and continues to beat Earl with
punches, kicks, knees and elbows! Earl blocks another head butt, and
gives Din one of his own. Earl gets even more dizzy. He tries to fly, but
is unable to.

AUH: What's wrong?

AUM: He's losing consciousness. His vibratory rate is low.

On the device, a meter with the word "Vibration" under it appears to the right of the word "Wisdom."

AUM: of course, vibration is the nature of all things.

In Canada, Earl runs away on foot and Din pursues. Earl tries to create a laser beam to shoot at Din, but gets distracted by a random thought of nuclear explosion. Earl unintentionally puts enough feeling into the random thought to create a NUCLEAR BLAST which THROWS them both to opposite ends of the Earth! This also causes damage to both of their light bodies.

AUM: Now, what happened there?

AUH: He was about to shoot that laser. It somehow became an explosion. His creation wasn't clear enough⬚

AUM: His *intention* was not clear enough. The Creator creates with clear intention, and so can we. Add intention to your tools.

The word "Intention" appears as a button on Auh's device. Meanwhile, Din prepares a missile from a Russian military base. He uses his intuition to aim it directly at Earl who is preparing his own missile from an American military base.

SCOOTER: The cold war.

EARL: I never paid that much attention in history, but I know that you … will be … history.

(RECORD SCRATCHES)

SCOOTER: Dude …

EARL: Oh, man …

VINCENT: You get a cosmic "L" for that weak one-liner.

BINDIA: Even Mr. Lightman would be ashamed of that one.

Din feels powerful. He laughs and holds the large missile above his head using his mind. He stands under the missile, taking in the feeling of power flowing through his body and mind. He laughs maniacally.

DIN: POWEEEEER! UUUUHHHNNNN-LIIIIMITED POWEEEEEEEER!

AUH: Power is also used for creation.

The word "Power" appears on the screen of the device.

AUM: Power is to be used in order to create and serve others. Humility, along with balanced love and wisdom is required for the positive use of power. Power can be dangerous and corrupting if it is being used without grounding and balance, or by a being with a blocked heart center.

SCOOTER: They say, "Absolute power corrupts."

AUM: Power, intuition, logic, vibration, and wisdom. Hmm.

AUH: Thoughts, emotions, words, actions, desires and intentions are some of the basic tools that are used to manifest and experience reality in this dimension. How great is this device? I need a name for it.

SCOOTER: It looks like an iPad! It's a God Pad.

The name "God Pad" appears on the device.

SCOOTER: That's so cool!

Meanwhile, Earl and Din fly up above the Atlantic Ocean with their missiles prepared to launch at each other.

EARL: Might as well give up. It's over, homey!

DIN: I wouldn't be so confident!

EARL: Man, this is a game! My specialty! I ... don't ... lose!

DIN: This time you will. And ...

Earl FIRES his missile at a very high speed! This catches Din off-guard. The missile hits Din and EXPLODES, destroying his light body just as his awareness travels five seconds back in time. Din returns to the past and sees his future self just before Earl shoots his missile. Din teleports across the planet to where Earl is and hovers behind him. He molds a fireball and aims it at Earl. Just as he's about to shoot it, Earl does a back flip in the air and, while upside-down, shoots Din with a fireball which destroys his light body! The other Din, who has not been destroyed in this new timeline, fires his missile across the planet at Earl. Earl rotates upright again, catches the missile, and uses the momentum of the rotation to hurl it back at Din! This catches Din off-guard again, but he dodges the missile. He tries to catch his breath and gather his thoughts. He feels weak. The others sit in Central Park, loud and rowdy with excitement! Drool drips from Scooter's mouth as he shakes his head slowly and mumbles to himself.

SCOOTER: (Mumbling) Epic. Epic. Epic. Epic. Epic. Epic ...

KAREEM: Earl is very skillful.

VINCENT: That's my boy! Did you see that?! The boy is too nice!

As Din laughs, he notices that Earl's missile is going directly to Sudan, and is about to hit the village with Akeyo and the other little kids. In a panic, Din flies after the missile, grabs it from behind and tries to stop it. He's too weak. He realizes that the momentum is too much and the missile will hit the village. Just as he's about to fly away and avoid the explosion, he decides not to. He gets in front of the missile, pokes out his chest and takes a deep breath. This causes a giant sphere made of light to expand out of his spiritual heart center. The sphere swallows the missile. The missile explodes inside of the giant sphere. This saves the village, but destroys Din's light body. Din's awareness returns to his physical body in Central Park. He clinches his fists and screams.

DIN: Oh! Oh! Ahhhhhhhhhhhhhhhhhhhhhhhhh! That was —

VINCENT: Calm down!

DIN: That was —

SCOOTER: It was just a game.

DIN: That was the most fun I've ever had in ... my ... life!

He jumps up and down and celebrates.

DIN: Whooo-hooo!

VINCENT: Whoo-hoo? What are you, five?

DIN: That was great!

VINCENT: You didn't have to say it like a little girl!

Vincent scowls at Din and shakes his head in disgust.

Aum is appalled by Vincent's reaction to Din's celebration.

AUM: He mocks him for being too happy?

AUH: He allowed Earl to destroy him in order to save the village.

AUM: That should be the focus of this experience, but look at how he mocks the other and sends negative vibrations simply for being happy.

AUH: They're playing.

AUM: But the mentality, the words, the feelings are real. It causes more negativity. This is worse than I thought. These beings desperately need to change.

AUH: I don't think it's that big a deal. You can't force them to change.

Let them be for now. Give them time and let them learn.
AUM: You are correct.
Aum puts his head down.
AUH: Your vital energy has dropped to the lowest level since you've been here. Why did that upset you so much?
AUM: I'm beginning to experience stronger emotions like you are. It is coming in large bursts. Intense bursts of emotion. I do not know why. The fear ...
AUH: I know. That fear brings feelings of limitation. It can weaken and confuse us. It can slow us down. It can have its advantages though. It can be used to help us seek more intensely, to move faster, to be more accurate, to become wiser, more creative.
AUM: I feel it so strongly.
AUH: Fear can weaken our bodies also. You're feeling weariness.

Aum slowly raises his head and looks into Auh's shiny brown eyes. He sends her a powerful surge of fear, doubt and anger.
AUM: It hit me all at once. I have just realized how deep into the darkness humanity on this planet have gone as a civilization.

A few minutes later, Auh gathers the children around. She directs them to take their phones out and to open the Spyrit application again. They all press the number four and see the
R I P P L I N G E F F E C T in the New York City ground and sky. After the ripple, they see that they are still in the physical Sudanese desert near the ship.
SCOOTER: Whoa!
AUH: Your minds and bodies are vibrating at the third-density level again.
VINCENT: So, we did it?
AUM: We have all that was needed from the game.
AUH: No.
AUM: No?
AUH: I don't think so.
AUM: What is missing?
SCOOTER: That was so stupid, Din! You could've won! Why would you just give up?
DIN: I didn't give up. I just didn't wanna see the kids get hurt.

VINCENT: You do know it was just a game, right?

DIN: Okay. Who cares?

AUH: Unconditional love is the missing ingredient. Din loved the children unconditionally.

VINCENT: Ha, ha, ha! Din doesn't love anybody!

AUH: That's the energy we're looking for. Did you see his heart center open up?"

AUM: I did. Love. Of course.

AUH: Unconditional love, acceptance, and compassion. They bring freedom from this density. It is the literal opening of the portal within each third-dimensional being. Compassion, universal love, and service to others. This is the key to what you call Salvation.

AUM: I see. Well-done, Auh.

A meter with the word "Love" appears on the right side of the word "Vibration." The words "Christ-Conscious" appear in the top-center of the screen.

AUH: The Christic-consciousness is fundamental for the conscious evolution of those on the positive spiritual path.

AUM: As we evolve in our knowledge and experience, our thoughts, feelings, emotions, words and actions will be centered more and more on this Christic energy. This is the main key for activating the crystals. The young one called Din extended his unconditional love to the young ones in the small village. This love created a specific vibratory arrangement of energies in his heart. That vibration matched the vibration of the box. The Love you felt matched the configuration of energy that was required for the opening of the box.

NADIA: Wait. Where's my brother?

AUH: Unconditional love. Why was that not more obvious to us?

AUM: It does seem odd that we forgot that. On this planet, there is a great deal of it, but it has not been expressed in a way that would transform most of the social systems to a more evolved way of living. Most Terrestrial humans do not understand or value unconditional love. The love which they primarily express is based on specific conditions and often surrounded by fear. Many are pulled uncontrollably by strong emotional waves of love and fear.

KAREEM: Are we ready to go on the missions?

AUH: Yes, you are! Good job, guys!

NADIA: We did it!

They celebrate. Earl comes running in the distance. He dances as he gets close and joins the celebration.

EARL: I know, I know. I'm nice. I got skills. I don't lose. I said it. I showed it. I proved it. Y'all even started celebrating without me!

KAREEM: We found out how to activate the crystals!

EARL: The what?

KAREEM: The crystals.

EARL: I thought y'all was celebratin' my win.

NADIA: Boy, ain't nobody checking for you!

AUH: Let's get back to the mission. Let's get on the ship and figure out exactly how to activate Din's crystal.

AUM: I believe we have enough information.

AUH: It can't hurt to review what we've learned.

They all get into the ship and go up to the third level. The Arcturians use the God Pad to teach the children about some of the very basic laws and tools of manifestation. Aum explains that the laws are not actual laws. He explains that the device, and the tools and laws are for simplification and organization purposes.

AUM: During each mission, you will use your understanding of these tools and laws to create the frequency of vibration in your hearts, minds and bodies that matches the frequency of the crystals.

SCOOTER: I can't believe I understood that. I feel smart.

KAREEM: So, we have to show love and it will activate the crystal?

NADIA: Din showed love and his crystal didn't activate.

AUM: Hmm. Yes, the love caused the box to open.

AUH: Oh, yeah. What activates the crystal then?

NADIA: More love!

DIN: I did show a lot of love.

Vincent snickers.

AUM: Your love was pure, and yet the crystal was not activated.

VINCENT: So, we did all that just to end up where we started?

AUH: What's missing?

BEEP! BEEP! BEEP! The fourth vertical screen blinks its green light rapidly and the fifth blue screen makes an EMERGENCY BEEPING NOISE. Hathora speaks through the fifth blue screen.

HATHORA: Limits have been placed upon your journey.

VINCENT: (Shaking his head) Journey.

HATHORA: The time that you have to open the portal is limited. You must activate all seven crystals within this limited time.

VINCENT: Of course. Why not? (Laughs) How convenient it is. Now, if we don't hurry, we won't make it to Earth 5.0. I wonder if something will stop us from actually making it there.

DIN: I know. This is already hard enough. Now, we're timed?

AUM: Must the game be replayed in order to find the final answers needed to activate the crystals?

VINCENT: Well, I mean, we do have to learn all of it. I'm willing to endure the game again.

HATHORA: You have obtained all knowledge that was needed from the game. The final answers have already been given. Use your collective intelligence. Exhibit the harmony of the group and you will find the final answer. You will all have to rely upon each other in order to move forward. The strength of the group will depend upon the harmony of the group. Each has special knowledge, certain skills, and specific filters of reality. Yet all are one. Think together, talk together, share, give and take with respect to all others.

VINCENT: See? The whole point of this prank is to get us to learn how to work together and stuff.

AUH: How much time do we have?

HATHORA: You have enough time to activate all seven crystals, and to open the portal.

VINCENT: That doesn't answer the question.

AUH: Yes, it does. It's what we need to know. Thank you, Hathora.

NADIA: Thank you, Hathora.

They get together and try to figure out the missing ingredient for activating the crystals. They discuss it for a while.

AUH: You will need to forgive yourself, accept yourself, forgive others, forgive the world, and feel genuine unconditional love.

AUM: You must think positive thoughts which match the crystal's energy. And feel loving feelings that match the crystal's energy.

BINDIA: We need to use loving words.

NADIA: And loving actions.

Kareem, Scooter, Bindia and Nadia speak with Aum and Auh, trying to figure things out. Vincent turns to Din.

VINCENT: Stupid. You could'a killed Earl. You wanted to lose?

DIN: Get off my back about that! I didn't want the kids to get hurt!

VINCENT: It was only a game. You gave up your chance to see somebody finally beat Earl at a game. And to be that somebody!

DIN: I know.

EARL: (Dry laughter) Ha! I don't lose.

AUH: Din, what exactly were you thinking when you saw the missile headed for that village?

DIN: Um. I dunno. I just wanted to stop it from hitting the village.

AUH: And how did you feel?

DIN: Um. Scared? Scared for the kids.

AUH: You also felt compassion for them.

In their mind's eyes, Aum and Auh replay the moment when Din saved the village.

AUM: So, then, your general thought was, "I must save the children." And your emotion was love. Together, they formed feelings of deep compassion and a desire to help.

AUM: There is so much happening beyond the physical illusion.

AUH: There! The flash! When he had the thought and the feeling, his physical heart pumped faster and emitted a lot more electromagnetic energy. That worked with the energy of his spiritual heart. Your spiritual heart flashed as you radiated a very high amount of compassion. That's why you opened it up and took in the missile. Something happened there in that moment that we are overlooking.

VINCENT: Din, just tell them what you did! What did *you* do? You!

NADIA: Shut up!

VINCENT: It was his choice!

DIN: I told you! I just chose to save the children instead of —

AUM: You did what?!

DIN: I chose to save —

AUM: Shh!

DIN: You just asked me to —

AUH: Shh!

DIN: You guys are some rude aliens.

Aum and Auh close their eyes. They sharpen their signals to the higher light as they remember Dins heroic moment.

AUH: There it is!

AUM: I see — Choice.

VINCENT: I said it! I said it! I got it right! Wow! Just … wow!

The words "**Free Will**" flow into the God Pad, then dissolves into light. The light becomes a new button with the word "**Choice**."

KAREEM: Our freedom of choice.

NADIA: God gave that to us from the beginning! That's it!

AUM: Therefore, generally speaking, you will need to put unconditional love and Wisdom into your choices. All of the laws and tools we have shared with you can be applied into your choices. You must make the choice. Choice seems to be a, shall I say, wildcard in the equation.

   They review the God Pad for a while.

SCOOTER: It's like, an iPhone for … life. Imagine if we use the tools here like real tools. We could mix and match and do anything.

EARL: We already do, though!

SCOOTER: But we don't think about it like this.

AUM: Yes, this device may be used to learn and create and experience your life more consciously, purposefully, intentionally.

SCOOTER: Yeah, we do it randomly. We should learn this in school. This is crazy. I never looked at it like that — thought, emotion, feeling, words, actions, desire, choice. Love, wisdom …

There's silence for a while as everyone takes the information in.

AUH: You guys should appreciate what you've done here. You've helped to put together a fun and very basic system for the so-called "creating of your own reality."

AUM: You are much more prepared for your new life on Earth 5.0.

BINDIA: That's it? That's the big super powers of the universe? Thoughts and feelings? Big deal.

VINCENT: Yeah, that's … not that special.

SCOOTER: That's true. We already had thoughts and feelings.

AUM: Oh, young minds. You may sit in contemplation, in deep thought, about the power of a thought, of a feeling, of a word and a choice. If you cannot find the super power of a these tools in contemplation, you certainly will if you choose to use this power as you create and respond to life's challenging experiences. You will certainly know the awesome power of thought when you expand your awareness. You will learn the higher power and extreme value of these tools. You can learn to use them more carefully. You can learn of the dangers of misusing them. You can learn of their infinite powers, uses and combinations.

SCOOTER: It *is* infinite! Of course! It seems so obvious now! Plus the super power is in what we create with the thoughts. Not just the thoughts themselves.

AUM: By the end of this journey, you will hopefully appreciate the tremendous power of thoughts, emotions, words and choices, and how they help to create every experience of your life.

VINCENT: This whole thing is still kinda lame, though.

DIN: No, it's not!

VINCENT: Man, shut **uP!** It's obviously a prank to get us to learn some lesson. Every lame self-help spiritual person says, "Love is the answer." We didn't have to learn that. That's common knowledge.

AUM: So, why do you not live in a state of unconditional love?

DIN: Yeah. Why? Why don't you?

VINCENT: **Shut the hell uP! i don't need to rnow why!**

AUM: You are such an ungrateful child.

VINCENT: It's not my fault this stupid prank is so transparent. You're mad because **i'm too smart to fall for it**

AUM: You are a low-level being.

AUH: Don't get angry, Aum. They're evolving. Allow them to learn. No one ever taught them the divine value of their thoughts. To them, it's just a random, invisible thing going on in their heads. They have no appreciation of it because it is not valued in their society.

AUM: How could such basic parts of being not be valued? Do they know nothing of The Creator?

AUH: Be understanding, Aum. As a planetary social network, they've gone very far into the darkness. Let them learn.

VINCENT: Can't believe they made Din dance and show his soft side.

NADIA: Just stop.

VINCENT: Actually, I always knew he was soft.

Din clenches his fist. Vincent pats Din on his head. **din swings a hard fist at vincent,** barely missing his face. Vincent runs and Din chases him. **aum angrily turns his head away from them.**

AUH: Now you know that your thoughts are powerful. You know that every thought you have contains the power of creation. Now that you know it, you can't un-know it.

EARL: See, man, how you gonna un-know something?

AUH: Now, you have the responsibility of using your thoughts, and using all of this knowledge properly. As you evolve and progress in your process of awakening, there will be checkpoints and signposts that let you know that you've reached another level or a new arena of learning. And that you are ready to learn more. There will come a point where you have faced enough challenges and gained enough experience that you'll no longer be comforted as you complain about being a victim, and about the ills of everyone else in the world. You'll have to take full responsibility for your own thoughts, feelings, reactions, words, actions and choices. In many ways, that time is now. But you are young. You are born into an extremely ignorant society – ignorant to the ways of Unity and Genuine Oneness. You have time to make mistakes and to learn. On the other hand, as I said, you now know this information and can't un-know it. You will have to be more responsible for your own choices.

SCOOTER: Can we, like, write down stuff we wanna make happen?

AUH: Write notes. You can also write your intentions and goals.

Din catches Vincent. Vincent scrambles away and runs again.

AUH: You have much more knowledge now. You can change many major things about the way you experience your life from here on.

SCOOTER: Okay! That actually sounds like real super powers!

EARL: Yeah, to make big things happen.

KAREEM: Big changes.

BINDIA: I see it, too.

AUH: Use your phones to write your ideas down for now.

AUH: It's time for Din to go back to the village. Remember, you'll have to use unconditional love in your choices of thoughts, feelings, actions and words. I think you guys should start practicing that now with each other so you can be prepared to activate those crystals.

Din catches Vincent and they have a scuffle.

VINCENT: Chill! Din! Use love! Love and light! Love is the answer!

din punches vincent hard in his chest! Earl and Scooter break them up. It takes a while to calm Din down.

AUH: You have to start living in unconditional love.

DIN: Not with him!

NADIA: You have to, to activate the crystal! I feel cold.

DIN: I can't promise that … I'll try.

Scooter does an impression of Master Yoda from *Star Wars*.

SCOOTER: No! Do or do not! There is no "try!"

DIN: Vincent has to apologize for everything he's ever done to me.

VINCENT: You did stuff to me, too.

din: because you messed with me first!
vincent: it was after you started with me!

EARL: It's the chicken and the egg thing.

AUH: Wait! Quiet.

Auh feels cold. She pauses and closes her eyes. She feels a major disturbance in the flow of energy in the ship. She tries to stabilize her mind as she feels with hear heart.

C %E /A +S#* E!

Auh SCREAMS! The lights in the room get dimmer.

Aum stands up and spreads his arms for magical combat!

AUM: Warrior of darkness! Leave this circle at once!

NADIA: What?! Who is that?!

Auh closes her eyes and opens her heart. She feels a negative being in the room and extends her love to it.

AUH: In the love and light of The Creator, we ask you to please leave our space. My friend, you are one with us. I send you love and well-wishes. Go, darling, to a place of greater comfort, greater light, and more enjoyment for yourself. Receive our love into your heart.

BINDIA: What's going on?

AUH: We have a friend here in the room with us. Everyone, send him your love. Feel green or pink waves of love going out from your hearts and into our brother in the fourth dimension.

the negative being begins to feel uncomfortable as auh sends strong waves of love out from her heart center. the being leaves the ship.

NADIA: Who were you talking to?

AUH: It was a being who wanted to make sure that we don't learn more and spread this knowledge. To make sure we don't open the portal to the new Earth.

NADIA: What?! Like an evil spirit?!

AUH: The energy of love is the only thing that can keep us totally safe from those beings on the negative spiritual path. It was Vincent's negativity and arrogance, along with Aum and Din's anger that opened the portal to welcome our negative brother.

EARL: Killed the vibe. Had to mess up the Fung Shui.

AUH: These lower frequencies create an opening and a comfortable dwelling space for those on the negative path. Just like certain physical environments attract certain bacteria and viruses, emotional energies such as anger, resentment, hatred and arrogance, expressed enough, can create a comfortable environment for negative beings.

He's gone now. But, this is one of the reasons that we should go forward working together, in harmony with love as a group. His energy was dark,

293

but we opened our hearts to him in love.

AUM: It was your loving energy, Auh. Nadia and Kareem's energy of devotion to The Creator also created a field of very strong protection against this being who wished to harm us.

EARL: Okay, I don't play with evil spirits! Y'all better be loving or I'ma have to — to … love … y'all still …

AUH: We have to stay focused on our path — the positive path of healing, learning, and seeking greater awareness of Oneness in service to others. We don't need to put much focus on those who are on the selfish path. This was a warning. Aum, you have to shape up also. I know this planet and these physical bodies are uncomfortable. I know that humans, especially Vincent, can be annoying.

EARL: HAAAHHHHHHH!!!!!!!

AUH: But you can't let yourself get carried away with anger. You'll have to accept your anger for now. Understand it. Forgive yourself.

AUM: I shall correct this emotional misalignment. I forgive you all. I apologize, and I ask for your forgiveness.

NADIA: We forgive you.

AUH: Din and Vincent, make peace with each other.

VINCENT: Okay, Din. I'm sorry for everything I ever did to you.

DIN: You're just saying that because you have to. It's fake.

NADIA: Come on, Din. Everything was fine before.

DIN: I'm never gonna forget the crap he put me through.

AUH: You'll have to work on this unresolved anger. We can all move forward without putting too much focus on the deeds of our brothers and sisters who anger us. Including those you call evil.

NADIA: How do we defeat evil if we have to act like it's not there?

AUM: This is one area where a very basic balance of love and wisdom may be examined. By keeping your focus on others as an enemy, and putting so much of your attention into your disdain of them, you dis-ease your own energy fields of mind, body and spirit. Wisdom may help you to see how you may protect yourself and deal with the ones who oppose you. Wisdom may teach you, "I must protect myself from my enemy." Love may teach you, "I have no enemy." We have no need to resist the darkness.

NADIA: That's what Jesus taught – *to not resist evil.*

AUM: It is a balance which will challenge you all on the transitional Earth. Think upon this balance. The idea that you must protect yourself against an enemy, and the idea that you have no enemy, for they are one with you, and together, both are The Infinite One.

As the children discuss this and all they've learned, Aum and Auh call on Hathora. She commends Auh on realizing that, in this case, the radiation of love was the fastest and most effective way of sending the negative one away from the ship. She lets them know that it's best to not create the negative environment for them in the first place. She lets them know that they should remain positive, remain harmonious as a group, to keep their hearts open, to appreciate the positive experiences, and to keep their primary focus upon seeking and knowing The Creator within themselves and each other. Hathora lets them know that the energy in the ship at this time is very positive.

They celebrate and speak among themselves for a while.

Earl raps the lyrics to Kid Cudi's, "By Design" again.

EARL: "The satellite that sits in frame to illuminate this shaded place" …

He dances around the room.

EARL: "Moments don't pass me up, no, no 'Cause I seize them in stride. Tell them winnin' never gave me in when I eternally have faith. And the choices you made, it's all by design. Go with it, mmmm. Come on, don't wreck the Fung Shui" … "I see every thing with new beams, I do dream." … (Dancing in front of Bindia) "When you think too much, you're removing what's moving."

He sneaks up behind Nadia as she sits in her chair. He uses his two index fingers to poke the left and right side of her ribcage. The ZAP causes her to SHRIEK and JUMP to a standing position. The others burst out laughing. She laughs.

EARL: "The universe never steered me wrong, the universe never lied" …

Earl wiggles his fingers smiles. She runs around the room.

EARL: "Free from where you don't belong in the concept of time. New levels."

He chases her, grabs and hugs her. She laughs and tries to tries to get him off.

EARL: Ooooooh, tap into the frequency, love. Ooooooh, tap into the frequency, love."

About the Author

This work is dedicated to my loving and supportive Mother.
As well as my close relatives and friends who have supported me through the
process of writing these books.

Kivar Dhawan, birth name Kerin Gomes, is a 33 year-old Author living in New York City. He has ghost-written articles for independent clients, and has written articles for Constant-Content. He was born in George Town, Guyana. From the age of four, Kivar was obsessed with the mysteries of God. He compulsively sought answers from his elders, asking questions about God, nature, The Sun, Moon and stars. He was fortunate enough to have a loving mother and a very dedicated father who provided everything that was needed to survive and live comfortably. This gave Kivar the peace of mind to daydream and focus a lot on childish things. Kivar was fascinated by the look, feel, and smell of soil, plants and flowers. In the towns of Tucber and Canjee, Guyana, Kivar spent many days as a child sitting in silence and trying to observe the growing process of these beings. Kivar moved to the United States at the age of seven. In his teens, he became jaded and cynical after realizing the hypocrisy of many of the people who considered themselves to be "the good people" of the world — particularly many religious people. Around seventeen, Kivar developed a very close relationship with the Father God figure Yahweh, and began to read the Bible. After a few months, he became very empowered and focused. He wanted to be a Martial Arts Fighter and a great Writer. After reading some extremely troubling verses in the Bible which included Yahweh commanding men to the murder of children, rape, and terrorism, Kivar wrote a few questions on a piece of paper and carried them around with him. (Deuteronomy 2:34, Isaiah 15:15-18 are two of many.) He presented the questions to those who claimed to have an understanding of the Bible. He was almost always met with the same reaction: A denial that the violent verses were even in the Bible, and then after reading them, a very poor attempt to justify the violence as somehow "Godly." Having an obsessive and vivid imagination, Kivar dwelled on visions of the specific people involved in the attacks. He imagined the children having their arms and legs chopped off, mothers watching blood spew from their decapitated child's neck, and husbands watching their wives being raped by multiple men, all in the name of God. With all the adults around him confirming this as a good thing, his already-sensitive mind became warped. After finding no satisfying answers, Kivar lost faith and lost direction. With the help of comic George Carlin, he became brave enough to speak out about the dangers and absurdities within organized religion. He cursed the jealous, angry, murderous God, seeing no difference between Yahweh's violent armies in the Bible and the hijackers on September 11th, 2001. He became cynical, dark, and used this as an excuse to just not care too much about anything. He enjoyed violent movies, profanity, and dark humor. He was never violent or directly mean-spirited towards others, but in his ignorance and laziness, he generally figured, "If God approves of mass murder, slavery, terrorism, genocide, and rape, what's the point of trying hard to do the "right" thing?" From the ages of 18 to 23, he spoke out on the subject, ridiculing religion while becoming as arrogant and judgmental as the ones he spoke against. Like many young men, he was focused on sculpting the physical body, making money, wanting to be the alpha male, partying, the night life, and over-stimulating the body & ego with the sexual attention of women. On his 23rd birthday, he took on the general Agnostic position of "I don't know what the truth about God is." He continued on a destructive road of heavy drinking and trying to not give a damn about anything. He pulled away from his family. He enjoyed and cherished the company of people on the outskirts of "polite" society who were considered to be "weirdos," "outcasts," "those people." Being called "strange" and "weirdo" genuinely became a compliment to him. He put all his trust in mainstream science, rational thinking, and being a skeptic. Although he rejected all spiritual and religious ideas, he always held Jesus Christ up high due to the obvious good-hearted nature of his teachings, and his overwhelmingly positive actions in the Bible. As an agnostic, he watched the movies "Jesus," "Jesus of Nazareth," and "The Last Temptation of Christ" repeatedly. It was as if he was still trying to find something. Between the ages of 22-25, Kivar became clinically depressed to the point of thinking about suicide. At 25, after discovering the movie "What The Bleep Do We Know?" he learned about quantum physics and the strange behavior of physical matter and consciousness. It was enough to open his mind to an infinitely bigger reality, and nudge him in the direction of spiritually seeking again. He bought a book by Dr. Daniel Amen called, "Change Your Brain, Change Your Life." He began to organize his life, change his eating habits, and try to get out of the deep depression. Dr. Wayne Dyer became his primary teacher at this point. Kivar read Dyer's work, downloaded his video/audio presentations, and slowly applied the teachings to his life. He was primarily focused on the more "realistic" and practical spiritual teachings. He also read two books given to him by his mother: Napoleon Hill's "Think and Grow Rich," and James Allen's "As A Man Thinketh." He became focused on the power of thoughts, compassion, forgiveness and being a nicer, gentler person. In 2009, Kivar earned his Personal Training certificate, slowly cleansed his body from excessive alcohol use, began more research into the metaphysical, and began to write a (different) novel about teenagers discovering spiritual knowledge. He began to practice celibacy, conservation of semen, sexual transmutation, deep meditation, and an inner seeking of The Source. He became very distant from those around him, and had periods of prolonged solitude and deep inner seeking. In late 2010, he discovered a simple technique for stimulating the area between the eyebrows. This was about activating the indigo-ray energy center often referred to as the third eye. After practicing this technique for a few months in meditation, he became aware of a faint etheric light between his eyebrows when he closed his eyes. This led him to seek the aid of his Hindu Landlord. He described seeing "like, glittering stars" when he closed his eyes. The Landlord only confirmed that it was "The Light." He directed Kivar to The Bible, and said Kivar needed the discipline of The Father. Kivar did not want to hear that, but took his mother's Jehovah's Witness "New World Translation" Bible into his room. He didn't read the Bible, but this was the beginning of an extremely profound, astounding, magical, mysterious and fantastical series of synchronistic events or meaningful co-incidences that changed his life forever. The details of these experiences are presented in a written piece titled, "Testimony of an Inner Seeker." All of his profound spiritual experiences are subjectively accepted by Kivar as "real" and meaningful. The experiences will have meaning to others who are open to such ideas, and have no meaning to those who reject such ideas as foolishness.

Two of the most life-altering experiences occurred on the two days after Kivar brought The Bible into his room. One was an experience of transcending the ego for the first time. The other was a tear-inducing experience with what Kivar accepts as a major message from The Universal I AM Presence; I AM THAT I AM. On the day after bringing The Bible into his room, Kivar meditated. During meditation, he looked deeply into The Inner Etheric Light for the first time. He paid attention to the texture and the movement of The Light. He noticed that The light flowed and changed in patterns as he breathed. He noticed the connection between his breathing, the movement of The Light, and the feeling in his torso. He had strong sensations all throughout his brain. Upon further exploration, he realized that The Light was not in front of him, but all around him. After a few more minutes of meditation, Kivar realized that The Light was him and he was The Light. He felt ridiculous that he didn't realize that earlier. He remembered the work of Dr. Suzanne Lie, and accepted The Light as his Soul Self. It was his expanded Identity. During the next meditation period, Kivar went into The Light again and was able to consciously identify with It as his real self. He was able to tap into a state of genuine transcendence of the illusion. He played with this idea and was able to feel and perceive reality through the energy center above the head which some call the Soul Star Center. This was life-altering. He perceived his room and physical body as being "out there" or "down there." This was one of the coolest experiences, and it greatly altered Kivar's sense of Self. Of course, he was not able to consciously live as this expanded Identity all the time. The everyday challenges of the third-dimensional matrix create the natural challenges which usually prevent all awakening ones from fully living as the many expanded levels of Identity twenty-four hours a day. Kivar experienced direct Soul awareness primarily through meditation, and was guided by the Soul for the next few years.

Two days after bringing The Bible into his room, Kivar watched a video about the power of vibrating certain words. Later on, Kivar meditated. He let The Light pour into the center of his head. He breathed in The Light for almost an hour. This had been the longest he had ever meditated without stopping. He went in deep, beyond the chaotic mind and the usual random thoughts. He suddenly decided to vibrate The Name "JEHOVAH." Immediately, he heard a bang outside. It was Monday night, the night of garbage pickup. Kivar repeated, "JEHOVAH," and heard the bang again. He repeated The Name again and heard another bang immediately. Kivar enjoyed the feeling of the universe interacting with him through the garbage men as they did their job. This was becoming a normal thing in his life. And this is experienced by millions of awakening ones around the world. Where the world around you seems to interact with your peak experiences of oneness with All That Is. Kivar enjoyed the fact that this was really happening. He wanted it to be real. He felt that if he said The Name too much, it won't happen every time. So he stopped. He waited for about thirty seconds. In that time, there were no bangs. He assumed that the garbage men had moved further down the block, but didn't hear the loud truck drive off. After the distracting thoughts, he returned his focus on breathing. After a short time, he said, "JEHOVAH." There was a CRACKLING BANG OUTSIDE! That was one of the most intense and scariest moments of Kivar's life. He opened his bedroom door and went to the front door to see exactly what they were doing. When he got to the front door, he saw that there was no garbage truck. The garbage was still on the sidewalk. It was raining heavily. He heard the roar of thunder. He then realized that every time he vibrated The Name "JEHOVAH," the thunder blazed. Kivar doesn't remember the moments directly after discovering this. He does remember being in meditation later that night and receiving the thought that JEHOVAH wanted him to speak to others through his writing. He broke into tears. He cried and cried, which was something he rarely did. He experienced the feeling of the child Coming Home to his Father after hating Him and cursing Him, and having his Father accept him despite his flaws. Before this experience, Kivar would have thought of this experience as being too sappy and emotional. But the power of being a child of God sitting with his Father was too overwhelming for the thoughts of the ego to limit the power of this experience. It was life-altering.

As profound as the experience was, Kivar completely dismissed the idea that JEHOVAH came to him. The obvious feeling was, "Who the hell am I that this powerful presence would come to me?" He thought, "Even if it was true, there's no way I can handle that kind of pressure." The mental dissonance was intense. He ignored the experience, but accepted the fact that his books could help people and Serve The Totality in some way.

Kivar felt the power of JEHOVAH, but was still concerned about the jealous, murderous biblical figure. In 2014, Kivar discovered what he accepts as the truth about JEHOVAH, the original positive Presence who contacted Moses, and the negative entities who acted in JEHOVAH'S name to inspire the evil and elitist laws and behaviors that followed. This information was given through *The Law of One: Ra Material*, and *The Oahspe Bible*. This information also corresponds to the Gnostic ideas of the demiurge. These revelations cleared up a lot of confusion and fear concerning JEHOVAH. This gave Kivar an extreme sense of relief, and he opened his heart completely to JEHOVAH. After asking for more clarity, Kivar sought to learn more about JEHOVAH'S identity. He looked at the fact that the Being JEHOVAH was presented to the Jewish People and all of humanity as The One Creator of the universe. He noticed that other Higher-dimensional and extraterrestrial beings were considered to be "God", The One Creator by the human messengers who they communicated with. Upon further investigation, Kivar learned and accepted the idea that YAHWEH is 1) a Senior Higher-dimensional Angelic Being. (Not an angel. Not an extraterrestrial). 2) A social memory complex (Many beings who blend their consciousness to make up one being. As in "Let Us create man in Our image.") So YAHWEH can be Referred to as "They" as well as "He" or "She." Kivar learned and accepts the idea that YAHWEH is perfectly balanced as both male and female, but has been overly misrepresented as male only, due to the abusive and dominating nature of the male attitude over the female nature by humans themselves. Kivar learned and personally accepted the idea that YAHWEH has worked with many other angelic and extraterrestrial beings to aid the evolution of humanity on Earth. YAHWEH has changed name and presentation to perform certain duties from different layers of Their being. (As in "EHYEH ASHER EHYEH," "YOD HEH VAV HEH-ELOHIM," "EL SHADDAI," and "ADONAI.") JEHOVAH also seems to change name and presentation to communicate to a particular culture or person, or according to the particular times. It may be that the "Unutterable" Nameless Vibration of YHWH influenced Egyptian culture as the "Unspeakable" Nameless Vibration of Nuk Pu Nuk. Which is translated as "I Am Who I Am." Although the Being Itself is nameless, names are used in order to interact with physical 3D beings.

In 2016, Kivar began to relate to JEHOVAH by the Divine Vibration "AHAYAH ASHER AHAYAH," I WILL BE WHAT I WILL BE, which is commonly translated in English as "I AM THAT I AM." This name is believed to have been presented to Moses as it is written in Exodus 3:14 of the Torah. Kivar accepted this Divine Name as a vibration which *points to* Our Universal I Am Presence. YAHWEH, JEHOVAH, AHAYAH, directs us know I Am, The Identity/Self of Our Self, Existence Itself, The One Infinite Creator, Which Is nameless. I Am is universal identity and this is indicated by the fact that no matter what language a person speaks, verbal and non-verbal, I Am is the only Divine Name of God which every human being expresses every day of their lives. Upon even further devotion, contemplation, meditation, and absolute surrender to Universal Identity, Kivar realized the obvious idea of "The One I Am" Who becomes many "I Ams." He was then led to the vibration "ꜲHꜲꝪꜲH ECHꜲD ꜲHꜲꝪꜲH," "EHꝪEH ECHꜲD EHꝪEH." "I Am The One I Am." This is not a perfectly accurate translation, but can be used as a powerful mantra to consciously synch into Oneness.

Mainstream science has proven that there is no energetic separation of physical space and objects in all that exists. It's been thousands of years since humans have accepted the idea of One Source of existence. Kivar believes that this is what JEHOVꜲH and all other positive beings who have served planet Earth wants humanity to know and accept. And now that energetic Oneness is accepted by a majority of human minds through rational analysis, for those who are spiritually or religiously inclined, there's no positive value in serving a violent, immature, jealous god who is in petty competition with "other" gods. For The Creator, there is no "other."

The new revelations about JEHOVꜲH gave Kivar an openness to explore JEHOVꜲH'S Kabbalistic system in his own mind/body/spirit. It also led to a series of impulses that lead him to rewrite this novel and add primary lessons of the Law of One — a task that Kivar did not want to do.

A week after the JEHOVꜲH experience in 2011, during meditation, Kivar spontaneously and impulsively accepted Jesus Christ as Lord and Teacher. Although he noticed that this was a fundamental aspect of Christianity, Kivar did not personally accept this as a "Christian" act in any way. This occurred because of a very strong and "random" feeling that The Christ, a State of Being which goes far beyond religious interpretation, and far beyond Jesus, was guiding him. As a proud agnostic at the time, there was some initial discomfort in calling someone "Lord," but due to the occurrence of the other synchronistic experiences of the previous few weeks, it felt right and he accepted Christ through Jesus.

As the etheric light intensified in brightness, it led to the beginning stages of violet-ray, crown chakra activation. This led to a phone call from a stranger during an intense crown chakra meditation session which resulted in the introduction of Victor. Along with the JEHOVꜲH experience, and the word "Chosen" being delayed on the television's closed caption at 11:11 pm for a full minute, the Victor phone call was the most astonishing experience in Kivar's life up to that point. Victor is accepted by Kivar as an expanded, higher-dimensional aspect of himself. Victor also connected him to the Arcturians — an extraterrestrial civilization spoken of by Edgar Cayce. Kivar began to see the number 144 popping up in unexpected and unbelievably astonishing ways. For the next two years, the repeated sighting of the number, the etheric light, and a feeling of being guided by powerful higher forces led Kivar to a higher level of soul awareness and self-mastery. The 144 Victors were only *subjectively accepted* to be a portion of his expanded consciousness which has been referred to as The Atma, or Higher Self in spiritual teachings. As he held onto his agnostic label and revered many atheists as personal heroes, the metaphysical experiences pulled and pulled at his rational mind. As he faced many challenges, he continued to try very hard to ignore and rationalize the daily co-incidences away as meaningless. The persistence of the experiences changed him forever, and provided more-than-enough proof that something momentous was occurring, and that The Creator was more than just present in his life. Further research and personal development has allowed Kivar to make peace with all major religions, and to truly appreciate their many positive qualities. Kivar's novels are a result of his burning desire to know The Creator, his inner seeking, his research, and his desire to share the information with others who resonate. Kivar affirms that he is always a student before anything else. Writing this book series has been the greatest learning experience of his life. He has worked non-stop and has not yet given himself the time to truly be still, silent, and properly integrate the knowledge he's taken in over the past five years. The rigorous writing process was performed in a chaotic environment with many distractions, and very few periods of prolonged silence. Kivar believes that many lessons were learned, but too many went unlearned. Kivar has followed the inner light for step-by-step guidance, but has not yet embraced the inner light in a more balanced and disciplined way. It is Kivar's goal to now take time and go deeper into meditation; to better know himself as The Light behind the man, and the consciousness behind The Light. This is needed in order to develop a more mature and disciplined mind as he attempts to take on the honor/duty of teaching others who are open to his message.

Conscious Synching & Channeling Atma/Ka/Higher Self

It is my honor/duty to pledge my life time, deeds and service to The Creator and to all seekers who vibe with this information. The Creator I speak of *Is* The Source, the Infinity, Unity, Allness & Oneness of Existence Itself." It *Is* What It *Is*. *It Is* All That *Is*. *It Is* The One That *Is* no thing and all things. It *Is* the sum of All of Us. There are many positive and useful spiritual, mystic, religious and scientific systems of teaching that point towards It, but no one owns It more than any other. In Its Totality, It *Is* beyond name, gender, philosophical idea, religious interpretation, scientific theory, and New Age belief. Since we all agree that there's a creation, we can agree that there's a Source of creation. However, if ever, one decides to define that is only up to the individual.

My primary inner teacher is my Higher Self. I also accept the radiation of Master Yod Heh Shin Vau Heh, an incarnation of The Christ. I vibrate highly with the information given to humanity by Ra – The channelings by L/L Research, as well as Ra's particular method of helping adepts to explore the archetypal mind through use of the original Egyptian Tarot. I'm also exploring the mystical Kabbalistic system given to the Hebrews by ꔄꔄꔄ ꔄꔄꔄ ꔄꔄꔄ. This is a very, very large and important area of study that I have mostly only explored in relation to my own mind/body/spirit, and communion with JEHOVAH. I also vibe with some practical and joyful aspects of African, Egyptian, Hindu & Buddhist teachings related to the deeper knowledge of body/mind, and also related to seeing, feeling and using etheric Light/intelligent energy. I'm nowhere near an expert or guru on any of these systems of teaching/learning. I've only used them in ways that are practical and directly related to whatever is going on with my body/mind at the moment. I believe that mainstream science and all of the major religions point to The Creator, but it's up to the individual to seek The Source for themselves in an individual way. There have been many lies, edits, deletions, additions, perversions, tricks, innocent mistakes, and misunderstandings of many sacred religious teachings and texts, as well as much of our accepted mainstream scientific information. I've done my share of cursing and hating organized religion. And I see the damage they continue to cause. But, in general, I think the gathering of like minds of any religion in devotion and service to The Creator is a good thing.

The Group Mind

When I'm able to tune in with focus and balance, it feels like I'm writing as a group of individuals. Over the years, the process of tuning in has gotten much easier and feels much more natural. Now, I'm able to get into "the zone" with simple stretching and basic meditation. I personally enjoy the conscious union of mind/body/universe/Creator during the physical exercise, stretching, massaging, and stimulation of certain muscles, joints, and nerve endings. This part of it is related to reflexology, hatha yoga postures, pranayama breathwork, and some of the physical aspects of the Archetypal Mind. This goes along with simple mental and verbal tuning to the higher/deeper vibes through prayer, affirmations, music, toning, images, audio/video presentations, devotion, and appreciation for the presence of The Creator. This is more related to the mental and spiritual aspects of the Archetypal Mind. On the worldly, rational level, it just feels like I'm living and working from the deeper roots of my mind, and my True Personality. Metaphysically, I personally accept that there's a lot more going on. For me, the vibration of The 144 Victors include conscious imprints of my personality, AHAYAH ASHER AHAYAH, Ra, Yod Heh Shin Vau Heh, Akhenaten, Tehuti, Saint Kabir, West African Shamanic influences, the Arcturian Collective Consciousness, and The Universal Spirit of The Christ.

As far as how real this "collective mind" is and how it works -- Stillness and silence allows the logical mind to step aside and relax for a while, and allows subconscious, biological, universal, and metaphysical energies to work with the will, intent, and personal distortions of the individual. Peace, laughter, playfulness, excitement and love in its many forms can be directed to STIMULATE the mind, raise it to new heights, and tap into what has been called intelligent infinity. Sound and music has to be considered one of the most, if not the most powerful ways to elevate the mind and literally stimulate the soul. For those who are open to it, deep, genuine, heartfelt praise, worship, appreciation and reverence for The Creator/creation can, among other things, expand the mind and raise awareness to monumental heights. Most children, many of us average folks, and geniuses like Albert Einstein have can find their own ways to tap into this universal intelligence. Napoleon Hill takes away some of the religious and/or superstitious descriptions of this process in Chapter 14 of his 1937 Classic, "Think And Grow Rich."

Hill writes, "The thirteenth principle is known as the SIXTH SENSE, through which Infinite Intelligence may, and will communicate voluntarily, without any effort from, or demands by, the individual."

"The SIXTH SENSE is that portion of the subconscious mind which has been referred to as the Creative Imagination. It has also been referred to as the "receiving set" through which ideas, plans, and thoughts flash into the mind. The "flashes" are sometimes called hunches or inspirations."

From the generally accepted point of view of Western culture, my spiritual experiences are all subjective and exist only in my mind. As far as my definition of "reality" goes, I won't argue with that. For now, all that matters is the theoretical and experiential use of the information coming through, and the ability to share it with others who resonate with it.

The Information and The Flow

As much as I like teaching, I'm always a student first, then I attempt to teach what I learned according to my interpretation. Obviously, in most ways, I'm just as lost and confused as everyone else is. Like everyone else, I have an area of knowledge and talent that I'm especially skilled in and grateful for. This information is for all who feel that it's right for them, and not for those who feel it's not right for them. This information mainly comes to me from my burning desire to know who/what God is. The writing and the books are secondary. There's inner seeking, outer research, applying what seems to fit into my life, letting go of what doesn't, and then expressing it through writing and art.

Much of the information is gathered through research, childhood memories, experiences, dreams and many, many spontaneous mental and behavioral impulses. The impulses usually come during or just after meditation, or after I've consciously asked for higher/inner guidance. Some of the most unexpected impulses came during the day after sun gazing. I credit my Higher Self as an Author of the novel because of the complex arrangement, simplifying, presentation, and delivery of vital ancient spiritual knowledge through juvenile humor, action-adventure, gripping drama, and lovable characters. The main reason

I feel Higher Self deserves credit is for the large amount of information presented in this book that was not gathered from any outer research. Also, as I asked for help and moved forward, things outside of my deliberate conscious control seemed to create circumstances that helped me to block out many of life's distractions and worldly desires. I believe that my Higher Self also helped me to avoid a lot of unnecessary research into less important subjects, and to sincerely seek The Creator within myself in a very personal way. Higher Self helped me to gather the information from the work of many others, to apply it, organize it, and present it in an entertaining and easier-to-understand way. Through prayer, meditation, other forms of yoga, and a whole lot of spontaneous impulses, I was able to put the novel together while primarily keeping my focus on personal conscious evolution.

This information is presented with the limits of my current understanding, my many blind spots, my particular mind/body filters & distortions, and my many personality flaws. This is only my perspective.

Automatic Writing - Tuning Body/Mind to Spirit

Everyone's process is different, but I hope the information in this section can be helpful to others in some way. Clear and continuous connection with my Higher Self is only made when my individual intentions are purely focused on knowing The Creator, writing, learning, healing and empowering body/mind, doing creative work, or serving others in some way. As far as I know, Higher Self answered the call I sent out at the beginning of every writing session. In the very beginning, as I wrote the first book in 2009, I purified body, mind and environment. Before I sat down to write, I always asked, "God, please give me the words." And then, I meditated. I had no knowledge of automatic writing or the Higher Self. I had no understanding or expectation of anything spiritual occurring. I just always said that before writing anything important. After I asked, I meditated. I'd almost never get to "finish" the meditation. During meditation, the "perfect idea" would always come to me and I'd have to stop meditating to write it down. That was always the end of the meditation because ideas would bombard my mind at an extremely uncontrollable and uncomfortable pace. I would write sloppily with a pen or type compulsively for 1-3 hours without proper spelling, grammar or punctuation. I did interrupt the flow many times because I felt completely out of control. The same thing occurred in 2011 when I started writing this novel. It got frustrating at times because the book I had planned was a 30-page story with simple lessons. The way this novel unfolded felt out of my control, but I couldn't deny or reject the amazing automatic fusing of spiritual, scientific, and intuitive information flowing through an entertaining plot, characters and themes. After the automatic writing, it usually took twelve hours to a few days to sort out what was written, neatly put the pieces together through outer research, and try to tell an entertaining and educational story.

Now that I understand the process better and know more of what's happening, it's nowhere near as chaotic as it was in the beginning. Again, Higher Self syncing doesn't have to be viewed metaphysically. Physically, it's just about high mental efficiency, neurological synergy within the brain, accessing the more expansive geography of the mind. Everyone goes into the "channeling" state when they slip into "the zone" during really good music, great conversations, or as they perform any activity that involves a natural, non-resistant flow of experience.

These days, I do the tuning before any important spiritual, literary, or business-related work. The tuning used to be done after calling on The Christ to guide me. Now I tune to my Christed Self, which is a higher portion of All Of Us which is The Universal Christ. The tuning usually includes prayer, pledging & devoting my service to The Creator, physical exercise, stretching/hatha yoga, pranayama breath-work, meditation, spontaneous feelings of appreciation for the simple things, laughter, Inner-Light/Indigo-ray meditation to connect to intelligent infinity and use intelligent energy, and a natural devotion, reverence and appreciation for the glory of the feeling of the presence of The Creator. There's the mental connection to higher aspects of my Self, connection to the collective mind of humanity, the consciousness of The 144,000, the Earth, Atmosphere, Moon, Sun, Arcturus and the Galactic Logos. There are Kabalistic works which help me to feel more centered in the program of my inner universe. Not all of this is needed every time.   Over all else, I need a very strong, here-and-now awareness of the most natural, deep-down feeling of just Being...Alive. That comes from Silence and Stillness. Being a Being. For me, That Is The Creator without the religious/spiritual undertones. Even the terms "Creator," "Source," and "God" don't match this direct experience. It's a feeling/knowing I used to have around age five in Tucber, Guyana as I observed plants and flowers in the back yard. It's what toddlers and children feel before being given the more artificial definitions about God and reality. It's what we all feel and know at our core. The ingested substances in my body are vegetables or vegetable-based foods, green or black tea, as well as supplements of some basic vitamins and minerals. Whatever "high" I feel comes from the physical, mental and spiritual practices — the exercise, music, laughter, prayer, meditating, stretching, etc. After the tuning, I communicate with Higher Self, feel and live as my most natural Self, and get to work. This process is not for everyone. Others can enter the same state without these methods. This is my process; a fun and natural way for me to enter God Mode.

My Teachers and Inspirations

My primary teacher is The Creator, which Is every thing — My Self, body, nature, family, friends, fans, detractors and technology. Every situation, challenge, and experience is The Creator and our primary Teacher. From higher planes, I am guided by my Higher Self. I am guided and Guarded by THE ONE I AM, Ra, and Archangel Michael. I've been guided by Master Yeshua, Lord Krishna, and Siddhartha Gautama. In 2015, much of my very personal mind/body/spirit Revelations came from the radiation of Tehuti A.K.A. Thoth. When the noise, distractions and limits in work time increased, and focus on the editing process became difficult, I called on Thoth to watch over me as a supervisor. Mainly to help me avoid making unnecessary mistakes, and to help me catch the ones that I had made. This calling was done in somewhat formal ritual at first, and then involved the setting of certain configurations in my own mind. I was contacted and aided by Saint Kabir, The Poet. This was another experience that blew my mind and changed my life. I also feel comfort and aid from the constant presence of an unknown African Shamanic Ancestor. As of now, these are the metaphysical energies I get the most inspiration from and feel an extremely personal connection to. Krishna, Heru, Thoth, The Buddha, Yeshua, and many others are Christic Brothers and Sisters dedicating their services to us. They are not competing over who the "right one" is. It's understandable that many people are angry at the dark ones for using organized religion to co-opt ancient sacred information and hide many truths. And there is a need for these truths to be known *now*. But, we should be careful not to project our anger and ignorance onto these higher-dimensional teachers themselves. They are way beyond the "us vs. them" mentality. Any being inspiring you to revolt with violence, anger and hatred towards another group of people is an entity on the negative spiritual path. Negative beings use the sacred names of positive teachers while preying on the anger and resentment of positive humans who feel they have been wronged by the negative ones. They've used Christianity, the Bible, and organized religions to create lies, and have perverted the story of the life of Yeshua. They've used Yeshua's name for control, terrorism, thievery, genocide, slavery and discrimination in many forms. Don't let your legitimate anger towards the negative ones lead you down the negative spiritual path. All positive higher-dimensional teachers give their service to all who call on them sincerely with an opened heart, a desire to learn, and positive intentions in service. Their main message is what it has been from the very beginning — Love is the way. God is Love.

My Hindu connection relates to, among other things, my birth place in the West Indies, the yoga postures, breathwork and movements I learned without being taught, and my affinity for Indian women and culture.

Many awakening ones feel the movement of etheric energy through their bodies, but don't know how to manage and balance it. Learning some basic yoga postures or basic stretching of major muscles groups will help in grounding and balancing your physical and subtle bodies. Many awakening ones and children do many natural movements that allow energy to flow easier through the body. If you learn and practice some basic stretching moves, your higher intuition and animal instincts will kick in. You can do the techniques exactly as instructed, and also use intuition to follow what feels right, what feels good for your body. Use Bashar's advice of following your highest excitement and you will stretch and exercise the muscles in a way that cause your body to *just feel better.* When there's less tension/stress in your muscles, your mind immediately feels better. The path ahead gets clearer, and your life's mission becomes so much easier. You did this before. You know this stuff. You'll modify the movements and make them your own. Many of the movements you have or will learn on your own are documented in Hindu, Egyptian, African, Native-American, and other spiritual traditions.

As for the research on spiritual/metaphysical information, some of my teachers are Manly P Hall, Dr. Wayne Dyer, Gregg Braden, Deepak Chopra, Napoleon Hill, Bashar, Abraham Hicks, and Dr. Suzanne Lie. I thank James Will Power for helping me to make monumental breakthroughs in my awareness in 2011 through his videos. The teachings that have been the most fundamental to my experimental and experiential seeking of The Creator within have come from the work of 1) Alan Watts. 2) Matias De Stefano. 3) L/L Research. 4) Rysa Perisanna - creator of The Goldring: Game of Enlightenment. 5) Glenn Pendleton with The Sons of The Law of One Podcast, and all contributing beings of the information presented. Thank you. As a teenager and young adult, I was cynical and in the darkness. I rebelled hard against what I saw as an unbearable hypocrisy in so many of the supposedly "good people" of society. I didn't care about right and wrong. I had an "F the world" mentality. I was ready to die at any moment. At that time, I found brotherhood and inspiration through the works of Earl Simmons (DMX), Marshall Mathers (Eminem), George Carlin and Tupac Shakur. I can say that their work collectively kept me alive. Marshall helped me to vent and to see more of the hypocrisy in society. He helped me to be vulnerable, to accept and embrace my flaws, and to express myself in a more blunt way. His slim shady character helped me to laugh at myself and at the darkness all around me. Slim also helped me to release a lot of built-up anger in a comical way. The album, *The Eminem Show* holds a special place in the soundtrack of my life and my mental evolution. Marshall's ability to create complex rhyme schemes and to bend words to his will fascinated and inspired me to want to be great with words. Earl's album, *The Great Depression*, changed my life as I was goin through clinical depression. The song, *A minute for your son* was dedicated to God. As a teenager, I thought it was so dope to see a respected rapper dedicate music to God in such a way. The song *Damien 3* helped me to look at the demons in myself. Tupac's rap career was before my time as a rap fan. I always enjoyed his music, but he also inspired me through interviews documentaries about him. The documentary *Resurrection* played on a loop in my DVD player for a few months straight. His activism and desire to find solutions for the ills of society really spoke to me. The song,

Brenda's got a baby is the number one most inspiring song that guided me towards writing about serious social issues.

George Carlin is one of my personal heroes for many reasons, and by far my all-time favorite human being that I've never physically met. He helped me to see that it was okay to speak out against the negative qualities of organized religion. His greatest gift to me was guiding me towards leaving my family's religion and getting rid of the damaging psychological residue caused by rigid religious dogma. Carlin, who was a proud Atheist, spoke out against the absurdities of organized religion, but respected the mysteriousness of Existence Itself.

"I think we're a part of a greater wisdom that we'll ever understand. A Higher Order. Call It what you want. You know what I call It? The Big Electron. It doesn't punish. It doesn't reward. It doesn't judge at all. *It just Is*. And so are we." — George Carlin.

Bill Maher's standup comedy and his stance on religion just as big a part in freeing my mind from religious dogma in my early twenties. I played their music and comedy shows every day. I wrote detailed notes on their use of language. The slick wordplay, aggression, anger and intensity helped me to release and direct a lot of built-up energy. These men helped me through my darkest days. Being a word nerd, their poetry inspired me to speak out and channel my anger in a creative way through storytelling. I wrote a dark religious comedy screenplay at that time and shared it with friends. Their honest critique boosted my confidence as a writer. The past seven years have been filled with overwhelming positivity, joy and growth through facing challenges head-on. These have been the greatest years of my life. I don't personally vibrate with the anger and the negativity in the work of these men anymore, but I salute them for giving a voice to many young people who are angry, fed up, and ready to check out of this world. Their music, shows, books and interviews continue to inspire me. Their work helped to save my life, and continue to do so for others.

In late 2010, Dr. Martin Luther King came to me in dreamstate and told me to focus on writing positive information much more than negative. This shifted the attention of my writing a lot because I was always drawn to focusing on controversial topics, and having characters use malicious speech that would purposely enrage people on both sides of every issue. I believe that the more aggressive approach of facing challenges can be useful for positive individuals who are soldiers of light. There is a place for a more aggressive approach. This will be displayed in future books with older characters and more mature subjects. The message from Dr. King changed my approach to informing and educating through my work.

Richard Pryor is another personal hero. He's helped me to look at my own flaws, and to critique myself in an honest and crude way. This has lead to me consciously catching myself more and more in those moments when I act or speak in a way that is not in accordance with the positive spiritual path. I continue to face and change bad habits, judgment towards others, deep-rooted beliefs that no longer serve me, and little mental programs that keep me from expanding and expressing myself in a more clear and honest way. The ability to be brutally honest with myself about my mistakes, my ignorance, and my darkness has lead to a lot of growth.

I continue to be inspired by young scholars, inventors, social activists, volunteers, educators and counselors. To see others offering themselves in genuine service to others helps to fuel me as I move along my path.

Creatively, I've been inspired by low-budget independent films and documentaries. The better known names who have inspired me creatively are Russell Simmons, Chris Rock, Dave Chappelle, Larry David, Jerry Seinfeld, Bill Maher, D.L. Hughley, Louis C.K., Dwayne Carter, Will Smith, Vince McMahon, Quentin Tarantino, Ian Fleming, John Singleton, Tyler Perry, Spike Lee, Vince Russo, Charlie Kaufman and Stanley Kubrick. Thank you all.

Adonai Vasu Borragus

www.ingramcontent.com/pod-product-compliance
Lightning Source LLC
LaVergne TN
LVHW051541080426
835510LV00020B/2803